The Playing Fields of Eton

The Playing Fields of Eton

Equality and Excellence in Modern Meritocracy

MIKA LAVAQUE-MANTY

THE UNIVERSITY OF MICHIGAN PRESS

Ann Arbor

2012   2011   2010   2009   4   3   2   1

A CIP catalog record for this book is available from the British Library.

Library of Congress Cataloging-in-Publication Data

LaVaque-Manty, Mika.
   The playing fields of Eton : equality and excellence in modern
meritocracy / Mika LaVaque-Manty.
      p.   cm.
   Includes bibliographical references and index.
   ISBN-13: 978-0-472-11685-0 (cloth : alk. paper)
   ISBN-10: 0-472-11685-1 (cloth : alk. paper)
   1. Equality.   2. Merit (Ethics)—Social aspects.   3. Elite
(Social sciences).   I. Title.

HM821.L39   2009
305.509182'1—dc22   2008051145

for Danielle

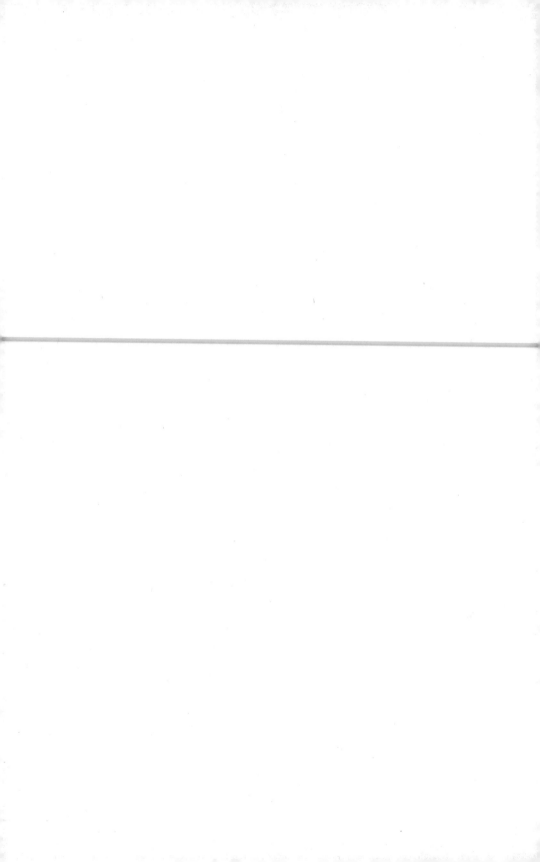

Contents

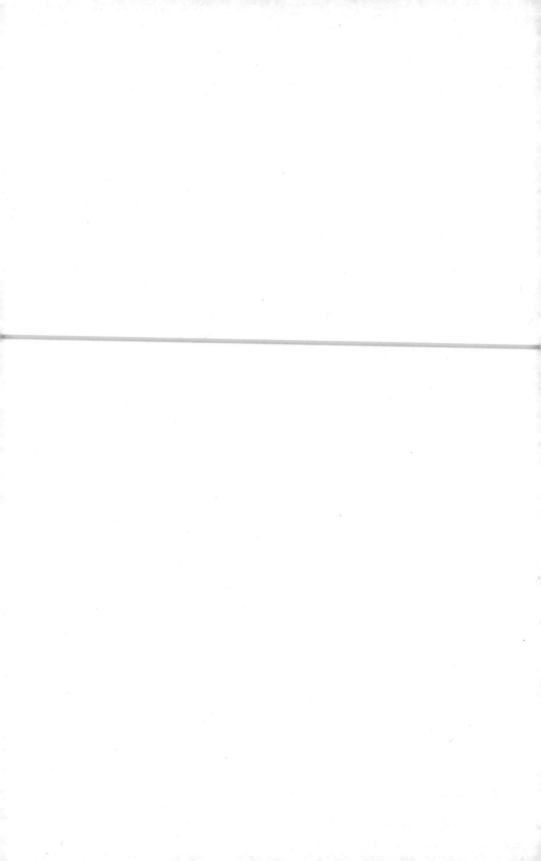

Preface

This book is about tensions between equality and excellence that have arisen in Western culture since the eighteenth century. Meritocracy—the idea that careers are open to talent, that the best man wins the game, that the race is to the swift—is one of the most important modern ideas invoked to solve these tensions. It does so in principle, but as I show over the following chapters, we moderns remain puzzled about what it might mean with regard to the details. What is talent? Does the best woman win any games? Why is the race to the swift and not to the dexterous or smart? How do you get talent? Speed? Smarts? Underneath those questions is my assumption that modernity is meritocratic—or at least sincerely tries to be—and that the value is worth pursuing.

The book came together during the 2004–5 academic year, when I was the A. Bartlett Giamatti Faculty Fellow at the University of Michigan's Institute for the Humanities. This aspect of the book's genesis has a fortuitous connection to its substance: The second known occurrence of the adjective *meritocratic,* the *Oxford English Dictionary* tells us, appears in Giamatti's 1989 book, *Take Time for Paradise.* Not only does Giamatti's book appear in the following pages, but what he says about the role of sports in modern culture significantly informs my argument about why it is worth paying attention to sports and physical culture when we think about enduring questions in political theory. So it is thoroughly appropriate that my first debt is to the memory of Bart Giamatti: it was an honor to hold a fellowship in his name. This isn't cheap talk, either: chapter 2 shows that I take seriously the idea of honor.

Still, there's honor, and there's everyday reality, but here those, too, came together: my year at the Institute for the Humanities was the best year of my professional life so far. I owe much thanks to director Danny Herwitz, both for logistics and for intellectual substance: his comments on the chapter on dueling were extremely helpful. The other fellows made intellectual life generally rewarding; George Hoffman and Sue Juster became friends who have helped make this book what it is and certainly much better than it would have been. Each has read much of the book and has remained supportive and offered invaluable suggestions.

The University of Michigan Press has offered a good home for this book and treated it well. Jim Reische was such a committed editor that he remained involved with the book even beyond his tenure at the press. The book is much better for his involvement. Jim also found two excellent anonymous reviewers, whose comments I found extremely valuable.

The ensemble of people who have helped me is so large and their influences so varied that I cannot name them all, although I am nevertheless grateful to each one. I acknowledge my gratitude to Elizabeth Ben-Ishai, Mary Dietz, Lisa Ellis, Linda Gregerson, Barbara Herman, Katherine Ibbett, Steve Johnston, Sharon Krause, Roger Michalski, Rob Mickey, Scott Page, Claire Rasmussen, and Bernie Yack. A conversation with Jasjeet Sekhon late in the process helped me better formulate my conclusions.

The political theory faculty at Michigan have been wonderful colleagues, interlocutors, and friends. Don Herzog, Arlene Saxonhouse, and Elizabeth Wingrove read and commented on parts of the manuscript and offered great support. Elizabeth deserves particular credit for helping me realize what this book is about; she is perhaps the most incisive reader and commentator I have known, and I am proud to have her as a colleague.

I have the luxury of sharing a home and a life with a brilliant theorist and even better writer. I cannot possibly enumerate the ways in which Danielle LaVaque-Manty has contributed to this book, so let me just acknowledge my debts by dedicating the book to her. Also on the home front, Zook, Plug, and Gertie have been a source of inspiration, energy, and perspective.

Parts of the book have appeared elsewhere: a paper related to chapter 1 was published as "Kant's Children" in *Social Theory and Practice* in July 2006; a version of chapter 2 was published in *Political Theory* in 2006; and parts of chapter 5 came out in the *Disability Studies Quarterly* in June 2005. I gratefully acknowledge permission to reprint the work here.

Introduction

The Indispensable Fictions of Equality and Excellence

This book explores a tension between two values, equality and excellence. Does a fundamental conflict exist between those values? Perhaps the more equal we become, the more we dumb down our hopes of real excellence. Or is it the other way round? Someone can be excellent only in comparison to a group of peers, which means that excellence depends on some sense of equality. This is one of the enduring dilemmas of modern politics.

The answer this book offers is that both equality and excellence are products of our imagination. Don't get me wrong: that's a very good thing. Just for comparison, consider a few other products of our imagination: moveable type, the *Goldberg Variations,* steam engines, antibiotics, airplanes, the iPhone. Imagination and the ability to shape the world accordingly separate humans from other animals. There are also, of course, iron maidens, machine guns, gas chambers, and Windows Vista, which ought to remind us that we shouldn't just pat ourselves on the back for being human.

To say that equality and excellence are fictions, then, is not to devalue them, but it is also not to do away with the tensions between them. Make them up as we do, we want them to do something in the physical world in which we find ourselves. We are constrained by the world's physical laws: we can imagine a lot more than we can realize. We differ from other animals in some rewarding ways, sure, but we are also like them in many more ways. So we make up our values with an eye toward the constraints that keep us from levitating and exercising telekinesis. But while it is true that our imagination can take us well beyond what is possible for us, the opposite is frequently also true: much more is realizable than we might currently imagine. Until 1954, when Roger Bannister broke the four-minute mile, highly competent physiologists doubted that a human being could run that fast. Yet we do know that there is some limit to human running speed, even if we have learned to adjust our view of what that limit is. So, what we can do is limited by the physical world; what we can imagine is limited by our social world. And as the four-minute-mile shows, the limits don't come just from some knee-jerk prejudices but even from the best knowledge of the day.

This gets us to politics and to the argument of this book. Ever since the made-up idea that some things people do are excellent came into conflict with the made-up idea that people should be seen as equal, people have tried to reconcile those ideas. These attempts have been limited and fostered by the physical and social worlds, by what people can do and what they think they can do. *Both* of those things, as Bannister's achievement shows, can change, and they have changed radically over the past couple of centuries, although they do remain anchored by the fact that we are physical animals. That is the first part of the thesis of this book. The second part is that at least since the introduction of the political value of equality, excellence has always required some understanding of equality to be meaningful. For us moderns, the two concepts are necessarily related. The final part of the thesis is that the mutual dependence has worked the other way, too: conceptions of excellence have helped people create equality.

This book's answer to the worry about equality dumbing down excellence is, then, that the worry is confused: something can only count as excellent against some basis of equal comparison. But making things more equal or equal in new ways changes what we mean by *excellent*. There may be some kind of excellence you now appreciate that further equality will undermine. That may be, from your perspective, a real loss.

With a thesis this complicated, the argument has to be more complicated still. But it isn't so abstract. Let us get to the concrete themes by considering historical incidents.

First, in 1999, a group of wheelchair athletes sues the organizers of the New York City Marathon for discrimination under the Americans with Disabilities Act. Their charge? Although they are allowed to participate in the marathon, they are not treated *as athletes:* their participation is not a competition.[1]

Similar demands to make competitive pursuits more accessible—more "democratic," many say—have also generated a backlash: critics claim that our ideas of excellence and achievement are being dumbed down. Second, on U.S. college campuses, athletic programs—in particular, when faced with financial difficulties—shut down nonglamorous men's teams such as wrestling, diving, and gymnastics.[2] The cause behind this, according to an increasingly vociferous group, is Title IX, a 1972 law that provides for gender equity in education and that has come to be associated with college athletics in particular. Third, embattled baseball star Barry Bonds breaks Hank Aaron's record of lifetime home runs under enduring suspicions that Bonds owes his prowess to steroids. The majority of Americans believe his achievement should be recorded with an asterisk next to it, indicating at least suspicion if not a proven taint.[3]

What to make of these cases? One answer might be, Boy, how well off we are! We can afford to worry about essentially trivial questions and call them political. Many people think that in our world, far too many things become political. The view among some parts of the (old-fashioned) political Left is that such "cultural" politics distract from more important, genuinely political questions of the distribution of real goods: income, health care, educational opportunity, effective legal rights, political power. And the view among some parts of the political Right is that the cases show what happens when you mix the legacies of the civil rights movement with envy, discontent, and fear of hard work: every malcontent now turns her gripe into a claim of oppression. What follows, our skeptics believe, is that an increasing number of social practices get dumbed down and that the "natural" contours of societal differences don't get appreciated. (Women just aren't as interested as men in sports, they say, so it is silly to require, as Title IX does, that athletic opportunities be proportional to the overall gender ratio on a university campus.)

The story isn't as simple as any of these caricatures would imply. First, we are *not* dealing with anything new under the sun; similar controversies on the fringes of politics have regularly arisen ever since equality talk became common in the West. At the turn from the eigh-

teenth to the nineteenth century, members of the German bourgeoisie begin to duel, even though one might have expected them to
reject the practice as a feudal relic. Why would recognizably modern
political actors be sympathetic toward dueling? The bourgeois benefit
most when merit and wealth replace birth as the signs of status. Perhaps they just want to be aristocrats, as some have suggested. But
maybe not; maybe they just want respect. Dueling is a practice that
deals in respect-worthiness and requires equality from its participants.
But can it be a source of respect if everyone gets to participate?
(Many contemporaries say no, and I will explain why they are partly
right.) On what grounds is it a source of respect? (Because duelers are
honorable, the argument goes.) Not quite a century later, European
working-class movements debate what to do with sports. Some workers point to the nineteenth-century ethos that infers moral character
from physical prowess and argue that mass sports are a way of gaining political respect: if ruling classes think that being a good athlete
shows you are worthy of respect, they say, let's get some respect by
beating them at their poncy games. Others agree on the value of
sports but worry that accepting competitiveness means buying into
capitalist values. They urge the working classes to embrace noncompetitive models of physical exercise and thereby egalitarian modes of
human flourishing. Still others find the whole business a dangerous
distraction from politics and lament workers' delight in spending their
newly established leisure doing and watching sports. None of these
positions wins the day, which leaves working-class sports both thoroughly political and politically ambiguous: Is it a means of equality or
a means of co-optation? Or both?

This question about the tension between equality and excellence is
a political question because the two values reflect different systems of
personal status. Excellence is comparative and hierarchical; equality is,
well, egalitarian. Now, the textbook story is that according to those
norms that constitute what we call modernity, *political* status is egalitarian; hierarchies of excellence are supposed to be apolitical and in-
habit a social space we call civil society, voluntary aspects of social life
between the purely private and officially political. Treating political
status hierarchically was an organizing principle for the ancien régime,
and modern egalitarianism has replaced it. Where it still helps organize social relations, the same story continues, we are dealing with

aberrations, injustices, symptoms of modern failure. Your boss may have more money than you, and that's fine. But if his money or power gave him two votes or the right to tell you how to vote, we'd balk.

This book challenges the view that compartmentalization solves the tension between hierarchies and equality. Politically relevant hierarchies continue to exist and do so in some cases for good reasons, alongside but often uneasily with equality. Moreover, the idea of the equal dignity we have by virtue of our being human is necessarily abstract and becomes concrete only in historically contingent ways. One of the things "we" moderns have tried to do over the past few centuries is sort out an acceptable balance between what we might call the hierarchical and egalitarian kinds of social order. The hierarchical kinds aren't always a premodern hangover but are often a necessary though imperfect tool for trying to realize our political ideals.

In the academic subfields of political theory and political philosophy, one conventional way of understanding the tension between equality and excellence has been to frame it as tension between liberty and equality.[4] Our commitment to freedom, the argument goes, means that people should do what they want. When they do, some will be more intrepid and gain more resources than others; they will pass what they gain onto their children, who will start off better than the children of the lazy or the unlucky, and then it's curtains for equality. If, however, we try to keep things equal, we will in some ways limit people's freedom: we tax the energy and incentive out of the intrepid and the industrious. Political theorists have traditionally tried to reconcile that tension. That is not what I do here, in part because the liberty/equality framing is arguably overexplored: there is not a lot one can add to the multiple ways of spelling out the deep contradictions or reconciling these values. My main reason, though, is that we gain more political purchase by being sociological: the political tension is not between two *abstract* modern conceptions but between value systems embedded in historical social practices. That is, I am interested in how actual human beings in some specific moments in time try to understand what it means to be free or equal or excellent. The question can be framed as a tension between liberty and equality, but it is illuminating to explore the historical on-the-ground controversies out of which the philosophical tension arises.

The idea is that status and the goods that accrue from it are maintained and cashed out in social practices. You must *do* something to demonstrate and maintain your claim to some particular status.[5] Consider an absurd example from the real world. When I was in fifth grade, spitting well earned you high standing among your peers. (I spat badly, which is why I remember this.) "Well" had something to do with length of the trajectory as well as with the consistency of the projectiles, but even for preteens, this kind of excellence wasn't about some "social utility": it wasn't a means to some other end. Rather, it was a kind of proxy or a marker for characteristics that really mattered (some kind of vague coolness, in this case). Later, excellence in spitting gave way to other status markers, and most of us are grateful that it retains virtually no social cachet for adults. In fact, even in fifth grade, it was far from universal. It was very gendered, and, for all I know, a 1970s phenomenon or something only kids in Finland did. The general idea is that a person's standing in a reference group depends on what or how well he does or doesn't do something and that what will count as salient markers varies radically.

Status, in this sense, is thoroughly social: your status depends on what others believe about you and how they relate to you. Your way of affecting the others' beliefs is through a kind of communication that *shows* them what they ought to believe. It isn't that what you say doesn't matter—it does. But we are all familiar with what philosophers call the other minds problem: we can't get inside one another's heads and so cannot know whether others really mean what they say. Behavior is a way of cashing this out; it is the evidence—confirming or falsifying—for what has been said.

This sociological commonplace butts heads with the modern value that your political status depends *not* on show but on tell: our fundamental political principles, enshrined into institutions such as laws, declare that we are equal by virtue of our humanity alone. In this sense, status isn't social but intrinsic. The institutionalized principles, in the modern conception, don't create the status but merely acknowledge what is already there: "We hold these truths to be self-evident," the moderns say—for good reasons, too, most of us think. But intrinsic dignity is also, as novelist J. M. Coetzee has observed, an "indispensable fiction." It is indispensable: we have good reasons and even evidence to think that most of the old ways of denying some people respect—by race, gender, nationality, religious faith—are unsustainable because they simply get the facts wrong. If you say that the "lower orders" don't have courage, for example, you are simply making a false claim, just in the same way you are when you say "Girls can't do math." As I show in this book, there has been a kind of snowball effect in these arguments that has also chipped away at rearguard attempts to defend old hierarchies. It has become increasingly implausible to say, "Ah, okay, so, yes, I was wrong about the lower orders, but I'm certainly right about women or blacks or Arabs or people with disabilities: *they* can't do what (white) men can." But the snowball effect hasn't been an avalanche; at every step of the way, new arguments have still had to be made. It has nevertheless been a losing battle for the defenders of the old, so we tend to have a sense that there are fewer and fewer grounds for denying people's intrinsic value. Thus also our sense of dignity's indispensability.

But the assumption of intrinsic dignity is a fiction all the same, I claim with Coetzee. "Nor do we inherently possess dignity. We are certainly born without dignity, and we spend enough time by ourselves, hidden from the eyes of others, doing the things that we do when we are by ourselves, to know how little of it we can honestly lay claim to," Coetzee has written.[6] He is after different game from me, but this passage points to the central idea animating this book.

We don't inherently have dignity. It is false to claim that nonwhite peoples or women don't have dignity while whites or men do because on close scrutiny, that claim doesn't hold up in the face of the facts, however we construe them. But it is also false to say that we all inherently have dignity. Coetzee is playing with the dual meanings of dignity—*dignity* means a value we have, and *dignity* means appearing dignified—but those two are related, and the play is significant. For both meanings, at issue is whether someone is worthy of respect. As this book argues, being so depends on what we *do,* not solely on what we naturally are.

This is going to be controversial. Stephen Darwall has argued that there are two kinds of respect: recognition respect and appraisal respect.[7] The former depends on my recognizing that you merit respect solely on the basis of what you are: Ah, you are a human being! I may not just kill you even though you stand in my way. Ah, you are a professor. I had better call you "Professor Smith," even though you just belched. The latter depends on your doing something I value: Ah! You donated a million dollars to a charity; that is an impressive show of generosity. Ah, you did the Hawaii Ironman while on the tenure track; that is an impressive ability to work hard and multitask. While Darwall's distinction is valuable, the argument here is that those two kinds of respect have not been historically as distinct as we would like to think.

How does our dignity depend on show and not just on tell? A crucial reason is that we take someone's being a doer to be perhaps the key aspect of what makes her person.

What Is Enlightenment?

One powerful idea of the eighteenth-century intellectual movement we like to call the Enlightenment was that all humans have the equal dignity I have been talking about by virtue of their autonomous agency.[8] In Immanuel Kant's representative formulation, to be an autonomous agent is to act on reasons you give yourself, as opposed to being the vehicle for some other force—your body's urges, say, like an addict, or the will of someone else, like a slave. The idea is attractive, but one serious question facing Enlightenment thinkers was how to reconcile the ideal of autonomy with social reality. To many Enlighteners' eyes, people neither enjoyed the respect their supposed dignity warranted nor acted in ways that would have suggested they were autonomous. If the eighteenth century was the Age of Enlightenment, many people didn't act their age. Intellectual and political elites called this people's "immaturity."[9] Part of the problem was political in an institutional sense: absolutism, feudal vestiges, and religious authoritarianism—often through well-intentioned paternalism—made it difficult for people to be autonomous. But Kant and others thought that ordinary people themselves were part of the problem: their immaturity was also "self-incurred." This was a theoretical and practical dilemma. Imagine yourself in the Enlighteners' shoes: if another person's autonomous agency is your goal, you had better be careful about what and how much *you* do for her. Or, as John Dewey put it, "[P]ersonality cannot be procured for any one, however degraded and feeble, by any one else, however wise and strong."[10] A real tension exists between paternalism and respect for autonomy. There is also a risk of

elitism in concerning yourself with others' autonomy. What a person does doesn't tell you whether she chose to do it. Some people autonomously choose stupid actions and ends or actions and ends that might look stupid to you.

Call this Enlightenment's *autonomy problem*. It serves as my point of departure in this book, which is also why the eighteenth century is, roughly, the historical point at which I begin. The book is divided into three parts that correspond to the eighteenth, nineteenth, and twentieth centuries. This first part describes a historical moment in which people confront the autonomy problem and the related tensions between equality and excellence. The confrontations produce a set of themes that recur throughout the book. They are *the relationship between individuals, the state, and civil society;* the surprising and persistent *importance of physical culture and even sports* in our consideration of those political relationships; and, finally, *gender.*

Coming Attractions; or, From *Zweikampf* to *Klassenkampf* to *Kulturkampf*

One of philosophers' many occupational hazards is that they like to show off their erudition with ugly German polysyllabic words. Here I beg your indulgence for the bad habit: "From Dueling to Class Struggle to Culture War" just wouldn't capture what connects the seemingly different sorts of practices I focus on in this book. You don't have to know German to notice that *Kampf* is part of all those words; you probably do have to know German to know it means a couple of things: "battle," "struggle," and "competition." The multiple meanings are connected.

The underlying theme of part 1 is attempts to reform existing practices to realize the new ideals of equal human dignity and human autonomy. In chapter 1, I focus on the education of children. This is politically significant in various ways: one of our ideas about equality is what is called, with a sporting metaphor, a "starting line equality of opportunity": we are equal when we all begin with (roughly) equal opportunities to pursue our various ends. It is an appealing idea because it well reconciles the tension between equality and excellence. It is also a difficult idea to realize: it is seldom clear what the equal starting line

would look like. In the early twenty-first century, we tend to think it at least means roughly equal educational opportunities. That idea sees one of its first modern realizations in the eighteenth century in the ideals of German pedagogue Johann Bernhard Basedow. He significantly influenced, among others, Kant. Kant will make more than an occasional appearance in part 1. This is not a coincidence: this book aims to show political theorists as necessarily engaged with the problems of the day, and Kant is a very helpful example partly because his philosophy is so often read as entirely disconnected from its social and political context.[11] He serves as a helpful fulcrum for those moments in which theory and practice come together. His analyses help reinterpret and even occasionally shape others' understanding of the values they claim or hope to live by.

From the cradle we move near the grave, if not the grave you reach by longevity: debates on dueling follow the debates on education. Chapter 2 focuses on a peculiar phenomenon that is roughly contemporaneous with the previous chapter's debates about the education of children. In the early nineteenth century, the German bourgeoisie begins to duel, and we see elsewhere in the Western world a kind of "democratization" of dueling: people whom you wouldn't expect to want to duel embrace the aristocratic practice with surprising enthusiasm. One of the reasons they shouldn't want to duel is that the reforms chapter 1 discusses should be making it easier for people to ignore birth as a sign of status and instead focus on merit and achievement. Some contemporary commentators see the democratization of dueling as just that—as a means for essentially democratic claims. In this view, people are using an oldfangled idea—aristocratic honor—as a way of realizing a modern ideal of equality. Many other commentators just see it as a degeneration of old values: "There goes the social neighborhood." Bourgeois dueling and nonlethal dueling, they argue, make a mockery of masculine honor.

Part 2 traces the legacies of part 1 in the very long nineteenth century. In chapter 3, I explore a period during which the questions about equality, achievement, excellence, and competition for the praise of others crop up again. In the West, the nineteenth century grew obsessed with physical culture. This was in part because of developments in science and medicine: an increasingly sophisticated understanding of human biology, hygiene, and psychology meant that the

whole human body became the window to the soul. Victorians and their continental and transatlantic counterparts thought a person's moral character was exemplified by his [*sic*] physical prowess. This influenced, among other things, theories of education. But there were also disputes about what "proper" physical prowess meant. The chapter shows how these controversies reflected and shaped more general preoccupations about social, political, and economic change. For example, whether the emerging ideal of the modern professional—both in the office and on the playing fields—was an ideal worth aspiring to was not an idle question, as we will see.

Chapter 4 focuses on the emergence of mass sports, particularly socialist and other working-class sports organizations at the end of the nineteenth century and the beginning of the twentieth. The chapter begins with a puzzle about these political organizations' inordinate interest in sports. I argue that one reason for this was exactly the nineteenth-century obsession with the physical: political actors saw physical culture as a promising site for a kind of practical political rhetoric. As I suggested at beginning of this introduction, fierce debates occurred in and between working-class organizations about whether this preoccupation was a good idea. Central for my purposes are debates about the nature of competition, on the one hand, and the extent to which the social space of physical culture was political, on the other: Was it within the unavoidable control of the capitalist state, or could it help change the state?

Part 3 takes us to our own fin de siècle and to more familiar political debates. Chapter 5 explores the general question of how difference matters for ideas about equality of opportunity and excellence. It focuses on two categories, gender and disability. The chapter turns to broad questions about how we—a liberal democratic society at the turn of the twenty-first century—understand excellence. How does someone whom society *defines* as "disabled" exemplify excellence? What does it mean to pursue excellence? What might an equal opportunity to pursue excellence look like? If equality of opportunity is guaranteed by a boundary drawn between groups of people—women and men, say—what principles do we use to draw the boundaries? If Casey Martin can't walk, can he play professional golf at the elite level? Can you run a marathon in a wheelchair? What kind of wheelchair? Does it matter how you got in the wheelchair? If Marla Runyan is blind but still as fast as sighted athletes, should she participate in the Paralympics or the Olympics? I suggest that disability rights activists intuitively realize that access to sports—a form of physical flourishing in our culture—is necessary to count as a citizen.

Chapter 6 focuses on the contemporary obsession with athletic doping. I argue that the current salience of athletic doping reflects not only contemporary partisan divisions between "liberals" and "conservatives" (although it does reflect those) but deeper tensions about individual achievement and fair competition in an age that is increasingly called the age of biopolitics. The chapter refuses a choice between a "reductionist" analysis (which says that our questions get answered when we solve the nature/nurture debate) or a "macropolitical" one (which says modern sports are just a form of global capitalism) or an individualist-moralist one (which says that the problems with doping have to do with morally unsavory characters in sports). Instead, it takes all these analyses seriously and charts the relationships among them as enduring puzzles about how to understand the moral and political values of fairness, achievement, and human flourishing.

Continuities

How do the various *Kämpfe*—struggles, battles, competitions—these chapters describe form a coherent whole?

Individuals, the State, and Civil Society

All of the episodes illustrate changing relationships among individuals, the state, and civil society. One general characteristic of the modern state is that it can no longer do what the premodern could (at least pretend to) do: provide salvation. One reason the state has gotten out of the salvation business is the emergence of what the philosopher John Rawls called "the fact of pluralism": people have apparently irreconcilable disagreements over what salvation would look like.[12] Insofar as the state professes to be the guardian of one kind of salvation, it risks the sort of violent religious strife that marked the sixteenth and seventeenth centuries. If the state cannot promise salvation, and if *ought* implies *can,* as moral philosophers think, then *can-*

not implies *need not,* and the state needs something else to promise its members, be they subjects or citizens.

We can think of two kinds of purposes for the modern state. One is that the modern state promises its members a secular version of salvation. The other is that it promises justice. Although there are famous attempts at going for secular salvation—we find them from Rousseau to Marx to Lenin and Mao—states that embrace justice as their purpose tend to have been more successful. The fact of pluralism, it turns out, goes beyond disputes over religious salvation. To borrow from Rawls again: the disputes are about the conceptions of the good life more generally. In other words, we have learned that we disagree on so many important things that a state that promises a single vision of a good life, whatever it looks like, will have to rub someone the wrong way. In such a case, dissent, unhappiness, or strife are likely to ensue.

What the modern state tends to promise its members, then, tends to be justice, not salvation. A relatively prominent modern idea is that to count as justice, justice under the fact of pluralism has to be agnostic between the competing conceptions of the good that exist in society. This is why in modernity, democratic or liberal ways of organizing the institutions of the state are usually successful. You can involve people in their own governance to make sure different perspectives get represented (democracy), or you can grant people rights to pursue their lives without interference from others (liberalism), or both (liberal democracy). This need for a neutrality among competing conceptions of the good generally has meant that modern justice must include the promise of autonomy: citizens should be not only permitted to but *capable* of setting their life goals and participating in governance.

This is not how the actual modern state came about or how it functions. If I just sketched what we might call the general "normative" conception of the modern state (that is, it is how thoughtful people, on reflection, would describe the ideal modern state), people who study actual states and their histories describe the state as the institution that consolidates *power* so it has monopoly over it in a given territory, particularly over coercive power.[13] Pluralism may indeed be an empirical fact of the post-Reformation northern Atlantic world, but a sufficiently powerful state doesn't have to be neutral between conceptions of the good: repressing unsavory views is also always an option. You can—*if* you can—always transport pesky dissenters into colonies or the gulag. You can (try to) impose your secular salvation.

But however different the normative and empirical perspectives might look, a connection exists. First, the normative conception isn't just some naive pipe dream conjured up by philosophers with too cheerful a vision of humanity and too much time on their hands. Rulers have almost invariably been concerned with legitimating their power, however much of it they might have had and however insincere their claims to legitimacy. Second—and this may be one of the reasons why everyone seems interested in legitimacy—out-and-out repression tends to be costly. For strategic reasons, even Niccolo Machiavelli and Thomas Hobbes, the two supposed defenders of straightforward power, urge rulers to pay attention to the feelings of those they govern. Sure, there can be a wide gap between the appearance of justice and real justice, but the normative (the ideal) and the empirical (the real) are related.

We can see one of the ways the two are related if we think of the issue from the perspective of persons. One way to understand the historical emergence of pluralism is to see it as a result of early modern individuals simply having more power than they used to have. Sociologically speaking, societies have always been to some extent pluralist—Can you really imagine you'd agree with your most like-minded friend all the time?—but what is necessary for pluralism to become social force that needs be reckoned with is, well, force. The disagreements must be momentous enough to matter for people, and the people must have enough power to give others notice. Early on, historically speaking, power wasn't anything like the political power modern citizens enjoy: people didn't share it equally, and it was almost never sanctioned by an authority. It was a power that emerged, for example, out of structural economic changes: think of the creation of a class of "masterless men" that emerged in early modernity when feudalism could no longer sustain all the people it had sustained and forced many of them to move.[14] It was also a power that came from changing notions of religious authority and religious hierarchies: just think of the Protestant slogan about the "priesthood of all believers." That this power is not clearly defined or its authorization, if any, identifiable was exactly what made it a political problem. The power

was the power to wreak havoc, to disrupt the existing order, to desta-
bilize. The early modern state's power might have sufficed against
some disruptions, but not all. The state might have been able to re-
press the poor clamoring for bread or better wages, but it often
needed the help—specifically, the purses—of other people (historians call them the bourgeoisie). That, in turn, increased the political
power of the bourgeoisie.

The early modern state, in other words, faced possibly restive and
increasingly powerful groups of people. It could naturally try to placate them. The promise of justice was one such way. Whether such efforts were sincere or literally just attempts to placate, the means could
be the same. That is why the normative and the empirical conceptions
of the state merge. They merge uneasily, this book argues. It is a structural feature of modernity. To demonstrate it requires attention to
both the ideals and the practices; hence my interest in theorists and
the worlds in which they find themselves theorizing.

The politics this book explores is always related to but necessarily
outside the "official" institutions of the state. This is because it requires that individual people themselves demonstrate their claims to a
political status: the state *cannot* stipulate a person's respect-worthiness,
I argue; it can't make a person autonomous by fiat. The extrastate political space where these practices happen is what we now call civil society. Civil society itself looks radically different at the historical moments I cover: we can hardly talk of civil society in the eighteenth
century; it exists uneasily alongside the weakly democratic state in the
late nineteenth and early twentieth centuries; and at our own fin de
siècle, the liberal democratic state and civil society mutually reinforce
one another. *Whom* civil society includes also changes radically in the
period. It is no coincidence that it is social space with more and more
people in it: mass politics and mass culture are two of the phenomena
social theorists regard as textbook features of modernity.

One currently popular way of thinking about civil society is that it
serves as a school for the political virtues a democratic citizen needs.[15]
That is occasionally true, but I show here first that civil society can be
political in its own right and second that the nature of civil society
varies radically depending on the kind of politics that take place in it.
Can civil society be a site where we sort out what equality of opportunity means or where we challenge the problems that arise in capital-

ist society, for example? Or can it instead just be a place for free but apolitical associational life? The answer is yes and no: there can be apolitical, free, voluntary practices and pursuits in civil society, but it is also—and necessarily—a site for political activity. It offers resources for making things political; moreover, it is the only place where some kinds of politics by autonomous citizens can take place.[16]

Getting Physical

The debates this book explores reflect not only abstract ideas about what it means to be a person and a citizen but also the idea that personhood and citizenship are fundamentally physical. For example, whether you are autonomous, it turns out, depends on what you do as a physical being. This may seem trivial, but it is anything but. Physical culture both serves as a metaphor for political culture and *is* political during the episodes I describe. It is a kind of normative playground or moral laboratory for society. This remains true today. In modern society—most of the period I cover in this book—the most common aspect of physical culture is the wide world of sports.

In a general way, sports reflect society's broader ideas about merit and excellence, fairness and norms. They are profoundly conventional—which is to say, cultural—creations of human agency. A. Bartlett Giamatti suggests that sports, like the arts, reflect two of humankind's highest aspirations: self-knowledge of one's freedom, on the one hand, in a community shared by mutual agreement, on the other.[17] You don't have to agree with Giamatti's formulation to think sports are indeed an important cultural site in which at least our modern society tries to sort out many of its broader value commitments.

Let us specify these dimensions. First, sports are a social practice the whole point of which is the idea of achieving something others value as praiseworthy. Second, in sports, this praiseworthiness depends on *competition:* to the extent that some people do something better than others, those achievers are ranked as more praiseworthy than those others, and whoever is better than everyone merits the most praise. This competitive dimension is a *constitutive* norm—that is, it makes the practice what it is. There are many other social practices that are about the pursuit of excellence but where competition is not constitutive: the arts, for example. Further, in sports, the standards of excellence are supposed to be as clear as they come. This isn't quite true: sure, there are objective measures, but their application depends on what categories are salient, as we will see later. And sports are an important set of practices in civil society: engagement in sports either as a participant or as a spectator is almost entirely voluntary. Citizens can choose between different kinds of engagement in sports—spectator or participant, golfer or a gymnast—or simply choose *not* to engage in them at all.

Finally, the focus on sports and physical culture gives us purchase on the enduring question of what role nature plays in politics. The scientific picture about what is and isn't "natural" is different at each of the different moments. That profoundly affects what kinds of differences between human beings we count as salient. Is the human body the window to a person's soul, as the Victorians thought? And how are supposedly natural differences between, say, men and women, salient? Salient for what? Where is the boundary between natural and nonnatural differences?

Be a Man?

The natural and social differences we have come to call sex and gender, respectively, aren't the only differences that matter in this book, but they crop up with surprising regularity. The crude but in the first instance helpful way of thinking about sex is that it is a biological category about primarily reproductive differences between males and females, whereas gender is about the social roles of men and women as well as the social norms appropriate for those roles. Those are the norms of masculinity and femininity. Most species of animals have sexes; very few—possibly only humans—have genders. One of the enduring questions in the study of gender has been about the almost universal overlap of sex and gender, of the roles of men to biological males and the roles of women to biological females, with all the attendant (and problematic) assignment of norms and values. It's a problem simply because we no longer take the "natural" (biological facts about ourselves) as "normative" (as something that ought to be so). Just because you were born with short-sightedness doesn't mean you should die by the age of six because you can't see the scorpion in your shoe: we invented eyeglasses to prevent that. Ditto for antibiotics, fluoride, and breast pumps. So why should anyone think that just because your plumbing makes it possible for you to give birth while mine doesn't you should be making the coffee and I the decisions?

But clearly we have not done away with the effects of these biological differences for the ways our lives turn out. Partly it is because differences make a difference, as I argue in chapter 5. But the way they make a difference needn't mean endorsing sexist prejudices. This is, in large part, a book about gender, even outside chapter 5. It could be a book solely about gender, so important is that social category, I believe, for how we continue to organize our lives together as human beings. How to capture that importance while attending to other relevant factors, given the limited resources of the author and the limited patience of the reader? (You didn't want a book that had 1,642 pages, did you? Not on this topic, not written by me.) First, there is a difference in what people say and do, on the one hand, and what a scholar writing about them says, on the other. Gender could be what we call an analytic category—a useful lens through which to look at the world—in all my cases. At the same time, it doesn't always register *at all* for the people whose views and practices I explore. For example, I show in chapter 2 that gender explains a lot of Kant's thinking about dueling, even though he hardly notices the social category. That's because the differences we now know are social seem like a given to him, a bit of the furniture of the world not worth analyzing. (No one writing about the median voter theorem begins with an analysis of why the sun rises.) That's roughly why Kant—like so many of his contemporaries—remains inattentive to gender as something to analyze. This remains true even and particularly when he writes about men and women, which makes his analyses tortured but interesting. He is taking the eight-hundred-pound gorilla—the social category of gender—in the middle of the room for a piece of furniture.

But the question was how *I* should deal with gender in this book. My approach is twofold. First, while gender is a helpful analytic category in all the cases I explore, it is helpful to varying degrees. For example, it is crucial for my argument about dueling; it is important but not central for how I discuss the education of children. Second, gender sometimes does matter as a political category for the people I explore: they themselves, and not just this retrospective scholar, are aware of its importance. This is true, for example, to some extent in chapter 4 and to a great extent in chapter 5. This approach may not fully satisfy either the reader who would want to see gender as more central than it currently is or the reader who sees it as irrelevant, but as I suggest in the conclusion, it does very much reflect our age's uncertainty about how gender figures and should figure in our political thinking.

It's Not Just the Economy, Stupid

During Bill Clinton's 1992 presidential campaign, his adviser, James Carville, coined a slogan that soon acquired a life of its own: "It's the economy, stupid." It was a reminder that what really mattered for Americans was the condition of the economy. Carville thus joined an illustrious pedigree of politicians and political thinkers: politics is about the distribution of economic resources. In contrast, this book is quite silent on economic matters and resources more broadly, even though competition and political economy seem closely connected. Here is an explanation for the silence.

Why do we compete? The usual story, which students of political theory learn from Thomas Hobbes or David Hume or Adam Smith or Karl Marx, is that when there is a relative scarcity of resources, we start competing for them. That seems intuitively plausible. But, in fact, it's not at all obvious that the fact of scarce resources automatically makes us compete. After all, Hume added our "confin'd generosity" as a reason for the competition.[18] If we all loved one another, we might respond to relative scarcity by recognizing a problem of distribution: How do we make sure that we have enough for everyone? In other words, something has to make us want to compete for the resources. That is, something has to make me see you as a potential antagonist in search of the same resources and think that my getting what I want is *so* important that it should motivate me even in the face of the knowledge that you might not get what you want or need.

It is not obvious that we think that way. Ethicists and economists differentiate between relative and absolute scarcity for precisely the reason that they think different norms apply depending on whether there would be enough for everyone as long as we figured out a way to distribute things (relative scarcity) or whether there simply isn't enough for everyone even to survive (absolute scarcity). The instances of the latter are rare enough that they deserve their own name—lifeboat ethics—and an entirely different set of considerations.

Another question we might ask is whether competition for *stuff* is really quite as primordial as Carville and other political economists like to think. In some ways, it obviously has to be: if you don't have any stuff—food, say—you aren't going to be around to compete for scholarships, gold medals, Academy Awards, and your friend's acclaim. But modern economists have pointed out that what we need depends in part—though of course only in part—on what we *think* we need. And that thinking, in turn, is informed by what we think we deserve.[19] "Really, Mom, to keep my title as Poughkeepsie's pie-eating champion, I *need* to eat three peanut butter pies a day." So competition is never just about stuff. It is, instead, about social things and in particular about meanings.

Hobbes knew this.[20] He said that we are driven to quarrel with others because we seek glory.[21] Sure, glory is a form of power and so ultimately a currency convertible to stuff. But if that were all, we'd stop seeking glory once we had our bellies full. And we know that is not true. In fact, the classical political economists—who include both Smith and Marx—knew that what we want goes far beyond what we actually need. And what we need, recall, depends on what we think we need, which depends on what we think we deserve.

Things begin to look a bit circular, and indeed they are. This isn't a vicious circularity; it is an interesting one that tells us that it is very difficult to claim that competition for stuff is primordial. Instead, competition is highly contingent on a host of things, only some of which are the sorts of resources that make us survive. Thus it should come as no surprise that what *competition* means and what we think we compete for and win varies—culturally, historically, linguistically, and in all sorts of other ways, as we will see.

Family Quarrels and Snapshots

Michel Foucault turned Friedrich Nietzsche's idea of genealogy into a method in the late 1960s, and since then, it has been trendy for a social theorist to claim that what one is trying to do with one's work is to provide a genealogy of this or that set of ideas and practices. The principle of genealogy is straightforward and is most easily illustrated by taking the metaphor seriously. When you engage in a genealogy, you trace the history of a family. There might be a couple of main lines, the Smiths and the Joneses, say, and you might notice how little Jane Smith has Grandma Jones's nose but also those famous Smith blue eyes, despite the recessive blue-eye gene. So little Jane has something from both main lines. That's complicated enough. But cousins Emma and Wilbert Jones are actually adopted—and from different birth mothers, no less—and isn't it shocking, really, how Archibald Smith looks more like the mailman than his father? Like the Smiths and the Joneses, concepts and practices retain family resemblances to earlier ideas in the same family tree but aren't the same thing. And sometimes there's some entirely new blood, bastards and adoptees.

To stick to the kinship metaphors, what I do in this book is not genealogy but an exploration of the quarrels that arise in families. I take sets of issues at different historical moments and try to sort out the relationships and issues between those concepts. They are never entirely straightforward, and the effort is anyway retrospective, so the best I can do is a good-faith effort at understanding why Aunt Pullet just couldn't stand little Maggie and why Uncle Joe had such an uneasy time at church. The different historical quarrels I study might also suggest that they do involve the same family—or at least some distant relatives—all throughout my episodes. As I have suggested in the previous section, there are certainly good reasons to think so. But for the most part, showing that there are connections is not my brief here; it remains possible that the resemblances are coincidental, that it's just another Joe Smith, no relation, that we encounter a hundred years later.

Another metaphor captures how I explore these family quarrels. Over the next several substantive chapters, I provide wide-angle snapshots of sets of political disputes at different historical moments. They are snapshots: they can't begin to cover everything about a historical moment or even everything about the political issues at the moment. At the same time, they are wide angle: they capture quite a bit of ground with pretty good depth of field but also some distortion toward the edges. In other words, although the specific disputes and attendant practices have to do with education, dueling, physical culture, and sports, there will be other recognizable elements related to those practices: the institutions and the building of the state, civil society, broader mass politics, familiar disputes about gender.

Because of the importance of Immanuel Kant in grounding my overall argument, I have tried to make the book friendly to Kant scholars without having those features get in the way of a more general reader. In my discussion of Kant and the other German Enlighteners, I give the relevant concepts in German as well as English. I also cite Kant using the scholarly standard of citing the *Akademie Ausgabe* (the academy edition) of Kant's collected works. This may not interest nonspecialist readers; it should not, I hope, distract them, either.[22]

Although I don't want to make too much of the metaphor of family quarrels or snapshots, it seems appropriate to begin the substantive exploration of such quarrels with children.

::: *part one* :::

one

Kids and *Körperkultur*

On the Difficulties of Fostering Civic Independence

Most citizens of modern liberal democracies endorse equality of opportunity as a fundamental political value. Many people don't think that it is enough—for them, equality demands more than opportunities—and others aren't quite sure what exactly equality means or requires, and for good reason. As I argue throughout this book, those questions are not easily answered. But all the same, many people take this view.

At one time, not all that long ago, equality of opportunity wasn't universally endorsed. It is of recent provenance, a feature of the modern era. The early instances of the demand for equality of opportunity included calls to make "careers open to talents." That simply means that offices and positions should go to those who are competent to hold them and that if there are competing candidates, the offices should go to the most competent people. That someone should have to make that demand sounds baffling to us—What, we might ask, would the alternative be? But alternatives abounded. The two most common alternatives were the aristocratic inheritance and the sale of offices and positions.

We now know that the obvious virtue of the meritocratic principle over the nepotistic and economic principles prevailed, at least theoretically. It wasn't an easy victory, and the difficulties didn't result only from recalcitrance, corruption, and venal selfishness. The people clamoring for careers open to talents immediately recognized the difficulties in the concept, and many of those difficulties are complications in the general concept of equality of opportunity. One of them—the one this chapter addresses—is the question of the *creation* of talent. In the first instance, to make competence a job requirement at all is a great improvement over a situation in which Freiherr von Adlerkreutz's imbecile nephew Karl Heinz gets to be the undersecretary of mine administration just because of who he is, but people soon come to realize that talents themselves are partly social: they depend on background conditions that either have or have not fostered those talents. Or, put in another way, once it is obvious that Karl Heinz should not be the undersecretary, people begin wondering about how best to foster the talents in general that make someone good at the job.

This points to the larger complication that equality of opportunity is very sensitive to: equality at what point? If Joe has a Harvard MBA and Jack dropped out of high school, it may be entirely fair, on a careers-open-to-talents basis, that Joe is hired at McKinsey Consulting and Jack isn't. But if Jack dropped out because he had to take care of his family while Joe enjoyed the benefits of his billionaire parents' wealth, we might wonder whether they were equal in terms of other opportunities and whether equality of opportunity really existed. Most people in the eighteenth century—and quite a bit later, for that matter—weren't terribly exercised about this further complication. After all, almost anyone other than the imbecile Karl Heinz *was* an improvement. But people in the eighteenth century were not entirely blind to this issue, either. It cropped up as a question of education: how to provide the necessary talents not only for the existing set of offices and positions but for the increasing number of increasingly complex offices and positions. The even broader autonomy problem that I identified in the introduction arose in this context, too: the talk of talents and merit only makes sense against a background picture in which sufficiently many people enjoy some kind of civic independence in which *they* are the authors of their choices. There is a difference between "careers open to talents" and "careers assigned to talents": the former allows for the possibility that you should also want the job you are competent to do, while the latter allows for someone—Plato or the East German state, for example—to engineer everything from above. But that very difference also reminds us of a common paternalistic desire even many of us moderns have, against our better judgment, to interfere in people's lives for their own good and ours: "Son, it's great that you want to be a rock star, but your math skills just point more toward accounting than heavy metal."

This chapter explores one of the settings in which these questions about the creation of talent and the fostering of civic independence come together: the increasingly numerous eighteenth-century debates about the rearing and education of children. Such debates were numerous because contemporaries considered the question of children pressing for political reasons. At base, those debates involve the questions of who should be educated and how. They are more generally if a bit more abstractly about conceptions of autonomy, merit, achievement, and the roles of nature and nurture. We should not be surprised when, as I show, the question of *physical* education emerges as an important part of the debates about education as soon as theories we'd recognize as modern arrive on the stage. One of this book's arguments is that such modern ideas as "moral personhood" and "intrinsic dignity" and "equal citizenship" not only are *about* embodied physical beings—we already knew that—but are necessarily physical themselves.

This chapter shows how a dynamic relationship between the upbringing of real children and metaphorical children—the currently immature masses—works politically. I concentrate on educational reformers, although I spend some time on conservative opposition to reform as well. As in chapter 2, I dwell on Immanuel Kant's treatment of these topics. His thinking of real and metaphorical children in particular is helpful: he was a theorist with a penchant for metaphors, and children and child-related images crop up in his works frequently and give us a sense not only of how he and his contemporaries thought about the autonomy problem but also of how a focus on children might help solve it.

Little Creatures

One curious feature of seventeenth- and eighteenth-century portraiture of children is that they tend to look like miniature adults. They often wear adult clothes, and even when they don't, the proportions of their bodies, the expressions on their faces, and their activities suggest that they are not children but small adults.[1]

There are debates about whether modernity invented childhood—that is, whether something we now recognize as childhood existed before the modern period—but something like an obsession about children clearly developed during the eighteenth century.[2] Particularly interesting for our purposes was this mutual dynamic: on the one hand, children stood in for adults—they are the future, after all— but, on the other hand, childhood-related metaphors often described the adult world. Just think of what I called Enlightenment's "autonomy problem" in the introduction: contemporary masses were seen as "immature." To call someone immature is to imply that she is not acting her age: she is like a child. This suggests that if you are concerned about putting an end to the masses' immaturity, you might look to the development of children to see how they become autonomous. The obvious problem with that strategy is that children don't just turn into autonomous adults. They need to be brought up. They need biological and particularly social nurturing. And how they are nurtured affects the way they turn out.

This was well known in the eighteenth century. Enlightenment era thinkers hadn't yet heard Ernst Haeckel's claim that ontogeny recapitulates phylogeny—that is, the biological development of an individual goes through the same stages as the development of the entire species—but it would have been a good metaphor for how many of them thought about individual psychology and historical anthropology. Jean-Jacques Rousseau had suggested that the process whereby humanity had developed and (in his view) been corrupted was more or less recapitulated in every (male) individual during his formative years. And as Rousseau had explicitly spelled out in his hugely influential works, most importantly in *Émile,* education could stop the corrupting processes and instead foster healthy autonomy. There are always new generations to be brought up, and it doesn't take much beyond ordinary common sense to realize that insofar as one wants to effect permanent change in prevailing attitudes, beliefs, and types of personhood, childhood might be the place to start.

You don't even need to be a social reformist to endorse part of this view. Because children are the future, the maintenance of ways of life also requires attention to children: if you are a conservative and want to reproduce not just future generations but future generations that sustain the things that you find worth sustaining, you had better pay some mind to children's upbringing.

None of this means that you must *educate* all children. If a society's continued way of life seems to require the passivity and ignorance of its majority and you are hoping to preserve that society, then you will try to ensure that future generations remain passive and ignorant and make your educational policy pretty selective. Or if you believe humans differ from one another in systematic ways in terms of potential capacities, you might think that education policies ought to acknowledge that and be appropriately tailored. It's called tracking. Varieties of conservatives and elitists have often subscribed to the former view. The latter view has been held by as diverse a group of thinkers and policymakers as Plato and the East German educational authorities, with many perfectly respectable, sane, well-intentioned, and even possibly right-headed folks in between. The very novelty of what we call comprehensive education shows that we didn't always think that people required the same basic education, and mainstreaming special-needs students remains controversial.

The general questions eighteenth-century people asked remain with us: Who should be educated? Who *deserves* to be educated? (This is a tricky one: if education is supposed to generate genuine merit, how can desert enter into the question *before* education?) If there are differences in how people should be educated, what causes those differences? Nature? Nurture? What would education be for? Whom would be it for? Whose responsibility is education?

One of the valuable insights we discover in the eighteenth- and nineteenth-century debates is a serious attention to *what kinds of creatures* the institutions of upbringing and education are supposed to treat. There were separate questions of who could and should be educated and how. Many answers were importantly attentive to details. The debaters' understanding of the details was often wrong, theories of physical and psychological development then being what they were, but that in part makes the discussions so interesting to us.

Although these debates took place all around eighteenth-century Europe and North America (in Benjamin Franklin's writings, for example), I focus here on the German Enlightenment in the late eighteenth century. That intellectual context is not just a good exemplar of the general trends but was particularly influential even beyond the Germanic world. For example, one of the main "educational products" of the late-eighteenth-century German Enlightenment was Joachim Heinrich Campe's rewritten Robinson Crusoe story, *Robinson der jüngere.* First published in Hamburg 1779–80, the book was immensely popular and was available in more than dozen languages before 1800. (I will return to the subject of Campe and his *Robinson*.) More importantly, for my purposes, some of the German educational reformers are the first moderns to introduce *Körperkultur* (physical culture) through physical education as an important part of a school curriculum, with an explicit pedagogical rationale for doing so. As we will see in chapter 3, this German influence will figure prominently even in the more famous setting for physical culture, Victorian England.

Erziehung and *Bildung*

First, a quick clarification of terms. German actually has two roughly corresponding terms for education, *Erziehung* and *Bildung*. The differences between the two are significant. When people talk of the educational models and ideals of the German Enlightenment, they usually focus on *Bildung*. In his answer to the question What Is Enlightenment? to which Kant's contribution is more famous, Moses Mendelssohn had *Bildung* go hand in hand with Enlightenment (*Aufklärung*) and culture (*Kultur*).[3] Although the idea is broad, its modern conception points to education as the cultivation of higher learning not for any instrumental purposes but as intrinsically valuable.[4] Furthermore, it is fundamentally a state of an individual's *inner* landscape—that is, his (or her) cognitive, moral, and spiritual dispositions. *Bildung* does, to be sure, affect the person's actions and even physical way of being in the world but does so only indirectly. The word's etymology is what it suggests to an English-speaker: it is about building. The philosophical conception of *Bildung* is based on a late-medieval idea that *Bildung* describes the state of a person's soul. Although the modern conception is decidedly more secular than the medieval one, we can think of the modern idea in semireligious sense: a person with *Bildung* has a healthy, well-developed soul.

The idea of *Bildung* became particularly important for the so-called Romantics in the late eighteenth and early nineteenth century. Through them, it influenced not only German culture for much of the nineteenth century but also other areas of the continent, and it had a large impact on aesthetic pursuits in general, including fine arts and music. But although *Bildung* was the most famous aspect of Enlightenment education, it wasn't the only one. The other German term for education, *Erziehung,* connotes something slightly less highbrow than *Bildung.* There is no consensus on the exact relationship between *Bildung* and *Erziehung,* but the rough-and-ready distinction is that while *Bildung* culminates in higher education, *Erziehung* is something you might receive even in elementary or vocational school.[5] It may have an instrumental relationship to *Bildung,* but it may also have an instrumental relationship simply to making ends meet as a cobbler, welder, accountant, or lawyer. If *Bildung* is intrinsically valuable, as some of the Romantics thought, *Erziehung* is primarily useful to some other end. This meant that *Erziehung* was the proper education for a person who was not yet mature enough for the autonomy-emphasizing *Bildung.* The precise location of that line was—and remains—a matter of controversy, but at least for children, *Erziehung* was clearly the appropriate approach. So *Erziehung* precedes *Bildung,* for practical and philosophical purposes. But even *Erziehung* doesn't begin in the cradle, so let us backtrack even further: a child's development during what we call the preschool years affects what he or she looks like when she shows up on the first day of school.

Walking Carts and Leading Strings

Here is the story the early moderns—folks somewhat before our eighteenth-century Enlighteners—told of childhood:

> The Infant is wrapped in Swadling-clothes, is laid in a Cradle, is suckled by the Mother with her breasts, and fed with Pap.
>
> Afterwards it learneth to go by a Standing stool, playeth with Rattles, and beginneth to speak.
>
> As it beginneth to grow older, it is accustomed to Piety and Labour, and is chastised if it be not dutiful.[6]

This comes from the contemporary English translation of Johann Amos Comenius's influential illustrated 1658 encyclopedia, *Orbis sensualium pictus* (The Visible World). A woodcut on the opposite page

Fig. 1. Child *(left)* using a walking cart, from Johann Amos Comenius's *Joh. Amos Commenii Orbis sensualium pictus* (1659). (Illustration © The British Library Board. All rights reserved.)

from the text illustrates the *Societas Parentalis* (figure 1). Nothing this brief and general is the whole story of child rearing or even of the ideology of child rearing, but what interests me here is exactly that this short description includes, as a matter of course, the "Standing stool" as the device with which the child "learneth to go." Comenius's Latin has the device as *Serperastro;* his German original is *Gängelwagen* (the original, like its translations, was bilingual). According to the Brothers' Grimm dictionary, it was one of the first printed occurrences of the term in German. The more common English translation is "walking cart."

Closely related to the walking cart are leading strings (*Leitbande* or *Gängelbande* in German). Both the cart and the strings were child-rearing devices commonly used in Europe from the Middle Ages well into modernity. They show up in art and literature; you can see them in, say, seventeenth-century Dutch masters' works, and you can find them in Samuel Richardson's eighteenth-century novels. Metaphorical leading strings make an appearance as late as in E. M. Forster's *A Passage to India.*[7] They were tools to help children learn to walk while their parents tried to balance children's need for self-direction with concern for safety. One doesn't have to be a parent to understand what a crucial watershed learning to walk is. It is particularly crucial in terms of its scale: the entire physical object—that is, the child's body—is now under control of her self-direction in a way that allows her to move to new places and new heights. Her self-direction isn't perfect, of course, nor is it very reflective. Learning to walk thus comes with numerous risks: the child may hurt herself in new ways; in particular, the risks to her head from falling from new heights make things more dangerous. Thus arises the understandable dual pull on parents: walking has to be *her* activity and so ultimately unaided, but at the same time, she by definition does not yet have all the skills necessary to avoid the risks involved.

Gängelwagen is a child-sized version of what we know as a walker, commonly used these days by adults with disabilities and by the elderly. Leading strings are either a kind of harness or simply reins or a leash. Walking carts and leading strings can even serve slightly different purposes: leading strings remain useful long after a child has learned to walk as a way of controlling him. (In this latter use, leading strings still remain in the toolkit of at least the most cautious parents; as of this writing, OneStepAhead.com sells a modern version for $12.95.) But the overall purpose is the same: they are tools that try to balance safety, control, and assistance for someone who can't be trusted to move about by himself.

Perhaps the most important philosopher of autonomy, then and now, has much to say about these two devices. Immanuel Kant likes to use both leading strings and walking carts as metaphors for things he doesn't like in reality. The terms *leading strings* and *walking carts* occur in important places in his works, with sufficient frequency for us to want to explore his discussions. In his famous 1784 essay, "What Is Enlightenment?" both devices show up several times; the first instance is on the first page. Although Kant blames people themselves for their "immaturity"—people prefer not to make autonomous choices because it's easy and safe not to—well-intentioned "guardians" worsen the situation by their paternalism. As Kant makes this point, child-related metaphors get mixed with animal images: after guardians "have made their domesticated animals dumb and carefully prevented these placid creatures from daring to take a single step without the walking cart [*Gängelwagen*] in which they have confined them, they then show them the danger that threatens them if they try to walk alone" (WE 8:35). Soon we also encounter leading strings:

> A revolution may well bring about a falling off of personal despotism and of avaricious or tyrannical oppression, but never a true reform in one's way of thinking; instead new prejudices will serve just as well as old ones as the leading strings of the great unthinking masses. (WE 8:36)

As both passages make clear, the metaphorical walking carts and leading strings constrain thinking. A revolution might remove explicit political restrictions and still leave people unable to think for themselves because they rely on the support of knee-jerk prejudices and other shortcuts.

Elsewhere in Kant's works, the metaphors serve more or less the same rhetorical and philosophical purpose. In the preface to the *Critique of Pure Reason,* leading strings help make a point about the autonomy of reason. Reason should not try to find its principles under nature's guidance: Seventeenth-century scientific revolutionaries

> comprehended that reason has insight only into what it itself produces according to its own design; that it must take the lead with principles for its judgments according to constant laws and compel nature to answer its question, rather than letting nature guide its movements by keeping reason, as it were, in leading strings. (CPR B:xii)

Later in the first *Critique,* Kant notes that "examples are the *Gängelwagen* of the power of judgment, which he who lacks the natural talent for judgment can never do without" (CPR B:174). In both cases, the need for the devices suggests a lack of cognitive autonomy. In the 1786 essay "Conjectural Beginning of Human History," Kant makes a similar point: the development of humankind will ultimately free humanity "from the *Gängelwagen* of instinct to the guidance [*Leitung*] of reason" (CBH 8:115).

Some commentators, most famously Hannah Arendt, have taken

Kant to approve of leading strings and walkers.[8] But that is clearly a mistake. Only in two instances does Kant's use of the metaphors suggest anything even remotely positive. Those two cases both have to do with religion. When it comes to religion as a social phenomenon, Kant's ultimate goal is a situation in which people "believe" (whatever that means) in a purely rational way, without having to rely on organized religion or religious dogma—that is, on unquestioned beliefs. As things progress historically, Kant thinks, the leading strings of "holy tradition" and dogma (*Kirchenglaube*) may be necessary before humanity develops its capacities enough to move to the pure rational, nondogmatic, and noninstitutional religion.

> The integuments with which the embryo is first formed into a human being must be laid aside if the latter is to see the light of day. The *Leitband* of holy tradition, with its appendages, its statutes and observances which in its time did good service become a bit by bit dispensable, yea, finally, when a human being enters upon his youth [*Jünglingsalter*], turn into fetter. (Rel. 6:121; see also Rel. 6:135n)

> If the government were to neglect that great means [of treating the Bible as if it is divine revelation] for establishing and administering civil order and peace and abandon it to frivolous hands, the audacity of those prodigies of strength who imagine they have already outgrown this *Leitbande* of dogma [*Kirchenglaubens*] and express their raptures either in public churches devoted to theophilanthropy or in mysticism, with its lamp of private revelations, would soon make it regret its indulgence. (CF 7:65)

We can put this in slightly less abstruse terms: as long as there are people whose rationality we can't quite trust, dogma will keep them from turning into fanatics. Insufficiently mature people believe they can think for themselves and ignore the sober teachings of the church, but they are wrong. Even here, however, leading strings are only useful transitionally. By the time humanity reaches its metaphorical "youth"—whenever that might be—leading strings risk turning "into fetter."[9] But if Kant likes walking carts and leading strings as metaphors, it is exactly because he does not like the real ones. He thinks they are a bad idea.

The relevant place for such discussion is his very late treatise on education, the *Pädagogik*. Even there, though, it isn't at first glance obvious that he would find them noxious. The whole set of lectures is framed around the dilemma of the historical autonomy problem.

> One of the greatest problems of education is how to combine subjection to legitimate constraint [*den gesetzlichen Zwang*] with one's facility to exercise one's freedom. For constraint is necessary! How do I cultivate freedom when there is constraint? I must accustom my pupil to put up with a constraint on his freedom and to direct him to use his freedom well. (P 9:453)

On its face, this solution suggests that Kant wouldn't have a problem with paternalistic constraints on freedom. But this is really just statement of the abstract principle Kant and most other liberals endorse: freedom, as opposed to license, is intelligible only against some constraints. In the following paragraph he writes that the foremost principle of child rearing is that

> one must grant the child from its earliest childhood freedom in all things (except where it might harm itself, as for example when it tries to grab a knife), as long as this happens so it doesn't impinge on others' freedom—for example, when the child screams or is too boisterously cheerful, it begins to annoy others. (P 9:454)[10]

Later in the book, Kant spends several pages discussing the common methods of teaching children to walk and thoroughly condemns both walkers and leading strings. He especially singles out the latter for an attack; they are not only useless but are "in particular very harmful" (P 9:461). They can, in Kant's view, cause permanent damage to the child's upper body by distorting and deforming the still-soft bones of the rib cage. In general, such "aids" (*Hülfsmittel*) teach children bad habits: children don't learn to walk as steadily on their own feet if they get used to being helped. "It is best," Kant says, "to let the children crawl on the ground until they eventually start walking on their own" (P 9:461). He also thinks people have exaggerated worries about how hard children fall. And, he suggests, letting them fall a few times teaches them better to move lightly and to turn their bodies so that falling is not damaging (P 9:461). Furthermore, Kant wants to disabuse people of the particularly problematic belief that children should never be allowed to fall forward because they will hurt their faces. Quite the contrary: letting them fall forward, he thinks, teaches them to use the most important "natural tool" they have: their hands (P 9:462).

That gets Kant to his overall point: the more "artificial tools" one uses in teaching children, the more dependent they will remain on "instruments." "In general, it would be better if one used fewer instruments right from the start and just let the children learn more things by themselves. That way, they would learn things more thoroughly" (P 9:462). Children's free exercise of their bodies on their own terms and at their own pace makes them stronger, teaches them independence, and gives them ownership of their actions and behavior. The "foremost is that the child always help oneself" (P 9:466).

So artificial aids are bad, and self-direction—even when it means clumsiness and stumbling—is good. This is consistent with the familiar understanding of Kant as an advocate of autonomy, although Kant is interested in physical self-direction in the case of concrete walking carts and leading. But a connection exists between the importance of a child's physical self-direction and his theory of autonomy as "using one's own understanding," which the metaphorical leading strings might hamper. It is little remarked that Kant thinks physical self-cultivation—"gymnastics in a strict sense"—is a moral duty. The importance of the physical thus isn't limited to how children learn to walk; it extends to how children grow up and adults develop themselves.

I will return to this moral injunction to cultivate oneself physically after showing that Kant is far from alone in thinking this way. His views in fact reflect an important educational movement interested in not only making careers open to talents but reforming education in a way that more talent would be on offer and that its provision would be more equitably provided. The movement was called *Philantropinen,* and Kant was one of its many champions. Although his opposition to revolutions is well known, Kant explicitly rejects "slow reformism" and uses a rhetoric of a "speedy revolution" when it comes to changing education policies (APB 2:449). That rhetorical call comes in a pair of short essays—pamphlets, really—that Kant wrote in 1776 in explicit support of the *Philantropinen*'s experimental school in Dessau. I mean *explicit* support: Kant was peddling subscriptions to the school, and the end of the essay contains information on how to buy one from him (APB 2:449, 452). He continued to endorse the school and its ideas throughout his life: even the late *Pädagogik,* published in 1800, has Kant waxing enthusiastic about the school.

Child-Centered Learning, Eighteenth-Century Style

The *Philantropinen* movement emerged in the 1770s, when its founder, Johann Bernhard Basedow, opened his school in Dessau. The school, the Philantropinum, was based on the educational ideas Basedow had outlined in a 1768 pamphlet, *Vorstellung an Menschenfreunde* (A Presentation to Friends of Humanity).[11] Basedow's ideas, in turn, had been heavily influenced by the educational theories of John Locke and Jean-Jacques Rousseau, although Basedow wasn't just parroting them (even if he sometimes quoted both at great length). Rather, Basedow modified the earlier suggestions in many ways and even went against them.

Basedow's thinking had three central and very radical ideas. First, he saw education as a collective good that was in the state's interest and argued that the state, not the church, therefore should be in charge of it.[12] Second, he argued for a *common* education, almost (though not fully) independent of social status (MB 17). Finally, he and the *Philantropinen* in general favored pedagogy we might call child-centered: learning was to resemble play and was to be on the children's terms (MB 42–47; EW 259–60). All are very much in keeping with and inspired by Enlightenment ideals, and I will say a bit more about each before focusing on the final idea.

Basedow did not oppose religious education, but because the goal of all education was the happiness of the state and its citizens, its oversight had to be the state's responsibility (VM 12–19, 33–35; MB 21–27, 185–208). It was fine and in fact desirable that state religion be taught in schools, and schools had no obligation to offer religious education that criticized state religion. However, even state religion had to be taught tolerantly, and the children from religiously dissident families could not be kept from attending schools simply on the grounds of their religion (VM 35–38). Moreover, as we'll see in greater detail shortly, religious education should not begin until a child was capable of understanding it—after the child had already learned many other things (MB 135–47). At the same time, the development of patriotic feelings was an important goal of education (MB 42). But even this was not just for mindless obedience; its purpose was to ensure that all even minimally educated people would have appropriate civic virtues (VM).

The reciprocity between the collective happiness of the state, on the one hand, and the citizens who constituted the state, on the other, undergirds Basedow's second central idea: an education that is far more independent of social status than any previous and many later educational theories had it. Although Basedow thought that the children of the "great masses" and the children of the bourgeois and the gentry might go to different schools, their education would be the same. "Because people of every estate are still people, and children children, the beginning of instruction [in the schools for the better-off people] can be nothing other than what it is in the large schools" for the masses, Basedow said (VM 61). The idea is that at an early age, it is impossible to tell whether someone is going to become more highly educated, so everyone must be offered the same basic skills for practical life (MB 17). In regions with sufficient resources, basic elementary education could be followed by *bürgerliche Schule* (citizen school) at what we could call middle-school level (VM). Even though this began to differentiate educational opportunities, it did so not on the basis of any given individual's resources but based on geography. And, again, even in these schools, the assumption was that whether a child would become more highly educated wasn't predetermined. The emphasis was also on education for practical life, not for further schooling. (VM secs. 23, 39; MB 42) Only at age fifteen, Basedow believed, enough evidence would exist to determine whether a child should be even more highly educated. Perhaps ironically, at that age financial resources came directly back into the picture: only absolute geniuses from poor families should be offered a free high-school and university education at state cost; all others had to show sufficient economic resources to be able to support themselves. Presumably Basedow wasn't after too radical changes in people's economic mobility. Furthermore, the state would strictly regulate the number of people allowed to pursue higher education—that is, schooling past their fifteenth year (VM sec. 19).

These were Basedow's ideas for the infrastructural organization of education. Bringing about such changes alone or even by a small movement, even if the ideas had been less radical, would naturally be slow and difficult process, and the early *Philantropinen* never saw these ideas realized on a large scale. However, the "microeducational" ideas—that is, the actual pedagogy—could be put into practice much more easily. Basedow argued for the immediate establishment of experimental schools, and the Philantropinum tried to fulfill this role. Although experimenting was important because it was impossible to know fully in advance what kinds of methods would work best at different levels, he did have important principles in mind.

These ideas were the most radical part of Basedow's program. I have already mentioned Basedow's idea of the first two stages of education as a preparation for practical *living,* not for school. Basedow didn't, however, emphasize the practical because it was all the common classes would need in the future. After all, these stages of education were for everyone. Rather, the idea was that the practical was something everyone would need, regardless of station in life and future plans. Basedow didn't mean this merely as an empirical observation about the world but as a proposal with its own causal efficacy: it *would* bring about a more egalitarian, republican state.

A set of key pedagogical principles would achieve the practical goals. The central notion was that learning—especially early learning in the common elementary school (*Volksschule*)—was to be on the child's terms. In general, all education should happen with means appropriate to the child's developmental stage. This meant that early teaching should resemble play as much as possible. A full half of a child's day in the *Volksschule* should be some kind of physical (*körperlich*) play or "work" (VM 59). The subjects of the *Volksschule* were the same for all: reading, writing, arithmetic, *Realien* (history and what we would now call elementary social and natural sciences), practical knowledge of nature and of the law. Rote memorization was absolutely banned; instead, children should learn through "real" remembering via playful exercises and practices (MB 95–100). Basedow opposed physical punishment but thought that physical education was important, through both simple gymnastic exercises and physical games (MB 62–65). This is significant and deserves its own discussion, because of both its importance in Basedow's scheme and its influence on later developments.

Here Comes *Körperkultur*

An anonymous 1796 book review in the *Neue allgemeine deutsche Bibliothek* began by calling the Dessau Philantropinum "one of the most beneficial phenomena of our century."[13] This high praise was remarkable—and screamingly controversial—coming as it did at the end of the century of the Enlightenment and a few years after the French Revolution. But it is an opinion very much sympathetic with Enlightenment, and it isn't crazy: of all the experiments inspired by Enlightenment thinking, it wouldn't be hard to argue that a peaceful school might on balance be more beneficial than, say, the terribly bloody revolution across the border.

In the reviewer's opinion, one of the benefits of the Philantropinum had been the introduction of physical education. The book under review was one specifically inspired by that aspect of the Basedowian philosophy: Johann Christoph Friedrich Guts Muths's *Gymnastik für die Jugend* (Gymnastics for Youth). Guts Muths had intended his book for children and youth who weren't able to attend progressive experimental schools or schools at all, as was the case with many upper-class and better-off bourgeois children, who often got their education at home from tutors. Guts Muths's book is a combination of philosophical justifications for exercises, detailed descriptions of those exercises, and discussions of their history and context. It reflected an increasingly popular appreciation for physical education, and Guts Muths made a career of such books: he also wrote *Games for the Practice and Strengthening of the Body and Mind, Intended for the*

Youth, Their Educators, and All Friends of Innocent Youthful Joy and *A Small Self-Study Guide of the Art of Swimming*. *Gymnastik* was quickly translated into other European languages, and as we'll see in chapter 3, it was particularly influential in Britain.

In general, whether or not they considered Basedow's egalitarianism too radical, most reformers agreed on the importance of physical education. Some differences existed, but on the whole, their accord is striking. People generally also thought that the physical was strongly connected to the rational and the moral. In 1790, Peter Villaume wrote in the *Deutsche Monatsschrift*,

> Of all the periods of a human life, none is as important as youth. At this time, the previously weak and undeveloped body receives its perfection and strength. Before this, one could say with a kind of hindsight that the child had only vegetated; now it begins to live. Reason awakens, feelings begin to rule, he rises to the dignity of a moral being.[14]

Bodily development, reason, and dignity—all of them together! And as I already mentioned, even Kant, the supposed paragon of the cerebral, argued for physical exercise as a moral duty:

> Finally, cultivating the *powers of his body* (gymnastics in the strict sense) is looking after the *basic stuff* (the matter) in a human being, without which he could not realize his ends. Hence the continuing and purposive invigoration of the animal in him is an end of a human being that is a duty to himself. (DV 6:445)

Part of the rationale for this injunction is simply the idea that the physical body is where moral personhood necessarily resides in the case of humans (as opposed to, say, angels), so it needs to be maintained. But Villaume's view is explicit, and even Kant is implicit about the existence of a stronger connection between human agency and the physical body.

Villaume's and Kant's points concern the need for physical exercise well into adulthood, but exercise should of course begin quite early. In fact, it begins literally with the child's first steps—leading strings and walking carts. Even budding and inchoate awareness of what my body can and cannot do plays a role in my developing a sense of myself as an autonomous person. Errors and failures are important for learning to understand the limits of that exercise, "for one cannot straightaway do all that that one *wants* to do, without having first tried out and exercised one's powers" (DV 6:477). This is true of all aspects of human agency, but again, when we think of children, it is particularly true of one's physical abilities. So it makes sense, if we return to the Basedowian *Volksschule,* that half of a child's day is spent on physical play and exercise: those are the ways in which the child can be self-directed on her own terms. Young children aren't yet fully rational agents, but they can be self-directed on their own terms: there are *some* things in which they can be the sources of their actions and in which it is only harmful to have their minds fall under the direction of others. So here we have the beginnings of a theory of agency—and of tyranny. Leading strings for the child, like rote memorization or physical punishment for the *Volksschüler,* are an externally imposed form of immaturity. However well intentioned, they are, in this kind of Enlightenment theory, a kind of tyranny.[15]

But even if a wide variety of Enlighteners agreed on the importance of the physical as a kind of baseline autonomy, plenty of room remained for intellectual and political differences. First, a commitment to physical autonomy as a baseline is perfectly consistent with deep social differences. That is, you might think that all humans, whether princes or paupers, have some basic physical abilities that their humanity requires, but you might also think that *other* differences make a prince a prince and a pauper a pauper, and appropriately so. Indeed, the Swiss variant of Enlightenment educational reforms, spearheaded by Johann Heinrich Pestalozzi, stressed the importance of physical education, but it emphasized tailoring education to the pupils' social status and likely future occupation: for some people, physical work would be the *only* appropriate mode of autonomy.[16] The larger background idea is that moral and civic autonomy still differs from the baseline physical autonomy of a "thinly" conceived human being. This view ended up informing the educational legacy of the German Enlightenment. We need to turn to the question of moral education to understand why.

Moral Education and Autonomy

In radical contrast to the prevailing practices and attitudes of the day and in keeping with child-centeredness, Basedow thought religious education could begin only in middle school, when the child had developed a sufficient understanding to make any real sense of it. Otherwise, Basedow suggested, the child's proper understanding and thus *real* faith would be threatened or impeded (MB 122). He outlined these ideas in eight lengthy pieces of advice to parents and educators (MB 135–47); we can get a good sense of their logic from a letter Kant wrote to Christian Heinrich Wolke, the director of the Philantropinum, in support of a friend's son's application to the school. The view Kant outlines is ostensibly that of his friend, Robert Motherby, but what Kant says captures the school's (and Basedow's) pedagogical idea.

> In matters of religion, the spirit of the Philantropin agrees perfectly with the boy's father. He wishes that even the natural awareness of God (as the boy's growth in age and understanding may gradually make him arrive at it) should not be aimed at devotional exercises directly but only after he has realized that these are valuable merely as a means of animating an effective conscience and a fear of God, so that one does one's duties as though they were divinely commanded. (C 10:192)

However, although religious education should be postponed, children's moral development was not unimportant. Proper moral development simply would be hindered by religious education undertaken too early, especially if it took the form of religious memorization—"mere words," as Basedow called it (VM 57). Instead, moral education should include experience-based learning and should proceed through relaxed play as well as through instructive moral conversations (MB 102–7). Perhaps the most famous example of this is Campe's reworked edition of Daniel Defoe's *Robinson Crusoe,* in which Campe interjects helpful instructional conversations between a teacher and a child reader between the narrative chapters.

Robinson der jüngere may strike a twenty-first-century reader as hopelessly clunky and patronizing. It may have struck its contemporary readers and listeners—at least the children—the same way, but it was hugely popular all the same. It was translated into more than dozen European languages within a few years of its publication in Germany in 1780. Because its point was to make its audiences think of it through a familiar framing, the "translations" were more than what we would expect of a translation. For example, one of the many English translations, this one via French and published in London in 1789, begins "at Twickenham," where a gentleman "of the name of Billingsley" has decided to "undertake himself the care of his children's education."[17] Another English version, translated and published in Germany in 1789 "for the use of those, which are learning English," has the relevant family living "in the country, not far from the gates of Hamburg."[18]

The overall point is for the book to model how parents should have conversations about "moral" matters while imparting lessons in morality and knowledge. In his translated introduction, Campe says that his "most important design was, to arrange the circumstances and adventures so, as to be productive of many moral remarks, and natural occasions for pious and religious sensations, adapted to the understanding and hearts of children."[19]

In the English translation via French, Mr. Billingsley is telling his children about Robinson's childhood. The one girl expresses ignorance, while the boys show greater moral and intellectual maturity.

> *Mr. Billingsley:* One day, when, according to custom, he was strolling about the the streets, he met one of his old playfellows, whose father was captain of a ship trading to Amsterdam, and who had just come down from Plymouth to see some his relations. . . . He told Robinson that he was to set off with his father in a day or two for Amsterdam.
> *Charlotte:* What, papa, by the stage?
> *Henry:* No, Charlotte, in a ship; for you must cross the sea to go to Amsterdam. Well, papa.
> *Mr. Billingsley:* He asked Robinson if he should like to go with him. "Yes, very well," replied he, "but my parents will not consent to it." "Pooh!" said the other, "come off with me

as you are, just for the frolick. We shall be back again in a month or six weeks; and as to your father and mother, you have only to let them know that you are gone." "But," says Robinson, "I have no money in my pocket." "You will not want any," replied his companion; "but if you should, I'll supply you."

Young Crusoe hesitated a few moments, at last, slapping his companion's hand, he cries, "Agreed, my boy! I will go along with you: let us set off this moment for Plymouth." At the same time he commissioned one of his acquaintances to let his father know (after the expiration of a few hours), that he was only gone to see the city of Amsterdam, and that he should be back in a week or two.

Richard: I do not like this Mr. Robinson Crusoe.
Edward: Nor I either.
Mr. Rose: Why so, Richard?
Richard: Because he seems to make nothing of leaving his father and mother without their permission.[20]

Using a conversation as a teaching device wasn't Campe's invention. For example, G. F. Seiler's 1772 *Religion der Unmündigen* (Religion of the Immature) had used it for a more conventional catechistic purpose. Whether Campe's tales—whose stakes get higher as Robinson's adventures progress—convinced the children is unclear. There is something slightly ironic in the double purpose of modeling the conversations parents should have with their children, on the one hand, and simply offering those conversations readily digested to the readers and listeners, on the other: if you are convinced by the moral conversations in the book, you'll likely not have them yourself. For imparting knowledge, the method may work, but for a child to develop his or her own moral sense, there would have to be genuine moral dilemmas. The book ultimately doesn't encourage children to think on their own.

Perhaps the Cobbler Should Stay at His Last after All

Whether Basedow would have endorsed this approach to helpful moral conversations is also unclear. Campe had associated with Basedow and taught at the Philantropinum briefly, but the relations of the two were severed in 1777, and Campe left the school, with a few other teachers. The causes of the break were more practical than philosophical: Basedow was by all accounts a terrible manager, particularly in a financial sense, and the school's management difficulties, exacerbated by Basedow's difficult character and drinking problems, made the Philantropinum's everyday significantly less exciting than its ideals.[21]

But philosophical differences existed as well. Despite his influence and despite the public admiration for him (an anonymous call for a Basedow memorial was published in the *Deutsche Monatsschrift* in 1791, a year after his death) the most radical elements in his educational philosophy not only remained unrealized but were either toned down or reversed very quickly. Basedow's 1893 editor, Hermann Lorenz, lamented that the educational ideals weren't anywhere near being realized even in late-nineteenth-century Germany.[22] Eighteenth-century conservatives predictably ridiculed Basedow: outright opponents of any reforms argued that the lack of social differentiation would serve primarily to elevate the common classes.[23] Such reforms would, in this view, give commoners' children skills that would make them uppity and demanding, at worst promoting revolution and at best leading to unhappy and frustrated commoners.

Even Campe and fellow Enlighteners maintained some distance from Basedowian ideas.[24] Campe edited in 1785–92 a massive compendium, *Allgemeine Revision des gesammten Schul- und Erziehungswesens* (General Revision of Common Schooling and Education), which became the overall statement on education in the German Enlightenment.[25] The *Revisionswerk,* as the compendium came to be called, defended the idea that all citizens (*Bürger*) should be educated, but their education should be appropriate for their status and occupation.

The difference is subtle but significant. None of these reformers, including Basedow, was a complete social leveler; even he accepted the predominant view that society is divided into different estates. But his view was more egalitarian than others: straightforward meritocracy ought to guarantee real social mobility at least for the greatest talents. In other words, *some* equalization of opportunity is built into his educational philosophy. The *Revisionswerk* instead takes the position that prior social position—in fact, a child's parents' social position, their class status—should affect in a very big way the way the child's life turns out. Part of the story is that even reformers (along with more clearly self-identified conservatives) think that social class ought to be longer-lasting than the most enthusiastic radicals think. So their education policy in effect affirms the idea that the cobbler should indeed stay at his last; he should just be as good at his work as possible. Careers should be open to talents, but that doesn't mean that careers should be open to all.

We can read the *Revisionwerk*'s position as a slide toward a position that is now identified as classical conservatism. But it isn't quite that or just that: The more conservative position of Campe and his kind reflects first a caution about the effects of too much social mobility, which wasn't an unintelligible concern from people who had witnessed the turmoil of the French Revolution.[26] This is familiar. But the conservatism also reflects a sense that perhaps education *cannot* fully shape people. It is one of the many recurrences of the nature/nurture problem. Even if one is committed to fostering civic independence by bringing up children to be self-directed adults, the question is whether differences should exist in what self-direction looks like in different people. Nature constrains the possibility of what a person can be. Of course, in the twenty-first century, we now tend to think more along Basedow's lines and even beyond: sure, we say, nature constrains and shapes what individuals can be, but such constraints don't track where the individuals find themselves at the start. Being born low doesn't mean you can't aspire to greater things; being born high doesn't mean you really merit the privileges that come with it.

However, I don't want to take our retrospective agreement with Basedow as dispositive that Campe and the other cautious Enlighteners are wrong. We have good reasons to think our position is correct, but it has been long time in the works, and even the caution and conservatism of the eighteenth-century thinkers is intelligible. For them, the origins of inclinations and potential are an open question, as is whether nature's constraints are generational so that they make social distinctions between different "classes" of people deep.

These difficulties about the relationship between upbringing and the ultimate social standing of a person were not solved in the eighteenth century—in Germany or anywhere else. They haven't been fully solved yet, although the terms and stakes of the debates have changed in important ways. One of the key tensions is between what I called the physical baseline autonomy and moral autonomy; it is a question that continues to haunt the nineteenth century, as I show in chapter 3.

Conclusion

First, though, I offer a set of observations on the basis of this discussion to ground the next chapter. All educational reformers I have discussed so far took one social difference—that between boys and girls—as so obviously natural that it wasn't worth much remark. For the most part, this assumption comes across as the silence about women with which we are so familiar from canonical political theory and history. But things are a bit more complicated. First, the German word for a child, *das Kind,* is in the grammatical neuter, and thus the third-person pronoun is also in neuter: when you refer to a child with an *es,* your reader can't know just from the language whether you are talking about a boy or a girl. Even more than grammar, though, what butts against the possibility of a complete silence on girls is sociology: the world of children is not uniformly the world of boys. As the illustration from Comenius's book or the passage from Campe's show, families tend to have girls as well as boys. After all, if family is the "private sphere," as much social theory has tended to think, and if the family is the realm of women and of the feminine, it should not be surprising that we encounter mothers and girls when talking about children in general. They have to be somewhere.

And reformers occasionally seem to have both boys and girls in mind. But as we saw in the Anglicized version of Campe's *Robinson,* presenting the girl as an ignorant ditz doesn't really open up doors for gender equity in opportunities. So, complications aside, the reformers clearly think that the gender difference is essential—boys and girls, like men and women, are fundamentally and unavoidably different. Even when the language suggests neutrality, reformers focus primarily on boys. In Kant's *Education,* for example, a large part of the education in the early teens is to prepare the boy for responsible sexual maturity and to take into account the troubles such maturity presents.[27] Similarly, for Kant, effeminacy in a child is a sign that education has failed him. Kant must, of course, have *him* in mind because effeminacy would be the appropriate goal of the education of girls, were Kant interested in it.[28] In the next chapter, we see the political consequences when a committed egalitarian takes masculinity as a given and believes that gender differences—which we now tend to think are social—are believed to be natural.

two

Dueling for Equality

The Master's Tools Will Take Down the Master's House

Meanwhile, back on the ranch, you can't always wait till the cows come home: Whatever hopes for the future educational reforms carried, they involved a definite delay. Also, the reformers focused on the first part of the autonomy/dignity equation. The question of a person's worth—dignity is a kind of worth, as the German *Würde* for both suggests—is different, if even related, question. This chapter directly addresses the question of worth and focuses on a very different social practice: dueling. The political changes that emerged as a result of political and theoretical debates weren't much more immediate than the outcomes of educational reforms, but the actual political dynamics in dueling were more direct: they weren't about the future generations but were about the actors themselves.

One history of Western politics has it that under modernity, equal *dignity* has replaced positional *honor* as the ground on which individuals' political status rests.[1] Now, the story goes, the dignity which I have by virtue of nothing more than my humanity gives me both standing as a citizen vis-à-vis the state and a claim to respect from others. Earlier, my political status would have depended first on who I was (more respect for the well-born, less for the lower orders) as well as on how well I acquitted myself *as* that sort of person. In rough outline, the story is correct, but it has important complications. One of the most important of them is that aristocratic social practices and values themselves get used to ground and shape modernity. This chapter explores one such mechanism and its consequences.

Dueling was one of the key practices in a culture of honor throughout the Western world: it was a means by which claims of honor were made, maintained, and understood. It emerged out of medieval "trial by combat" in the sixteenth century and was, despite some regional variation, a common phenomenon in Europe and North America until the nineteenth century.[2] Although dueling has been obsolete long enough to strike many of us a patently irrational, it took a long time to fade away; its story is one of slow decline, with odd bumps along the way. The contours of its fading capture an important aspect in the transition to modernity—that is, how the aristocratic conception of masculine honor can be deployed in a politics of equal dignity and how that deployment affects the conceptions of equal dignity. Two things about dueling make this possible. First, the practice distributes respect; second, dueling is necessarily an extralegal practice—that is, one that is outside the direct regulation of the state. This combination allows people to make claims to equality as individuals. That is the main argument of this chapter. But because the honor in dueling is *masculine* honor, presupposing a subordinate feminine honor that the masculine defends, it gives content to equal dignity in a way that forecloses, at least contingently, claims of gender equality. These are not independent of one another: many people in transitional moments want to preserve at the same time that they reinterpret some of the aristocratic values, in part because they worry about the ways some conceptions of equal dignity threaten what from their perspective is an ordered and meaningful universe.

This chapter illuminates one important mechanism in the shift from premodern, aristocratic value system to a modern one, focusing on the role of dueling in that transition. Social theorists, I argue, played a role in that transition; I continue to focus here on Kant, whose treatment of dueling not only helps us understand it as an intelligible practice in its own right but also offers a reinterpretation that makes the practice compatible with the modern value of equal dignity. This is because Kant's conception of a person requires that for someone to have dignity in social life, he must respond to challenges to that dignity, and the relationship of social equality that dueling involves provides a model for this theory.

I begin by describing dueling during the long transition between the decline of aristocracy and modernity. I then zero in on what I call the moral economy of dueling, doing so largely through Kant's eyes. Kant believes that some aristocratic values embedded in social hierarchies are worth retaining because the values help ground the values we associate with modernity. But he also believes that modernity itself threatens the coherence of aristocratic values. His solution to the paradox between these tendencies helps us understand what I call the path-dependencies of dueling in the service of equality: it remains necessarily masculine. Finally, the discussion of dueling helps illustrate the role of the state to dueling and why the state necessarily must keep a distance to some practices in civil society.

What Is Dueling?

Dueling, Francis Bacon suggested in 1614, was "a desperate evil." He listed the reasons: "[I]t troubleth peace, it disfurnisheth war, it bringeth calamity upon private men, peril upon the State, and contempt upon the law."[3] A few decades later, Cardinal Richelieu echoed Bacon. Dueling was, he wrote in his *Political Testament,* "pernicious evil [*dangereux mal*]" and a "disastrous madness [*une frénésie qui . . . cause tant de mal*]."[4] Many contemporaries and even more historians agreed. Bacon was cited with approval well into the eighteenth century, and he seems to confirm our own Enlightened view of dueling as an irrational throwback.[5] George Sabine, an American commentator, wrote in 1855,

> Duelling, as everybody knows, is a relic of the Dark Ages. Among the ignorant and superstitious people with whom it originated, and even under the institutions of chivalry, there may have been some excuse for it. But in the present state of civilization it cannot be justified; and this is the common remark.

But he is not merely reflecting on an antediluvian practice; he is lamenting its staying power.

> Yet it is still prevalent to an alarming extent, and simply because warworn veterans who are covered with scars, and judges in robes, and clergymen in surplices, and statesmen who lead legislative bodies or preside in cabinet councils, continue to afford it either example or countenance.[6]

Sabine is troubled because something putatively irrational appeals to social elites who certainly should know better: "judges in robes," "warworn veterans," "statesmen."

At the beginning of the nineteenth century, the German bourgeoisie began to duel.[7] We might have expected precisely the opposite: the bourgeoisie is the sociological avant-garde of the Enlightenment: it most immediately benefits from talent and wealth replacing birth as marks of status, and its ascendancy ought to extinguish rather than spread aristocratic legacies.[8] As late as 1910, none other than social theorist Max Weber was ready to challenge a man to a duel in defense of Mrs. Weber's honor.[9] That challenge never got issued, and at any rate, nineteenth-century German dueling was largely nonlethal, but the new enthusiasm for it remains a puzzle. Equally puzzling is the ambivalence of modern theorists, especially in the eighteenth century, toward it: for example, Montesquieu, Rousseau, and Kant are far more measured about dueling than are Bacon and Richelieu. If the sixteenth century could parody as absurd the idea that anybody but aristocrats would duel, the late-eighteenth- and early-nineteenth-century changes were significant.

In a way, dueling had been a source of social and political ambivalence almost from its emergence. Perhaps surprisingly, it is an early-modern phenomenon. It grew out of its medieval precursors, trial by combat and chivalric dueling, in the sixteenth century. In France, the last legally authorized duel occurred in 1547 under Henry II, and in 1550, he issued the first edict against dueling.[10] If its purpose was to curtail dueling, it failed miserably: the practice only gained in currency.[11] Specifically, it became dueling over "points of honor," with several key features.[12]

Dueling is a form of proof. Trial by combat was the earliest Western precursor to dueling. The idea was simple: victory in an officially sanctioned fight simply provided legal vindication. This was true of both criminal and civil cases, "criminal being waged for purgation of an imputed crime, civil when for deciding of controversie touching private wrongs or interests."[13] Because God was taken to have her fingers in these matters, fighting ability could be a proof of rightness because it was a proof of providential choice: "Heaven always gave victory to the right cause."[14] The idea that one simply proves oneself—that is, one's honor—remained a key feature of modern dueling.[15]

Points of honor are personal matters, even when they involve collectives like the kin or estate.[16] Although cultural and historical variation existed on these points, the core components were the same: "the Lie given, Fame impeached, Body wronged, or Curtesie taxed," as the earliest English historian of the duel lists them.[17] The accusation of dishonesty was one of the most frequent grounds for dueling.[18] A blow, which is a violation of one's physical integrity, was also a grave insult.[19] Claims of cowardice generally were important, especially among soldiers (a point to which I will return). Equally common grounds were threats to the man's kin, both in the abstract sense of sullying the family name and in the concrete sense of insults to family members. Among these, insults impugning the sexual integrity and general feminine honor of those women a man was supposed to protect were particularly important.[20] Finally, the question of precedence and broader challenges to a man's status as an aristocrat were significant reasons for dueling.[21]

Dueling is necessarily extralegal. Whether the state officially sanctions, merely tolerates, or tries to end dueling, the practice gets its cultural sanction from aristocratic privilege: the cultural ethos of aristocracy is that aristocrats are people who get to settle some particular disputes extralegally. When duels are no longer part of official procedure, tensions between the monarch and the aristocracy arise. This idea puts some pressure on Weber's conception of the state as the institution with a monopoly over violence: dueling shows that the state is not just delegating its coercive power here but giving away some of its *control* of violence. This is important for the politics of dueling, as I discuss later, and for modern politics in general, as this book shows: much that is political necessarily happens outside the official power and authority of the state.

While extralegal, *dueling is highly ritualized.* Challenges were generally formal, as were the negotiations over weapons, time, place, and the like. The negotiations were commonly done by the duelists' seconds, the use of whom was a shared feature of the practice. The most common weapon for early modern and modern duels was the sword; the pistol became important in many places with the development of firearms.

I now dig deeper into the practice and in particular into its new potential for egalitarian refashioning. The goal is to see how, as Rousseau put it, "[p]oint of honor changed principles."[22]

The Moral Economy of Dueling

In 1794, the new Civil Code of the Prussian States specified that a dueler who killed his opponent would be tried for murder or manslaughter and sentenced to death if convicted.[23] Like similar statutes elsewhere, this was controversial. We have some reason to think that Kant was, perhaps surprisingly, a critic of the statute.[24]

Kant discusses dueling, briefly, in two late works: first in the political part 1 of the *Metaphysics of Morals* (the so-called *Rechtslehre*), and a few times in the *Anthropology from a Pragmatic Point of View*. In the *Rechtslehre,* Kant discusses two kinds of homicide that deserve the death penalty but in which the state has no legitimate power to impose it: a mother murdering her illegitimate child and a soldier killing another soldier in a duel (RL 6:336). This is because legislation "cannot remove the disgrace of an illegitimate birth any more than it can wipe away the stain of suspicion of cowardice from a subordinate officer who fails to respond to a humiliating affront with a force of his own rising above fear of death" (RL 6:336) In the former case, Kant explicitly says the action turns on the woman's "honor of one's sex [*Geschlechtsehre*]," in the latter, on military honor. Both reflect "indeed true honor, which is incumbent as duty on each of these two classes of people" (RL 6:336).

Gender is important in the distinction. Arguably, *both* cases turn on "honor of one's sex," or, as we might prefer to translate Kant's ambiguous term, on *gender honor:* as we saw earlier, one key feature in dueling is that it exemplifies manly virtue in defense of women's honor. I will return to this idea when I discuss the limits to the egalitarian refashioning of dueling. First, I explore the relationship between true honor and the manly honor demonstrated in a duel.

In Kant's political theory, the purpose of the state is to create conditions in which humans can attain their full moral autonomy.[25] To put it in Kant's language, the state is to create the conditions of "external freedom," which are the preconditions for full "internal freedom." Under perfect conditions of external freedom, laws on the one hand and morality on the other would converge because people would have no morally valid reasons to act immorally; conversely, their sociologically bound *interests* would always converge with the right moral *rea-*

sons. Such perfect conditions did not exist in the Prussia of the late eighteenth century, and the political question for Kant's theory is to identify dynamics that would bring such a convergence closer.

Elisabeth Ellis has recently argued that a theory of provisional right is one centerpiece of Kant's political theory. Roughly, practices and institutions that are consistent with a transformation to a perfect republican order are provisionally legitimate; those that are inconsistent with such a transformation are illegitimate.[26] In a way, this principle is a historical-political version of the categorical imperative in Kantian ethics. The categorical imperative enjoins moral agents to act only on those maxims—principles of action—they could at the same time conceive as universal laws. This way, lying cannot be permissible because a principle of action relying on lying cannot be universalized without its becoming self-defeating. Analogously, the historical-political version proscribes principles that would defeat the possibility of a transformation to a social order in which everyone's external freedom is fully realized. Kant thus comes to think that a hereditary aristocracy is provisionally legitimate even though the principle of inherited merit is incoherent and theoretically indefensible. "Since we cannot admit that any human being would throw away his freedom, it is impossible for the general will of the people to assent to such a groundless prerogative [of hereditary title]," he says (RL 6:329). But the state has "a provisional right to let these titled positions of dignity [*Würde dem Titel*] continue until even in public opinion the division into sovereign, nobility and commoners has been replaced by the only natural division into sovereign and people." He later says that a "nobility is a temporary fraternity [or faction, *Zunft*] authorized by the state, which must go along with the circumstances of time and not infringe upon the universal right of human beings which has been suspended for so long" (RL 6:370).[27]

But why, we might ask, should a "titled position of dignity" be respected even provisionally if it does not make sense? Part of the answer is that respecting it *does* make sense if people, through "public opinion," believe it does. And people may be, at least to some extent, right. Here, Kant's discussion of the dueling soldiers illustrates why. The point is not that the dueling soldiers are aristocrats; they might be, but by the late eighteenth century, they likely were not. Rather, it is because the reasons that make it illegitimate for the state to punish them reflects the reasons titled positions of dignity may exemplify real dignity.

The overall argument is that the dueling soldiers may have acted on a legitimate moral incentive and chosen the appropriate action to demonstrate it. When someone challenges your claim to dignity, you must somehow demonstrate that you do indeed have it. Not to do so would mean forfeiting it. *You* must do the demonstrating because you have to show you are a respect-worthy person. So it does not really matter whether the person who challenges my claim to dignity is mistaken; my response to the challenge proves it to be false. The response cannot be easy, which connects the issue to real honor. The analytic value of dueling is therefore twofold. First, it is a system that already has connected a person's *worth*—that is, his dignity—to *autonomous activity* through the *character* concept of honor. Kant does not change that fundamental set of relations in his reinterpretation of the dueling ethos. But he does broaden the meanings of those concepts and how those relationships are properly expressed: after his reinterpretation, it becomes easier for social inferiors to challenge social superiors, for members of the bourgeoisie to challenge aristocrats, for noncommissioned officers to challenge commissioned officers. Second, dueling is useful because its ethos involves a relationship of fundamental equality: the eligibility to demand or give satisfaction to honor challenges (*Satisfaktionsfähigkeit*) requires a relationship of equality between the duelists. In slightly different words, it implies a kind of respect for the other.

This analysis deliberately blurs what might seem like psychological and moral registers, which, the textbook reading of Kant's moral theory insists, ought to be kept strictly apart. Kant is not confused about the fact/value distinction but is trying to solve a problem the fact/value gap creates: he explains the relationship first between an individual's *moral reasons* and *sociologically bound interests* and second between those two and the *causal powers* and the *legitimacy* of political institutions.

Dueling is a form of proof or, as we might say with anachronistic language, a signaling practice. What it signals in the first instance is a specific status; what makes that status legitimate are the honorable character attributes on which it is based.

Autonomy and Extralegality

First, the honorable dueler has to act autonomously. By "autonomy," I do not yet mean a full-fledged Kantian moral autonomy, although there is a connection, but simply the idea that an autonomous man acts for himself. (This is not a requirement for feminine honor; indeed, the proper expression of feminine honor is obedient dependence on one's father or husband.)[28] As I quoted earlier, law cannot "wipe away the stain of suspicion of cowardice from a subordinate officer who fails to respond to a humiliating affront *with a force of his own* rising above fear of death" (RL 6:336; emphasis added). An accusation of cowardice is a claim that you lack the most important trait your position as an officer requires and implies. The only possible response to such a claim is to disprove it with a demonstration: I must show that I am indeed willing to face death. Were I to sue you for libel, I would already have failed: it would demonstrate the truth of *your* claim. A British commentator had said the same thing somewhat earlier: "Courage is one great Ingredient of good Souldiery: And it might seem to Impeach their Courage should the attempt their Vindication by those formal Steps [of law]."[29] Dueling does not have to be illegal, but it does have to be extralegal in that it is up to me to do the demonstrating required.

So law should not punish where it cannot help—that is, where a stronger social custom overrides its regulatory force. Thomas Hobbes already thought that given the mixed standards of law and attitudes about men's conduct, if "thereupon he accept duel, considering all men lawfully endeavour to obtain the good opinion of them that have the sovereign power, he ought not in reason to be rigorously punished; seeing part of the fault be discharged on the punished."[30] In his "Letter to M. d'Alembert on the Theatre," Rousseau thinks that French attempts to end dueling by banning it are ill conceived.[31] Legal proscription involves "a shocking opposition between honor and the law; for even the law cannot oblige anyone to dishonor himself."[32] Honor is about *individuals'* necessarily extralegal incentives, and an external authority cannot as a matter of conceptual logic "impose itself" into conflicts involving honor.

For example, Captain Macnamara defended himself at the 1803

trial where he faced charges of murder after having killed his opponent, Colonel Montgomery, in a duel in London:

> Gentlemen, I am a captain in the British navy. My character
> you can only hear from others; but to maintain my character
> and station, I must be respected. When called upon to lead
> others into honorable danger, I must not be supposed to be a
> man who had sought safety by submitting to what custom has
> taught others to consider a disgrace. I am not presuming to
> urge anything against the laws of God or of this land. I know
> that, in the eye of religion and reason, obedience to the law,
> though against the general feelings of the world, is the first
> duty, and ought to be the rule of action. But in putting a con-
> struction upon my motives, so as to ascertain the quality of my
> actions, you will make allowances for my situation. It is impos-
> sible to define in terms the proper feelings of a gentleman; but
> their existence have supported this happy country many ages,
> and she might perish if they were lost.[33]

There may be some irony in the fact that Macnamara and Montgomery had dueled over their dogs, but Macnamara argued that it
"was not the deceased's defending his own dog, nor his threatening to
destroy mine, that led me to the fatal catastrophe; it was the defiance
which most unhappily accompanied what was said."[34] The argument,
perhaps buoyed by the character references from three of Macnamara's admirals, including Lord Nelson, got him acquitted. Character
references and Macnamara's argument may in fact go together: he is
an honorable man in general because he understands the nature and
respects the value of custom. This custom, as Macnamara pointed
out, goes to the heart of what it means to be a gentleman.

Even such a committed opponent of dueling as Sir William Blackstone understood this logic about why the particular custom trumped
law. He considered a duel an aggravating circumstance in a homicide,
an instance of "express malice," but nevertheless lamented,

> Yet it requires such a degree of passive valor, to combat the
> dread of even undeserved contempt, arising from false no-
> tions of honor too generally received in Europe, that the

strongest prohibitions and penalties of the law will never be entirely effectual to eradicate this unhappy custom, till a method be found out of compelling the original aggressor to make some other satisfaction to the affronted party, which the world shall esteem equally reputable, as that which is now given at the hazard of the life and fortune, as well of the person insulted, as of him who hath given the insult.[35]

What makes such a custom an "unhappy" one is exactly that it leads people into lethal encounters over words about their dogs, but it is nevertheless intelligible. Moreover, it is intelligible in a way that has it trump law: the social meaning of the custom is deeper than the rationality of law.

None other than the creator of modern police force, Sir Robert Peel, "distrusted the efficacy of legislative changes."[36] As late as 1880, Austrian politician Otto Hausner, reviewing European laws against dueling and the frequency of the practice, wondered whether "there can be any clearer evidence against the usefulness of these laws than the fact that in Holland and Norway, where duels are not punished, there are far fewer duels than in France, where it is classified as a manslaughter."[37]

Law fails because public opinion prevails. Rousseau hoped to bring about a change in *l'opinion publique* as a solution to the problem of dueling.[38] That change would require a separation of a man's respect-worthiness from his autonomous defense of his honor. To understand the possibility of the change, we first need to understand what makes such autonomous defense legitimate and, from Kant's perspective, even valuable.

Honor as a Legitimate Incentive: Moral Courage and Equality

Kantian morality appreciates our penchant for avoiding shame; in fact, avoiding shame is required by morality because shame threatens the self-respect we owe to ourselves (see, e.g., DV 6:420, 434–37; LE 27:349). This is directly related to courage. As we saw, courage is the key component of military honor. But military courage expressed by one's willingness to risk one's life is only one contingent realization of courage.

A more general courage is connected to real honor, maintaining the dignity we have by virtue of our humanity. At first, this seems paradoxical: Why would I need to *maintain* something that I have by virtue of my humanity, simply by being a Homo sapiens? There is no paradox: First, "humanity" is not a thin biological concept but points to our being "subject[s] of morally practical reason"—that is, beings that can reason autonomously and act on that basis (DV 6:434). It is "the capacity to set oneself an end—any end whatsoever" (DV 6:392). Second, just as you can disrespect me by denying my humanity, *I* may disrespect myself. One *can* forfeit one's dignity, Kant thinks, but one *may* not (DV 6:435). Morality enjoins me to live in a way that does not amount to self-disrespect. Although Kant explicitly says that a person's dignity as a person (as opposed to as a physical animal) is independent of time and place ("Someone who, a hundred years from now, falsely repeats something evil about me injures me right now," he says [RL 6:295]), it is also clear the meanings of honor and dishonor *and thus of dignity* are time-bound.[39] The duty of self-respect can be recognized in ordinary moral dicta: "Be no man's lackey.—Do not let others tread with impunity on your rights" (DV 6:436). To have courage, then, is to be able to live according to those dicta even when someone tries to make you his lackey or treads on your rights.[40] In a world in which refusal to respond to challenges to my honor would mean forfeiting my dignity as a person, morality requires that I respond. Dueling can stem from legitimate moral motives. But that is not all: the practice of dueling—that is, responding to *and even issuing challenges*—also models a worthy social relationship, Kant thinks: equality.

The idea of modeling is important. Whatever our ideals about metaphysically grounded reasons for regarding all humans as universally and necessarily equal, the sociological fact is that social relations are realized only contingently in practice. If we want to see our ideals realized, we need to look for practices that emulate them; we also need to understand which practices model social relations that are inconsistent with the ideals.

This kind of search is part of what is going in Kant's discussion of dueling in his *Anthropology*. There, an analysis of military dueling is sandwiched into a general treatment of courage, including "moral courage." Moral courage is displayed, for example, in a person's willingness to pursue steadfastly a worthy goal even when it *is being ridiculed* by others (A 7:257). This is not a trivial kind of courage: even "many people who prove their bravery in the battlefield or in a duel" might lack it (A 7:257). Why? Because, as Kant spells out in the *Doctrine of Virtue,* ridicule is a type of malice, and it models an unworthy social relationship: ridicule is holding up another person's "real faults, or supposed faults as if they were real," to "deprive him of the respect he deserves" (DV 6:467). The paralyzing thing about ridicule is that in so disrespecting a person, it invites a defensive response while denying the possibility of one. For you to mock a person in a humiliating way is to insult her and simultaneously deny that she can do anything about it. Dueling, in contrast, by its logic acknowledges the possibility of a vindication of the challenged honor. A challenge is, in other words, a form of respect.

We might interpret the emergence of dueling among the German bourgeoisie and thus the "democratization" of dueling in general against the backdrop of this aspect of Kantian analysis: Where the abstract rhetoric of equal dignity requires some way of making it practically intelligible, dueling is one available means, for two reasons. It is a practice with which a man proves his honor. In Kant's analysis, we now have a much closer relationship among honor, respect-worthiness, and general human dignity than was previously the case. Kant has shown that the physical courage of a dueler is a contingent realization of the broader worth of the autonomous person, *not* of the intrinsic worth of an aristocrat qua aristocrat. Second, the relationship in dueling presupposes equality between the duelers. This means that if a person successfully challenges a social superior to a duel, then, for that specific moment at least, the social superior ceases to be one and becomes an equal. To succeed in a challenge to a duel just *is* to enjoy respect as an equal.

These two dimensions have to go together for dueling to become a means for the politics of equal dignity. This is a conceptual point in the service of a historical fact: the democratization or social leveling of dueling emerged; it did not always exist. Inferiors may always have launched some challenges, but they were sufficiently few not to register as a social phenomenon. The first dimension that decouples honor from aristocrats qua aristocrats has to be understood well enough so that aristocrats cannot just refuse inferior challenges as contemptible category errors. At the same time, dueling must still be understood to exemplify honor so that social superiors cannot just abandon the practice, like they might abandon something as déclassé because it is tainted by parvenu enthusiasm. And because the honor involved in duel is courage in the face of possibly lethal violence, a refusal can be risky. A social superior may try to insist on the formal hierarchies ("You, commoner, are beneath my notice as a challenger"), but that refusal may leave a nagging doubt that it stems from fear and not from confident superiority. In other words, this ambiguity has to be palpable enough for inferiors to force their superiors into these acknowledgments of equality. I have suggested that analyses such as Kant's make that possible. And we have evidence of social inferiors exploiting this fundamental ambiguity as late as the mid-nineteenth century. Even after many German student dueling societies officially refused to have duels with Jewish dueling clubs, the Jewish clubs issued challenges by claiming that the gentiles just lacked the guts to fight.[41]

All of this might make dueling look a bit too promising. That is problematic for historical and conceptual reasons. Dueling is not a broadly recognized part of modern egalitarian and democratic politics; it does disappear. And there is something paradoxical in the idea that a social practice that exists to buttress a social order can smoothly be used to undermine that social order. With promise come complications, to which I now turn.

"False Honor" and Other Paradoxes

We get a sense of the difficulties about the modernized dueling by considering the most famous duel in American history, that between Alexander Hamilton and Aaron Burr. On the one hand, it well illustrates some of the mechanisms Kant describes, at least in Joanne Freeman's recent interpretation. She argues that despite his great opposition to dueling, Hamilton had to fight Burr exactly because aristocratic honor had become a marker for other worthy characteristics: it was a criterion of an early republic politician's professional integrity and competence. She quotes Hamilton's own apologia for the duel: "The ability to be in future useful, whether in resisting mischief or effecting good, in those crises of our public affairs, which seem likely to happen, would probably be inseparable from a conformity with public prejudice in this particular."[42] In other words, had he not fought, he would have undermined his professional legitimacy.

On the other hand, the outcome was ironic. That Hamilton died said nothing about who was a better politician or a man of higher integrity. Even though dueling generally signals both parties' honor, it is very costly, and the cost is importantly divorced from who is in the right. In the early Middle Ages, when actual fighting ability was the primary ground for political competence and when a dearth of other decision-making principles existed, trial by combat may have served as a reasonable procedural mechanism ("We probably should be led by the better fighter"). But by the time of Hamilton and Burr's duel, this clearly was no longer the case.

In fact, modern dueling becomes deeply ironic as soon as victory is not seen as a sign of God's favor. Montesquieu had already observed this in the early eighteenth century. "This method of decision was, of course, badly conceived," the fictional Persian traveler Usbek notes in Montesquieu's *Persian Letters,* "for it did not follow, just because one man was more skillful or stronger than another, that he had more right on his side."[43] In other words, death seems an arbitrary byproduct. Your dying and my living says nothing about you and me as individuals except that I am a slightly better (or luckier) swordsman or shot.

A tendency toward decreased lethality suggests that the deaths indeed struck potential duelers as an unnecessary and certainly unpleasant cost. Increasingly, too, it was enough to go through the motions. In one affair, recounted by late-nineteenth-century historian Ben Truman,

> In 1829, in England, the Earl of Winchelsea was challenged by the Duke of Wellington, and the distinguished gentlemen met with pistols. The Duke fired first without injuring the Earl, who discharged his weapon in the air, and subsequently acknowledged, through his second, that he had made expressions against the Duke which were not warranted by facts, which he greatly regretted, and for which he would amply apologize.[44]

(The Duke of Wellington was more generally an important figure in the transition to modernity, as we see in the next chapter.) And when the rifling of barrels in the nineteenth century made pistols more accurate than before, dueling lost even more of its appeal.[45] By the time dueling with swords became a fad among German university students, a scarring nick on the face was generally the most serious bodily harm.[46]

But to go through the motions and not risk life makes a mockery of the practice. The one thing that still had connected dueling to honor was a man's willingness to face death. If it was now probable that you would not get killed or if it was possible to calculate your risk, then it was unclear whether you deserved any respect for your courage. Neither an empty ritual nor a calculated risk quite seems to capture what dueling was supposed to be about.

At first glance, this might seem like grist for the mill of a familiar modern antiaristocratic sentiment ("Those aristocrats surround themselves with elaborate rituals that allow them to pretend that their position is legitimate"). But it is also importantly an *antimodern* argument, as these parallels illustrate. In his digression on dueling in "Letter to M. d'Alembert on the Theatre," Rousseau inserts a sarcastic footnote about potential duelers considering the various risks before engaging in a duel: "In this age of enlightenment, everyone knows how to calculate to the penny the worth of his honor and his life."[47] And in *Persian Letters* no. 59, Montesquieu's character Rica describes a conversation among several people who are debating whether things are better or worse than they had been in the recent past. One person who thinks things are better now adduces the prohibition on dueling, "with an air of satisfaction." Rica continues,

> "A judicious remark," someone whispered to me; "that man is delighted with the edict, and he observes it so well that six months ago he accepted a hundred blows with a stick, rather than violate it."[48]

In other words, the man supports the prohibition because he is a coward who prefers to risk the occasional beating to acting honorably— that is, to accepting challenges and risking his life. The dueling opponent's motives are no different from the calculating duelers: both lack the courage to say, "Here I stand, consequences be damned."

Despite the tendency toward fewer deaths, dueling remained, of course, potentially quite dangerous. This made it particularly rife for abuse, for engagements out of nonhonorable or even dishonorable motives.

We can understand the way nonhonorable motives work by returning to Kant's discussion of military dueling. The problem is that the "*military* has made dueling an affair of honor," he says in the *Anthropology* (7:259; emphasis added). Given the direct connection between dueling and courage in the face of death, it is easy to see why this would be in the military's interest. There is a kind of symbiosis with the state and the honor culture of dueling in the officer corps.[49] The problem is that the state's willingness to turn a blind eye toward the practice becomes terrible "because there are worthless people who play with their lives just to be somebody while those who endanger themselves for the sake of the state are ignored" (A 7:259). The state simply allows a perversion of the practice into something where distinguishing between legitimate incentives (honor) and illegitimate ones (ambition, self-conceit) becomes impossible.

Kant does not specify why this is a particular problem in the historical moment in which he writes, but we can make two conjectures. First, as the text suggests, two moral motives are perversely tangled in military dueling: an officer's honor depends on his courage to risk his life *for the state,* but to demonstrate that courage when challenged requires risking it for his *personal* status and, moreover, risking the life of another defender of the state. Second, Kant knows that sanctioned modes of honorable action, even valor in battle, can stem from a host of incentives. The combination of de jure prohibition and de facto sanction is a juicy forbidden fruit. It will attract the unsavory element interested in notoriety, and the mixed signals are exactly what make it attractive to some people. Further, Kant thinks, this situation is the state's doing. That is why the state is in no position to sentence the dueling soldier to death. At the same time, the officer who kills his fellow is condemnable: he knew it was legally and morally wrong to duel.

Things get worse yet. Straightforwardly dishonorable motives can become particularly appealing when duelers generally observe the norm that you only go through the motions but do not actually try to kill your opponent: if I am set on murdering you, I can relatively safely challenge you to a duel, assuming you will shoot in the air (as Hamilton is believed to have done in his duel with Burr) while I will actually shoot at you (as Burr is believed to have done).[50] Here, a cowardly calculus meets a sinister one, and although contemporaries adjusted their judgments of Hamilton (honorable) and Burr (dishonorable) accordingly, the tragedy was that the duel was unavoidable. It remains an excellent example of the troubling conflation of good and bad motives on the one hand and the causal forces that shape people's sociologically bound interests on the other.

One question is whether these tendencies are new developments in the eighteenth century or whether they are an integral consequence of dueling in general. Modern Marxist historian V. G. Kiernan claims that dishonorable motives are part and parcel of aristocratic dueling in general: "swarms of idle gentry" with nothing better to do would find the risk of dueling simply exciting.[51] But in more conservative views, the "democratization," "republicanization," or "vulgarization" (more or less the same thing to many contemporaries) of dueling specifically leads to its abuse by people with insufficient understanding of the demands of honor.[52] Widespread dueling in the antebellum American South is often cited as the extreme example of this perversion: there, critics observe, the practice had become completely separated from anything we might call real honor and had instead become empty, superficial thrill-seeking bravado.[53]

The conservative argument is likely right at least in this sense: as long as dueling is part of a broader system of aristocratic honor, or what Peter Berger calls static hierarchy, it is somewhat more probable that incentives and interests would cohere than they would in a society in transition.[54] After all, one of the grounds of honor in aristocratic dueling is, as we saw earlier, a man's defense of his status *as an aristocrat.* We can think of dueling as a collective defense of a social status. As Georg Simmel has observed, an important connection can hook an individual's sense of honor to the way that honor helps maintain group solidarity.[55] In Germany, for example, *Standesehre* (honor of one's social estate) was an important motive for dueling.

Its definition also denoted group solidarity over and against the lower orders, for in every "affair," or *Ehrenhandel,* the participants were representing not only their own interests but those of their class. The duel drew a strict line of division between "men of honor" (*Ehrenmänner*) and the rest of society, which enjoyed none of the psychic, social, or legal entitlements of honorable status.[56]

The duelers were, in Kiernan's words, "making a joint obeisance" to their social group by participating in a duel.[57] We might say, then, that the mistake in "republicanized" dueling for equality was to conflate the autonomous activity that dueling requires with the *value of* individual autonomy as a source of a person's honor. And inasmuch this becomes true, such individuals are likely to suffer from the condition Tocqueville claimed was endemic in democratic societies: on the one hand, individuals are feeble and need associations; on the other, they have a particularly difficult time forming those associations because they, unlike aristocrats, lack any immediately obvious grounds on which to unite.[58]

But even aristocrats' group identification is problematic. Kant thinks aristocrats a kind of faction or a fraternity, and where dueling bolsters a *Standesehre* rather than an individual's dignity simply as a person, it is not consistent with Kant's interpretation of what is honorable about it. The challenge to Kant and other moderns, then, is to find some ground on which to "defactionalize" the honor involved in dueling while retaining its social content in such a way that it would remain intelligible to contemporaries. In other words, once the kind of physical courage dueling involves has been decoupled from aristocratic status, there has to be some other way of defending its value. The answer Kant's discussion affords us may be theoretically compelling, but it comes with problematic baggage: it is to stress the manliness of the activity.

Path-Dependencies: Masculine Honor, Masculine Equality

The case of the dueling soldiers in the *Rechtslehre* has its feminine counterpart: a mother who murders her illegitimate child deserves the death penalty, but the state has no right to impose it. I have discussed the details of this example elsewhere; here I want to focus on Kant's point that each case involves gender honor.[59]

For Kant and many of his contemporaries, feminine honor is first importantly reputational. In unpublished reflections on anthropology, Kant notes that although true honor is more valuable than life, *reputation* for honor should not trump life *except for soldiers and women* (R 15:481; emphasis added). In a later note, he puts it even more starkly: "The woman's honor: what the world says. . . . Her honor: what people say; not what they think" (R 15:565, 566). The content of that honor had to do with specifically with chastity. Describing contemporary views that associated feminine honor with a reputation of sexual integrity, Ute Frevert has explained how it figured in practices of dueling:

> A woman who forfeited this integrity by giving her body to a man who had no "right" to it (or by being forced to do so) also forfeited her honour. It was only logical that women whose physical honour had been forfeited in such a manner could not restore it by their own physical efforts. Honour which had been "besmirched" by a man could only be "rehabilitated" by a man; either, in the case of unmarried women, by way of marriage, or, in the case of married women, by way of a duel between husband and adulterer.[60]

This is partly why the knowledge that a woman has had sex out of wedlock is a source of shame. And, in another note, Kant observes that although a husband may delegate the management of a household to his wife, "the honor and peace" of the home are his business (R 15:581). The Civil Code of the Prussian States notes in its statutes regarding aristocracy that aristocrats deserve their honor for the protection they provide; after Kant has decoupled honor from aristocratic status, a *man's* general obligation to provide protection can serve as the ground on which physical courage should be valued.[61] We might, then, say that one important component of masculine honor *presupposes* that there are women in need of protection. And if that is the case, we can follow later feminist analyses and say the relationship between the two conceptions of honor is a *necessary* one: masculine and feminine honor are necessarily relational and hierarchical.[62]

Although there are some reported instances of women's dueling in Western history, many of them are apocryphal and are often adduced as examples of the utterly freakish and the absurd.[63] A seventeenth-century account of *The Female Duell; or, The Maidens Combate,* attributed to Thomas Toll, exemplifies the perceived absurdity of women's dueling. The pamphlet describes the (almost certainly fictional) events around two women's love of one man. The moral of the story is that no sane man would wish to marry any woman capable of handling weapons: she would not be a woman properly understood.

After all, developing the courage to risk one's life in a duel is what it means to be a man, as an angry German defender of dueling writing under the pseudonym Leo argued in 1787. To give up those qualities, he further argued, is to become feminized: if the military were to prohibit dueling, officers would "little by little degenerate into sissies [*Weichlingen*]."[64]

Leo wrote in the conservative *Deutsches Museum,* but Kant and many other Enlightener-republicans shared the view that women have an honor appropriate to them, one that turns on their natural attributes and that presupposes a superior sex in charge of their protection.[65] This generates a way to defactionalize claims of honor from the aristocrats while still retaining meaning for the concept: the man who is able to defend a woman's honor and demonstrate this ability by his willingness and ability to fight a duel is indeed, on this reading, worthy of respect. But this means that if *Satisfaktionsfähigkeit* is a proxy for a person's being worthy of respect, women cannot be worthy of (that kind of) respect. And insofar as *Satisfaktionsfähigkeit* gets employed in the politics of modern equal dignity, women necessarily remain excluded.

Few examples illustrate this better than a delightfully ironic case involving Max Weber and his wife, Marianne.[66] In 1910, the forty-six-year-old well-respected professor was thrown into "white-glowing rage" after an article attacked his wife. Weber was ready to fight a duel with the author, a young docent at the University of Heidelberg, as an honorable "husband standing behind his wife." In the event, the pen eventually proved if not mightier at least more strategic than the sword: the Webers engaged the author in print and in private letters. But throughout the controversy, Weber stated his willingness to duel in defense of his wife's "good name." And the irony? Marianne Weber had been attacked because she organized a feminist conference. Weber seemed unable to appreciate the irony, just as Kant was little able to realize that his attempt to defactionalize dueling from the aristocratic monopoly still helped maintain a fraternity, albeit a broader one: that of all men.

Bringing the State Back In to Keep It Out

Where is the state in all of this? Dueling helps us understand the changing status of persons in relation to the state. How does it do so, given that the state itself is changing—sometimes radically—in modernity?

Dueling illustrates one enduring paradox about the modern state, as in Kant's discussion of the dueling soldier in the context of what Rousseau calls the "shocking opposition" between the incentives of honor and law. On the one hand, the modern state's claim to legitimacy turns on its promise of justice, as I suggested in the introduction. Yet on the other hand, the state *cannot* provide justice in these cases. The state may be able to provide *protection,* but that won't suffice. The modern police does not obviate the need for dueling. As we have seen, dueling is not a kind of self-defense that can be delegated; it is the defense of a *kind of person,* and the means of that defense is proof of one's being that kind of person. In theoretical language, some challenges to your autonomy can be met only by demonstrations of that autonomy. This paradox resembles the paradox of aristocrats' dueling and the state: the state grants you something that is in conflict with its powers. Part of justice is actually—and necessarily—realized outside the state, by individuals themselves. For that to be possible, there has to be a space for extralegal politics. The emerging civil society is such a space.

Things that work in practice might not work in theory, and theoretical paradoxes aren't necessarily problems on the ground. But this paradox can be a problem. Dueling certainly is, simply because it is in deep tension with the state's monopoly over violence. Changes in *l'opinion publique,* as Rousseau and others argued, can help solve that particular problem, although *l'opinion publique* is in no easy immediate control of the state, either.[67] But even after honor no longer motivates people to resort to private violence, the paradox about the modern state remains, as the rest of this book shows.

Conclusion

The University of Michigan Law School has a series of stained-glass paintings—cartoons, really—illustrating various virtues. The one depicting "Honor" has two white-clad young men at the end of a duel: one has just skewered the other with his rapier (figure 2). This is deliberately surreal: the clothing of the young men evokes at the earliest late-nineteenth-century sporting clothes; they are more likely representative of a typical sporting student from the 1930s, when the cartoon was created.[68] What is funny, in a macabre sort of way, is the creative anachronism. We are invited to laugh at the idea: "Think about it, folks: What if we still understood honor in this way? How silly is that?" In this chapter, I have argued that it wasn't so silly: dueling did have potential for modern politics of equal dignity, although that potential was limited. Why does the practice nevertheless fade away so quickly that this 1930s image works in such a way?

Historians of dueling argue that after the First World War, it becomes virtually impossible to insist on a duel as a way of maintaining a man's honor. This is in part because the carnage of a total war has a powerful effect on *l'opinion publique:* the bloodthirsty saber rattling of duelers is not merely quaint but looks thoroughly distasteful after Passchendaele and Verdun. But it is also quaint: the old trappings of military honor as successful officers' most important characteristics have been replaced by the skills about which the erstwhile dueler Max Weber famously theorized: efficiency, professionalism, instrumental rationality. Joseph Conrad's novella "The Duel," about two Napoleonic officers' decades-long set of duels, gets at this nicely.

> They were officers of cavalry, and their connection with the high-spirited but fanciful animal which carries men into battle seems particularly appropriate. It would be difficult to imagine for heroes of this legend two officers of infantry of the line, for example, whose fantasy is tamed by much walking exercise, and whose valour necessarily must be of a more plodding kind. As to gunners or engineers, whose heads are kept cool on a diet of mathematics, it is simply unthinkable.[69]

Fig. 2.   *Honor,* stained-glass cartoon at the University of Michigan Law School, ca. 1931–33. The cartoons were created as the law school's Hutchins Hall was being built. They were done under the supervision of architects York and Sawyer and created by the shop of Heinigke and Smith, both of New York City. (Photograph by the author.)

It is not that the Napoleonic Wars begin the causal process that the First World War ended. Modern warfare and other more benign trends clearly contribute to the demise of dueling during the nineteenth century: The fast-paced modern city makes it impossible to challenge everyone you bump into on a crowded sidewalk to a duel.[70] In general, aristocratic status decreases in social importance while socioeconomic status gains. Accurate pistols raise the stakes of dueling. As I have suggested, by the nineteenth century, the prospect of actually getting killed in a duel no longer seemed like such a great idea. But as I also have suggested, that is not just a consequence of technological change; it is a change in the ethos. And the tendency toward the nonlethality of dueling ultimately involves a contradiction that even the changed ethos cannot obviate: if it does not involve the risk of great bodily harm, then it is not a practice with which one's willingness to risk it can be demonstrated.

So although we may agree with Montesquieu that the practice of dueling is in fact "badly conceived," it is important not to draw the stronger conclusion that it is somehow objectively or necessarily irrational. Montesquieu and Kant do not think so. Dueling cannot be irrational on the theory that people rationally (universally? naturally?) prefer life to death. Maybe they do, ceteris paribus, but here the proof is in the ceteris paribus: it is about the conditions on which life is *life*— that is, worth living. As Kant made the point, "humanity" and "personhood" are not thin biological categories. Even in modernity, as we are well aware, we can *both* prefer life to death and sometimes be willing to die. Furthermore, for dueling to be meaningful requires an appreciation of life: I merit my claim to honor because I *so* value it that I am willing to die defending it. With honor gone, everything is gone, as seventeenth-century German writer Christoph Lehmann put it.[71] This more nuanced understanding also helps us understand some moderns' ambivalence about the practice. That, in turn, helps us see how it can coherently play a part in the shift to the kind of politics we consider modern and why that politics necessarily remains outside the state and at same time connected to it.

Should we share Kant's ambivalence about the changed ethos? Should we share his solution to the paradox? It seems to me we can answer *yes* to the former question without endorsing his gender-based answer to the second. Norbert Elias has famously argued that modernity is a story of "civilizing process" away from personal violence.[72] But he has also argued that some of the virtues associated with that personal violence can find a social and political space in other practices. Modern sports, which develop in the nineteenth century, offer one such space: they involve courageous perseverance in the face of physical adversity.[73] They, too, will for a long time remain a practice that is self-consciously but also ambivalently masculine—and a site for many other political puzzles. In the next two chapters we see how.

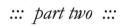

::: part two :::

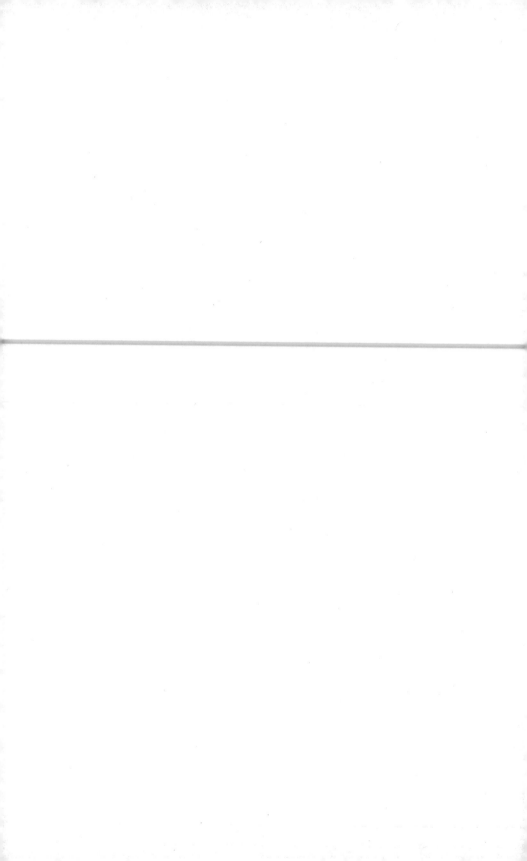

::: *three* :::

Mens Sana, the Playing Fields of Eton, and Other Clichés

In chapter 1, I mentioned Immanuel Kant's injunction that bodily cultivation—"gymnastics in the strict sense"—is a moral duty. There are good reasons not to be surprised about this. A central piece of Kant's moral, social, and political philosophy holds that humans are unavoidably physical beings—hybrids of angels and cattle—and one of his main preoccupations is to come to terms with that fact. As we saw in Chapter 1, he appreciates and even celebrates children's embodiment and physicality as the first important moments of their autonomy.

This chapter is about the nineteenth century, but this reflection of Kant's thought—expressed just a few years before the beginning of the nineteenth century, anyway—is helpful. Several very significant decades later, we find similar sentiments in thinkers very different from Kant.

For example, Herbert Spencer, best known for the dubious theory of survival of the fittest, wrote about education in 1861,

> Perhaps nothing will so much hasten the time when body and mind will both be adequately cared for, as a diffusion of the belief that the preservation of health is a *duty*. Few seem conscious that there is such a thing as physical morality.

Spencer concludes his *Education* by noting that "all breaches of the laws of health are *physical sins.*"[1]

The world underwent radical changes between the publication of Kant's and Spencer's texts, in 1797 and 1861, respectively. The period is a veritable era of revolutions—political (France in 1830 and 1848;

much of the rest of Europe in 1848; and the U.S. Civil War begins in 1861, for example), scientific (most famously of course Darwin's *Origin of Species* in 1859), and industrial. And these are arbitrary dates; if we go a decade or so in each direction, the changes will seem even more radical.

Yet the similarity of Kant's and Spencer's sentiments isn't a coincidence. One thing that remained constant throughout these decades—indeed, throughout the entire nineteenth century and beyond—was an obsession with human embodiment and physical culture. It wasn't the predominant cultural obsession, but it was important.

This obsession follows the social processes I illustrated in chapters 1 and 2 in two ways. Some of the practices to maintain physical courage as a sign of masculine honor get channeled into sports in the nineteenth century, as Norbert Elias and his coauthors have shown. And the emergence of physical education in Germany becomes an influential import. It is rare that one can plausibly point to the impact of a single person, but Johann Christoph Friedrich Guts Muths did become something resembling a long-distance guru to early-nineteenth-century Britons.

The obsession with the human body and physical culture gives us a wonderful lens on the bigger themes of the nineteenth century. My interests are primarily political, but they are inseparable from scientific and socioeconomic themes. Physical culture is one site where we see them coming together.

I focus on certain questions in this chapter: How did people conceive of the relationship between a person's character—or simply a person's personhood—and his (almost always his) body? This sounds like the philosophers' hoary old mind/body problem, and many contemporaries made the connection explicit.[2] But it wasn't just or even primarily a metaphysical question: it was a question in which practice and metaphysics blended together and had political consequences. So arises my second major question: How did people think about the political consequences of some of the answers? Specifically, what we see in the nineteenth century is the emergence of three closely related social phenomena: institutionalized physical education, modern sports, and spectator sports. Different ideas about how these practices should be—or should have been—arranged reflect different positions on the nature of equality of opportunity, masculinity, competition, science, and professionalism. For example, debates raged about whether modern sports were a social leveler and whether that was a happy circumstance. Some thought it was the former and so very decidedly not the latter: sports were bad because they mixed social orders—or, as they were increasingly called, classes—and so helped dumb down culture. Others thought precisely the opposite: the mixing was felicitous and the leveling upward: physical culture made the lower orders better than before and therefore more equal with their erstwhile superiors. Some specifically thought the social emphasis on physical culture served meritocratic goals, where plucky and disciplined individuals could pull themselves up from their previously low conditions.

But to say that physical culture affords us a handy lens through which to view nineteenth-century developments is a bit misleading: it isn't just a medium. It has its own effect on the political ideas and political values. For example, to say that modern sports in some ways help realize the ideals of meritocracy suggests that there is some prior well-understood idea of what merit is. In practice, physical culture and sports become a means through which people help sort out what merit might even *mean*. (Part of this book's argument is that we still do that.) And some decidedly modern values, now spread well beyond physical culture, emerge in the context of sports. The most important of them is the concept of fairness. Related to that is the slightly more specific ideal of amateurism, which raises important questions about the relationships among professionalism, competence, work, and leisure.

In what follows, I make two central points consistent with the earlier chapters. First, the emergence of new practices *and* the interpretations of those practices create new political values and open spaces for new types of social and political action, new conceptions of persons and social relations—for example, the value of fairness. Second, because the interpretations of the new practices are contested, the practices themselves can become means of political activity. We see this particularly in chapter 4; this chapter concentrates on the first claim.

Although some of the political rhetoric of the period (and thus some of my analysis of it) seems to reflect a world divided into two—the upper classes and the lower orders—it would be a mistake to think of the world in such stark terms. Nineteenth-century society was in transformation. Although the upper classes decidedly feared the lower orders, that fear didn't translate into the existence of widespread enthusiasm about aristocracy or all aspects of it. As befits a society undergoing a process sociological historians call *embourgeoisement,* most of the reform talk happened in the large middle ground between the highest aristocracy and the lower orders. For the most part, the social world that engaged, brought about, or tried to bring about social change was that world described in novels by such writers as Jane Austen, William Makepeace Thackeray, George Eliot, Anthony Trollope, and John Galsworthy: Whig aristocracy, country gentlemen, businessmen, emerging professionals.

This is relevant for my thesis. Those authors were trying to understand the mutual relationships among notions of excellence, freedom, status, and health. The complexity of those relationships generated internal tensions. For example, bourgeois challenges to aristocratic notions of what it meant to be a gentleman invited challenges: if professional competence should be the criterion for achievement, why should the access to gaining professional competence be based on *any* prior criterion, be it birth *or* money? Or, more directly relevant, if physical prowess was a sign of a person's moral character, why shouldn't really superior athletes, the kind of athletes we now consider elites or professionals, be seen as the most morally superior, which they weren't (and aren't)? These questions suggest that changing conceptions of honor and excellence were at stake.

I am not proposing either an inevitability thesis about social progress—that is, once you start equalizing even a little bit, things will snowball into total equality down the line—or that all developments resulted from careful planning. That is why the focus on physical culture is so useful here: it illustrates how some ideas about reform in one context can generate their own complications, unintended consequences, and new problems. People muddled through, arguing about this and that while generating new problems and foreclosing other options.

Most of this chapter focuses on Victorian England. From England—from the Victorian public schools, to be precise—the most recognizable forms of physical culture emerged and spread. England—and, to some extent, the rest of Britain—afford us, then, a unique perspective. At the same time, England did not remain unique:

the spread of physical culture and sports in particular was extremely broad and rapid. By the end of the century, the phenomenon was around the world, almost literally. I will not be able to explore the political uses of physical culture in the colonies, but as others have argued, there, too, the master's tools lent themselves to some creative attempts to chip away at the master's house, better known as colonialism.[3] None of this means that Britain is the sole source of the obsession; in some instances, indigenous forms of physical culture emerged independently of British sports, and those indigenous forms sometimes merged and sometimes competed with the anglophone imports. For example, in a 1881 speech, great German physiologist and neuroscientist Emil Du Bois-Reymond celebrates the indigenous German *Turnen*—a kind of gymnastics developed in the mid–nineteenth century—as far superior to the fast-spreading English invention, "sports":

> [T]here can be no doubt: the German *Turnen,* in its wise combination of theory and practice, is the happiest, indeed the definitive solution to the greatest problem that has occupied people interested in pedagogy since Rousseau.[4]

These local variations and their national popularity notwithstanding, the English case is richly representative for my purposes in this chapter and is therefore my primary focus, apart from occasional glimpses elsewhere.

Mens Sana in Corpore Sano

If there had been bumper stickers in the nineteenth century, the Roman satirist Juvenal's "Healthy mind in a healthy body [*mens sana in corpore sano*]" would have been one of the most ubiquitous. It became the contemporary equivalent of a bumper sticker: "A living article of faith to millions, *mens sana in corpore sano* was being preached in newspapers, in school chapels, and in the consultation rooms of doctors across the land."[5]

As early as 1776, an anonymous author in the *Spectator* used Juvenal's dictum to praise the value of exercise.

There must be frequent motions and agitations, to mix, digest, and separate the juice contained in [the body], as well as to clear and cleanse that infinitude of pipes and strainers of which it is composed, and to give their solid parts a more firm and lasting tone. Labour or exercise ferments the humours, casts them into their proper channels, throws off redundancies, and helps nature in those secret distributions, without which the body cannot subsist in its vigour, nor the soul act with chearfulness.

He concluded,

[A]s I am a compound of soul and body, I consider myself as obliged to a double scheme of duties; and think I have not fulfilled the business of the day when I do not thus employ the one in labour and exercise, as well as the other in study and contemplation.[6]

But like most bumper-sticker slogans, *mens sana in corpore sano* is if not bad, at least confusing. Its actual message is unclear, and instead of stating a firm position, it begs a question: What does "healthy mind in a healthy body" *mean?* Is it a *causal* claim: one causes the other? And if so, which way, as social scientists put it, does the causal arrow point? Or is it not a causal claim at all and instead perhaps just a statement of two independent facts or an expression of hope? In Juvenal's text, the latter is all it is. The whole line is *"Orandum est ut sit mens sana in corpore sano* [It's to be prayed that we would have a healthy mind in a healthy body]." So Juvenal says nothing about any causal connection; he just wants both, and the text is agnostic on the question of whether one helps bring about the other.

Of course, quoting someone's text doesn't require you to endorse the author's intentions. The ambiguity of the slogan probably helps explain its popularity: whatever your specific position on the relationship between the health of mind and body, the slogan becomes a handy expression of the importance of the relationship. The specific relationship is then up for dispute.

One view draws from the sort of logic that motivates Kant's moral command to cultivate one's body. Because a mind is embodied—that is, in a body—its site needs to be healthy enough for the mind to survive. The *Spectator* writer shares this view. This is trivially true at one extreme: kill the body, you kill the mind. By the early nineteenth century, even metaphysical dualists, who thought the soul was a different entity from the body, tended to be willing to admit this much about the mind.[7]

But because it is trivial, this extreme isn't particularly interesting. We would be very likely to say that Stephen Hawking has a very healthy mind indeed, but whether he has a healthy body is a different question. In the twenty-first century, I hope, we no longer automatically conclude that a "disabled" body is in some way unhealthy, but even if we did, it would be quite clear to us that the state of Hawking's body is very distant from the state of his mind. In chapter 5, I return to the question of the disabled body and to our conceptions of health. In the nineteenth century, though, the issue was pretty clear: what we would now call the disabled body most decidedly was not seen as a healthy body. That doesn't mean that the nineteenth-century notion of health was just narrower than ours; matters are more complicated than that, as we will see.

There is more content to it: the body has to be healthy, not just alive, for the mind to be healthy. The "healthy mind" is, to be sure, as ambiguous as the healthy body, and whatever it meant in the nineteenth century, it doesn't mean exactly the same thing for us. In the nineteenth century, the relationships among what we would call mental illness, intelligence, and even moral character were very much in flux. The nineteenth century saw the first modern attempts to grapple seriously (and scientifically) with those questions. It's not that nineteenth-century thinkers and practitioners didn't distinguish among health, intelligence, and moral character; they did. They were beginning to puzzle through the mutual relationships among those phenomena.

By the nineteenth century, people generally thought of the relationship as causal. This was not a radical departure from the past: a causal understanding of the mind/body relationship had begun to emerge with the scientific revolution in the seventeenth century.[8] But the development of empiricism—and in particular Humean and Kantian critiques of metaphysical dualism, which had seen the mind and the body as two fundamentally different *kinds* of entities, independent of one another—meant that in the nineteenth century, the causal story was the prevailing line of inquiry. Indeed, it led to some well-known excesses: phrenology, the theory that character traits necessarily tracked bodily features—the shape of skulls and noses and stature—was an understandable, however unfortunate, step along the causal investigation. Phrenology is obviously related to the *mens sana* belief, although most people who believed in the relationship between sound body and mind felt that things were a bit more dynamic than what phrenologists said. The phrenologists tended to hold relatively essentialist views: the physical features were if not immutable, relatively stable—even stable at a group level, as infamous and insidious caricatures about Jews or people of African descent remind us.[9]

Indeed, the central logic behind the talk of *mens sana* was that the relationship between mind and body is dynamic for any given individual. An unhealthy body can in many cases be restored to health, and a healthy body can be made healthier, all with the concomitant ameliorative effects on the mind. Very early on, people seized on the idea of physical exercise. As we saw in chapter 1, German educational reformers thought of physical activity as important; the anonymous writer for the *Spectator* also urges people to begin "that voluntary labour which goes by the name of exercise."[10] Others shared this view. Charles Caldwell wrote in 1834 that "physical education is far more important than is commonly imagined. Without a due regard to it . . . man cannot attain the perfection of his nature."[11]

So exercise is valuable. The *Spectator* writer thinks labor and "voluntary labor" are equivalent. The people who have to work with their bodies are better off than those who don't; those who don't are in fact "more miserable than the rest of mankind"—unless they exercise, of course.[12] It is true that manual work is a kind of exercise: it trains the body to do that very work better. By 1881, when one of the fathers of modern neurology, Du Bois-Reymond, gave the previously quoted speech on the value of exercise, he explained why these adaptive responses take place in the human body, and by beginning with the ubiquitous nineteenth-century example, the smith and his arm, he married an old intuitive idea with a new scientific understanding of it.[13] In a way, that *Spectator* writer is right: bodies at work do receive regular exercise of some kind, while bodies at leisure need to seek it.

But the view is politically and—we now know—physiologically naive: much manual labor is anything but good for the person who engages in it. It can be dangerous (the risk of accident outweighs its physiological benefit); it can be excessive (it results in what physiologists now call overtraining, which is damaging) or monotonous (it benefits some part of one's body while disadvantaging others); and, most importantly, the conditions under which manual labor has historically taken place are anything but conducive to psychological health. Even if shoveling slate were a good form of exercise, it is probably not healthy to do so inside a mine or a foundry.

In other words, the apparent equivocation of labor and "voluntary labor" ignore important political dimensions. I will later return to the question of the "lower orders" and their exercise; I now focus on the "voluntary labor" of the more leisurely classes, where the healthy bodies were particularly to yield healthy minds. Central among them were the youth of the upper classes—male youth, to be precise—and their schools.

The Playing Fields of Eton

The Duke of Wellington, the hero of the decisive Battle of Waterloo against Napoleon, is supposed to have said that the battle was won on the playing fields of Eton. Let's think about those playing fields for a moment. Eton is perhaps the most famous of England's public schools, which are anything but: they are private elite schools for the men of upper social classes. So the saying about the playing fields of Eton refers to the people who ended up as the officer corps, not as the rank and file: whatever happened on the playing fields, that's whom it happened to.

What happened was one realization of "*mens sana in corpore sano.*" Soldiering takes some physical prowess, but if that's all the playing fields were for, you'd think the rank and file mattered at least as much if not more than the officer corps. They didn't: to be sure, the future officers got physical exercise and so physical prowess on the playing fields, but more importantly, they developed courage and steadfastness—physical and mental—as well as loyalty to their fellows and pride in their home team. To learn to take pride in Eton or Winchester is training for learning to take pride, in the right way, in England. This was a civilized variant of what we saw in the previous chapter: here, the skills required would be inculcated in the officers without the destabilizing private violence of the duel. At least that was the idea.

Even though the Duke of Wellington was an alumnus of Eton, the claim about his mot is apocryphal—a myth. Not only is there no evidence that the duke ever said such a thing, but it really could not have been true: the educational reform in public schools that made the playing fields so important did not happen until well after the Battle of Waterloo. The reform movement is largely the work of Thomas Arnold, who as a headmaster of Rugby initiated an educational ideology and practice that was reflected on the playing fields. (Arnold's specific interest in physical education was weaker than the weight of his initial influence.)[14] But the mythical origin of the "Wellington mot" doesn't really matter. By the time the dictum came to widespread use in midcentury England, it reflected a popular ideology based on by then common practice. As late as 1868, Anthony Trollope took on a criticism by the lord rector of the University of Aberdeen that sports were "a national calamity" by ending his book on *British Sports and Pastimes* with

> one parting bit of advice to substitute for some portion of the metaphysical curriculum of the university which has placed him for a time at its head,—a slight modicum of cricket. It may teach his pupils one or two things they do not apparently learn at present, and it will, at any rate, contribute there, as it does here, to manliness, self-dominion, and modesty.[15]

The enthusiasm about physical education belies deep tensions about how contemporaries understood the practices related to physical education. Not everyone was on board with the idea at all; others had varying views on the relationship between human animality and culture, on whether and how the new "games" enthusiasm should be spread beyond the public schools and the upper classes, and on how anyone should relate to playing on the fields: Should sports be enjoyable or serious, a single-minded focus or a leisurely pastime?

Beasts or Gentlemen?

Herbert Spencer begins his chapter on physical education—the final chapter of his book on education in general—with a discussion of animals. He brings up animals to flag a missed opportunity: people—adult males, explicitly—appear to care much about the proper breeding, raising, and care of animals, he says, but forget about children.

> The fattening properties of oil-cake, the relative values of hay and chopped straw, the dangers of unlimited clover, are points on which every landlord, farmer, and peasant has some knowledge; but what percentage of them inquire whether the food they give their children is adapted to the constitutional needs of growing boys and girls?

He continues, "We see infinite pains taken to produce a racer that shall win the Derby: none to produce a modern athlete."[16]

It troubles Spencer that children are ignored at the expense of animals; he isn't troubled by the thought that what we learn about the care and cultivation of animals can be directly applicable to humans. It befits the father of Social Darwinism to think this way: the human is just another animal, subject to the same laws and regularities that govern the nonhuman animal kingdom. By the mid-nineteenth century, this view was widely but not universally held; by the end of the century, it had become even more popular. In 1896, German philosopher Karl Groos argued in *Die Spiele der Thiere* (The Games of Animals) that understanding animal physiology *and* psychology could be an important for understanding humans and that animals themselves played much like humans.[17] And even those who don't hold this view of the proximity of humans and animals with the enthusiasm of modern scientific materialists must admit that there are some important connections between the species.

All this generates a tension. On the one hand, physical ability should exemplify one's moral character and thus man's uniqueness in creation. It wasn't news that humans could behave like beasts, and the worry that some humans hardly exhibited signs of humanity was familiar. But the connection between *mens sana* and *corpus sanus* made this problem more acute: if physical animality and moral personhood are closely related, and if, in particular, the road to the latter goes through the former, how to avoid turning gentlemen into beasts, as opposed to the other way round? Or how to design modes of physical improvement that would not deny human animality but that would still lead to moral improvement?

Human animality posed another problem, with equally important political consequences: if we are all human in the same physiological way or at least within the same set of parameters, that might imply political equality. Rousseau already had suggested that all humans were similarly "perfectible," and if such was the case, those who advocated political equality might be right. One response was to deny similarity and stress differences: maybe innate differences existed within our human animality that overwhelmed the similarities; maybe our physical differences reflected moral ones. Roberta Park has pointed out that "it was widely believed that the physiology of the lower classes (the nervous system was especially indicted) qualitatively differed from that of 'gentlemen.'"[18] That was one prominent position, but it wasn't the only one. Together, the two questions about relationship between animality and moral personhood serve as an important framework for understanding nineteenth-century political questions.

Social Differentiation

One solution to *both* problems lay in social differentiation: *some* kinds of physical pursuits, the idea went, were appropriate for some types of persons and not for others.

The Curious Case of Rugby

We tend to think that brutality brutalizes and refinement refines and that brutal pursuits attract brutal types. Hence arise stereotypes about knuckle-scraping football players or thuggish hockey players. The stereotypes are false, but they point to something many people think is real: if you participate in a brutal pursuit or even just enjoy watching it, you risk your refined character and virtue; you may become brutal.

Many people in the nineteenth century shared that view, at least in some ways. Boxing, for example, was seen as a particularly low sort of sport, even by those hypocritical upper classes who might nevertheless have enjoyed it. By the second half of the nineteenth century, Trollope claimed in *British Sports and Pastimes* that professional boxing was dead: "Prize-fighting, which certainly would have been included in any list of out-of-door British Sports fifty years ago, still lives;—but it lives after such a fashion, and is so fallen in general interest, that we do not doubt but that we shall be thought to have shown a proper discretion in excluding it from our little volume."[19] Some of the opposition to dueling also took this form: instead of affirming virtue, opponents argued, engaging in duels was likely to degrade a person.[20] But significantly, a very opposite belief, now more surprising to us, also existed. This was the idea that only those whose virtues were of the highest quality could safely engage in brutal pursuits. For people of high virtue, brutality—violence, roughness—was not only safe (because they could handle it) but in fact good (a way of expressing their virtues).

One of the ideas of dueling was that the ability and willingness to engage in potentially lethal practice was the mark of the honorable gentleman. In the proper hands, in other words, dueling exemplified the right sorts of virtues and skills. In the wrong hands, it could get out of control and would encourage and promote—indeed, appeal to—bad characters.

It would be simplistic to say that sports fully replaced dueling. Dueling, as we saw, waned for a host of reasons and at varying rates, and the coincidence that dueling mainly seemed to disappear in the nineteenth century, when modern sports emerged, has no explanatory power by itself. But as I have suggested, others have remarked on such connections. Again, I am interested not primarily in the historical causes either of the disappearance of dueling or of the emergence of sports but in the attendant disputes and controversies and in contemporaries' interpretations of the phenomena.

One of the connections is, as Elias has argued, that sports represent the pacification of private violence and its transfer into the hands of the state. What was actually lethal and (thus) politically destabilizing had largely come under state control by the nineteenth century. But sports represented one area of social life where what people found appealing in practices such as dueling could to some extent survive. It's not that the emergence was planned: "Sport is, in fact, one of the great social inventions which human beings have made without planning to make them," Elias wrote. But, still, sports offer "people the liberating excitement of a struggle involving physical exertion and skill while limiting to a minimum the chance that anyone will get seriously hurt in its course."[21]

The question is what "seriously hurt" means. Nineteenth-century observers would not have agreed on one single answer, but the basic idea is that whereas in dueling the very logic *requires* a risk of death or dangerous bodily injury, sports shouldn't go that far. Sometimes they do, but those are accidents, not something that should happen as a matter of course.[22] At the same time, something must be demanding, both physically and in terms of a person's courage. If the playing fields help make honorable and courageous gentlemen and soldiers out of unruly boys, their games must not only enable the boys to accustom themselves to some pain to themselves but also teach them how to inflict pain on others—within limits. Rugby football is a particularly good example of this dynamic.

Developed at the public school with the same name, rugby was decidedly a sport of the upper classes. The development of all forms of modern football was rather amorphous for a while, but by early in the second half of the nineteenth century, rugby was clearly differentiated from the so-called kicking game, association football (soccer). Although on its face it looks like just a clarification of the constitutive norms of the practice—a clarification that resulted in two practices, rugby and soccer—it is very much about class.

In two different but closely related ways, rugby reflects the upper-class understanding of how sports can help make virtuous gentlemen and why they should remain the privilege of the upper classes. The first has to do with the nature of the actual play, the second with how it is organized.

There is no question that rugby is the rougher of the two British football games. Soccer can of course be quite brutal, but tackling and other full-contact physical attacks on opposite players neither are nor were part of its constitutive norms. So we might find it curious that the rougher game is in fact the upper classes' preferred game, the game supposedly conducive to gentlemanly virtues. The logic is quite simple: only the upper classes can be trusted to exercise a sense of proportion in such a game and to "leave it on the field"—that is, to understand that the game is a game and that good social relations between antagonists ought to prevail as soon as the game is over. At the same time, the brutality of the game is necessary: upper-class men, too, are animals; their violent instincts need some release, and they need to learn that those instincts might have to be used sometimes—in battle, specifically.

But the game wasn't just a venue for the release of man's natural aggression or a training ground for the skills with which those aggressions were put to use. It also provided exercise in moral skills. It is, in a way, slightly misleading to say that only upper-class men could be trusted with the violent practice: even they couldn't be trusted automatically. Thomas Arnold, for example, entertained no illusions about the natural moral goodness of anybody. Looking forward to his upcoming tenure as the headmaster of Rugby, he wrote to his friend, the Reverend John Tucker,

> At the same time my object will be, if possible, to form Christian men, for Christian boys I can scarcely hope to make; I mean that, from the natural imperfect state of boyhood, they are not susceptible of Christian principles in their full development upon their practice, and I suspect that a low standard of morals in many respects must be tolerated amongst them, as it was on a larger scale in what I consider the boyhood of the human race.[23]

So the point was to provide a way in which the natural unruliness could be safely exercised *and* developed into moral virtues, goals fostered by the organizational principles of rugby.

> Even though it was beginning to develop towards stricter control, the primary emphasis in Rugby continued to be laid on internalization of the rules, on self-imposed rather than external restraint. This can be seen clearly in rule xxiv which enjoined that "the heads of sides, or two deputies appointed by them, are the sole arbiters of all disputes." That is, it was felt that, as future "gentlemen," the captains could be relied upon to settle

controversies by discussion. Behind this lay the assumption that no player would deliberately contravene the rules and that, in cases of dispute, all would abide by their captains' decisions.[24]

In other words, the whole point was to have the players develop a sense of honorable responsibility *while* they were engaged in play that involved physical roughness, pain, and therefore easily heightened emotions. The desire to win, combined with excitement and the adrenalin rushes of the rough-and-tumble, created a setting in which a sense of honor would be more than mere words: the players' understandings of themselves as honorable would have to be the forces that kept them from turning the brawl of the game into real brawls. Of course, this practice was not always perfect, and it involved risks, but like the general public school disciplinary practice of "prefect-fagging"—where the oldest students rather than teachers were immediately responsible for maintaining order—the idea was that only the combination of power and violence would help foster a genuine sense of responsibility. As Eric Dunning and Kenneth Sheard have argued, "The structure and ethos of the reformed prefect-fagging system were thus reflected in the emergent Rugby game. That is, in its emphasis on self-restraint, its finely struck balance between force and skill, spontaneity and control, the individual and the group, Rugby football in the 1840s was a microcosm of its wider social setting."[25]

Whether this ideology worked better in the case of rugby than in the case of school discipline in general is in part an open question; rugby eventually became more externally structured and institutionalized but did so for many reasons, not primarily because the internal enforcement mechanisms of play failed.[26] But the ideal of autonomous self-development helps explain why resistance against the institutionalization of rugby was so intense and persisted for so long: control had to rest in the hands of the individuals and the teams, not of institutions and their representatives in the form of referees and umpires.

. . . and the Curious Case of Fox Hunting

Fox hunting is an equally prominent if different example. Most of us are loath to call it a sport any longer. Still, fox hunting involves aspects we would recognize as sporting: serious participation requires considerable riding skills, and the varied terrain and the likelihood of fence jumping can make it quite dangerous for the rider (and horse). For contemporaries, of course, it was a paradigmatic sport: in addition to the physical demands, it involved an exciting life-and-death pursuit, even though the only regular death was the fox's, with the odds heavily against it. In 1796, Peter Beckford offered his *Thoughts upon Hare and Fox Hunting:*

> Fox-hunting, an acquaintance of mine says, is only to be followed because you can ride hard, and do less harm in that than in any other kind of hunting. There may be some truth in the observation; but, to such as love the riding part only of hunting, would not a trail scent be more suitable? Gentlemen who hunt for the sake of a ride, who are indifferent about the hounds, and know little of the business, if they do no harm, fulfill as much as we have reason to expect from them; whilst those of a contrary description, do good, and have much greater pleasure. Such as are acquainted with the hounds, and can at times assist them, find the sport more interesting; and frequently have the satisfaction to think, that they themselves contribute to the success of the day. This is a pleasure you often enjoy; a pleasure, without any regret attending to it.[27]

But, Elias has argued, it was important that these matters of life and death were constrained and displaced. When the role of the hunters was just to ride after the hounds chasing the fox and, at the end, let the hounds do the actual killing, humans participated in a violent activity but did so at a remove that left the participants with clean enough hands (at least from their point of view). And these "[i]ncreasing restraints upon the use of physical force and particularly upon killing, and, as an expression of these restraints, a displacement of the pleasure experienced in doing violence to the pleasure of seeing violence done, can be observed as symptoms of a civilizing spurt in other spheres of human activity."[28] Still, the key idea *is* violence. Comparing fox hunting to fishing and "shooting" (i.e., hunting by shooting), Beckford wrote, "[F]ox-hunting is a kind of warfare;—its uncertainties, its fatigues, its difficulties, and its dangers, rendering it interesting above all diversions."[29]

Important differences exist in these two ways—rugby and fox hunting—of negotiating violence and being "civilized," but in both, participants' social status matters. The contrast is often to lower classes of persons who not only aren't able to balance refinement and violence but also don't even understand the value of the right sort of displacement. Describing the countryside of his youth and recalling how he had found its "unhunted" condition lamentable, Siegfried Sassoon noted that "[s]ome farmers made no secret of shooting foxes."[30] Not only did this practice further deprive the area of being good grounds for fox hunting—if the farmers shoot the foxes, they won't be there to be chased with hounds and horses—but the fact of farmers shooting shows the benighted nature of the region where poor young Sassoon found himself. In other words, it was appropriate that fox hunting was restricted to certain classes of people. Even more, the practices could even require this. Dunning and Sheard point out that "[r]ugby depended partly on the social homogeneity of the players. As future 'gentlemen,' most could be expected, most of the time at least, to play 'fairly,' i.e. to comply voluntarily with the rules."[31] From the participants' ideological perspective, this had to do with the "gentlemen" having the right moral character. We don't even have to agree with this elitism to see why homogeneity would have had the effect it did. The small social circles of homogenous elites would likely ensure that a blatant rule breaker would get a bad reputation and be remembered as such: if the people whom you'd likely encounter in your future social circles remembered you as a cheater or a bad teammate, your chances of advancement would be weaker than if you were known as a dependable and honest fellow.

What would happen, then, if sports got into the hands of the lower orders or if participants became heterogeneous? As the case of rugby suggests, people thought that different sports mapped onto social hierarchies: some were appropriate for gentlemen, others for common folk. Although the reasons that sports were—and are—socially stratified probably involve access, cost, and other material factors, Victorians blamed status-based moral differences. For example, Trollope attached moral categories to different sports.

We by no means grudge to Foot-ball the name it has won for itself;—but it is hardly as yet worked its way up to a dignity equal with that of Hunting and Shooting, or even with that of Cricket and Boat-racing.

And although his survey was supposed to be comprehensive,

> [t]here remains that wide word Athletics. Racing, Jumping, Ball-throwing and Hammer-throwing, and the like, have undoubtedly pushed themselves into such prominent notice in late years as to give them almost a claim to be reckoned among British Sports; but we have felt that they have fallen somewhat short of the necessary dignity, and have excluded them,—not altogether with a clear conscience.[32]

So, soccer—by 1868, association football was clearly the game recognized as "football"—and athletics ("track and field" in North America) were not quite dignified enough to count as sports. Trollope at least had the good sense to realize that he lived in a changing world; indeed, the proliferation of new sports and the "downward" spread and social leveling of some previously exclusive sports were a clear trend by the second half of the nineteenth century.[33] These mechanisms generated politically interesting debates about moral and political values and about new social categories.

Hierarchies, Old and New

One of the values in sports was the ability to sort the wheat from the chaff when it came to respect-worthy traits. In this, it indeed could serve the same function as dueling had served. According to Trollope,

> It is amusing to see how the characteristics of different men show themselves in [sports], and how opportunity is given for the exhibition of that which in ordinary life stands concealed. For instance, it has often been observed that a very conceited man, who seems to be shamelessly bumptious, is really the most nervous of creatures. At cricket this is detected to a certainty. More than alive to his own merits, but fearful to a degree that something will happen to mar their due exposition, the

brazen youth advances with his bat behind his back, under his arms,—a favourite attitude of this class,—or swinging it jauntily along as if he cared for nothing. Vain boasting! If you wish to see a real funker, look at him when the dreaded moment arrives, and Wootton prepares to put down one of his best. He must still feign calmness, or he is nothing; but you see by the twitch of the hand, the glove rapidly raised to the face, and replaced on the bat-handle, the jerk of the elbow, and perhaps the uneasy lifting of the foot, that his fear of a "duck,"—nought is called in cricket-play,—outweighs all other earthly considerations.[34]

Here we have a clear case of manly courage, tested and demonstrated openly. Pretense won't help, Trollope suggests. It is a modern answer to the laments by such explicit antimoderns as Thomas Carlyle and John Ruskin about the disappearance of "heroes."[35] Heroes, Trollope suggests, may still be among us, and their heroism is tested by their courage on the cricket pitch or on the hunt, for example.

In this world, heroes remain almost invariably men. Moreover, heroism itself is a largely masculine concept in the nineteenth century, much as honor in dueling was a necessarily masculine concept. Both got part of their meaning from the idea of protection of others. Women can, to be sure, demonstrate heroism on occasion, and some types of heroism are appropriate for women—protection of children, care of the vulnerable. The Victorians' Florence Nightingale cult is an example of the space for notions of feminine heroism. But even in these situations, few as they are, the heroism of women is different from that of men: the physical courage Trollope describes is a sign of masculine heroism.

This did not mean that sports remained beyond women's reach. The nineteenth century saw the emergence of women's sports alongside men's.[36] Part of the reason has to do with the idea of biology: the tension between our shared animality, on the one hand, and differences, sometimes imagined, sometimes real, between types of people, on the other, is quite obvious in the case of men and women. Women thus are seen as beings who can engage in sports, and they do. But they are also seen as different from men, so their engagement and the kinds of sports they do differ from men's. This tension doesn't go away; I return to it in chapter 5. Here I focus on a different tension that is complicated by the specter of gender.

While sports offer many possibilities for demonstrations of one's mettle, it is significant that Trollope's description of the cricket batsman is of a specific case. It doesn't follow that sports in general or as a system work the same way. There was a broader question about what physical prowess meant generally. Was it one's ability to acquit oneself commendably in any given athletic situation, be it facing a bowler in cricket or a fence while fox hunting? Or was it the sort of single-minded, focused brilliance in one pursuit that emerging elite athletes exemplified (and still do)? Or was that kind of focus actually a sign of dangerous monomania, fitting perhaps for the lower orders, just as expertise in shoemaking was fitting for the cobbler, but no sign of his general respect-worthiness? And was true physical excellence an athletic version of the Renaissance man: competent in many pursuits, superb in none, and appropriately detached from any one—much like the country squire's nonobsessive interest in fox hunting, art, literature, and music? According to Trollope,

> [H]ere is an old saying,—that whatever you do, you should do well,—which like many other old sayings is very untrue, and very dangerous in its lack of truth. But nowhere is this more untrue than in reference to our amusements. To play Billiards is the amusement of a gentleman;—to play Billiards pre-eminently well is the life's work of a man who, in learning to do so, can hardly have continued to be a gentleman in the best sense of the word.

Still more poignantly, he wrote,

> Even Cricket has become such a business, that there arises a doubt in the minds of amateur players whether they can continue the sport, loaded as it is with the arrogance and extravagance of the professionals. All this comes from excess of enthusiasm on the matter;—from a desire to follow too well a pursuit which, to be pleasurable, should be a pleasure and not a business.[37]

In the nineteenth century, *enthusiasm* still had largely negative connotations: people understood it to mean something very similar to fanaticism. It was a kind of pathology.

We saw this mechanism at work in dueling: a potentially commendable pursuit can also encourage various social pathologies. Here, though, the idea of competition generated the particular wrinkle. People became too interested in winning and so turned sports into something like a business, a single-minded, central preoccupation. Another example from the western side of the Atlantic makes the point further. In his 1892–93 report, Harvard president Charles William Eliot worried about what sports were doing to America's collegiate youth. An "inordinate desire to win and the attendant evils of commercialism, 'coarse publicity,' and 'hysterical excitement,' he insisted, had turned potentially healthy and beneficial activities into an aberration."[38]

Unlike antimoderns such as Carlyle and Ruskin who saw the new world of business as unadulterated badness,[39] Trollope and Eliot worried not because of some principled conservatism but because the extreme instances of these generally healthy developments turned against precisely the goals they were supposed to promote. These worries point to a deep tension in the contemporaries' values: on the one hand, meritocracy is on the rise and with it the idea of skillful competence, even excellence at some particular set of pursuits. Conversely, contemporaries also put a premium on broad competence: the ideal of the multitalented gentleman lives on in the emerging ideal of citizens with broad liberal educations. One of the places where this tension is at its most evident is in the differences between professional and amateur sports.

Consider two different sets of normative meanings of *amateur* and *professional*. In the first set of meanings, to be professional is to be competent and to be an amateur is to be a hopeless dabbler: "His advertising flyer for the conference was embarrassingly amateurish; he shouldn't have designed it himself but should have left it for a pro." This set of connotations is connected to the sociological conception of professional as someone who enjoys a relatively great degree of autonomy not only in his or her work but also in setting the standards of entry into the practice and the standards that govern the practice. Modern professional organizations such as the American Bar Association, the American Medical Association, and their international equivalents are textbook examples. The emergence of these kinds of professionals coincided with the emergence of the modern administrative state, and they replaced the hopeless amateurs of yesteryear: officeholders who had inherited or bought their offices, for example.

The other set of meanings for *professional* and *amateur* reverts the value connotations: to be an amateur is to care about something for its own sake and for its intrinsic rewards; to be a professional is to be a mercenary motivated by the wrong reasons, generally financial. We usually negotiate these two sets of evaluations easily enough by differentiating between the contexts in which it is appropriate to be a professional and those in it which it is inappropriate, when amateurism is fine and when it isn't. Sports are a pursuit in which amateurism and professionalism have coexisted even at the elite levels.

We twenty-first-century moderns have inherited many of the ideals of amateur sports and can be blind to many nuances in those ideas. Amateurism is, many of us tend to think, just as nineteenth-century ideology held: commendable and honorable exactly because people engage in amateur activities not out of greed but out of their admirable commitment to the fair game, to the noble pursuit, to excellence in its own right. They engage in it, as Trollope would have wanted, seeking the innocent pleasure of the game, not because they want to turn it into a business. Professionals, however, do it for money. We don't begrudge a poor guy's need to make a living, but given the ideals of sports, we think making a living with sports is somehow getting it wrong, somehow demeaning to those ideals. That is the ideology behind amateur sports, but their actual history is a slightly different. It doesn't make those ideals, however ideological, bad or false, but it does complicate things.

Amateur sports emerged as a way to carve out a social space for upper-class men to engage in competition on terms that would make it meaningful for them.[40] Many sports had professionals; aristocrats wouldn't have stood a chance in competition against such pros. Never mind the fact that such mixed competition would have required mixing among social classes; it simply would have demonstrated the upper classes as patently weaker and less competent. Rhetoric could of course help alleviate that a bit—Trollope's disapproval of the overfocused athlete—but it wouldn't do anything about the humiliation on the field. Historian Vray Vamplew reports,

The definition of amateur varied between sports but most had social connotations which reached their extreme in the Amateur Rowing Association's debarring from amateur status anyone "who is or has been by trade or employment for wages a mechanic, artisan, or labourer, or engaged in any menial duty."[41]

In the case of the rowers, the class-based logic is at its most blatant: it isn't even about professionalism in the specific sport but about keeping the classes separate. But it is inseparable from the question of how intensely or on what terms one should play sports.

So amateurism is a solution to concerns about the mixing of social classes and about the possibility for meaningful competition.[42] Entirely banning professionalism in some sports and creating different divisions for professionals and amateurs in others effectively kept the lower orders out of upper classes' games. In the sports where professionalism was banned, the lower social classes could not even rise to the necessary level of excellence: competence required a lot of time, and without compensation, they lacked the time to train. Even where sports included ways of making money, the existence of different divisions allowed the upper classes an opportunity for meaningful competition.

The point is not that the emergence of these divisions or amateur sports in general was bad. As I argue in chapter 5, sports divisions are a necessary means for securing meaningful competition for different groups and are desirable for precisely that reason. I also do not intend to deny the value of amateurism. There are many reasons to value it, and there are many reasons to lament professional sports, then and now. Still, the most immediate effects of the distinction were on social classes. Eric Hobsbawm even equates the "proletarianization" of sports with their professionalization.[43]

Working classes had their own reasons to worry about the professionalization of sports, as I suggest in the next chapter.[44] In a way, we have come full circle: the anonymous *Spectator* writer who had reintroduced the idea of exercise in 1776 had urged people to "indulge themselves in that voluntary labour which goes by the name of exercise."[45] Sports remained voluntary and thus commendable for those with sufficient means and leisure for it; it became just another job—and thus *not* voluntary labor—for many members of the working class. Hobsbawm's point also suggests that becoming an athletic professional wasn't quite like becoming a professional in the modern sociological sense of the term: professional athletes enjoyed relatively little autonomy, either as individuals or collectively. (Even today, where professional athletes are organized, they might on occasion have much collective power, but they still do not have not much autonomy to determine the nature and conditions of their work.) Still, if we focus on the way in which athletic professionalism differs from other kinds of professionalism, we lose sight of politically important similarities.

The idea of the modern autonomous professional is an outcome of political struggles, and in the nineteenth century, the professional was also a threatening figure. He—invariably he—represents social mobility. Much nineteenth-century literature has nothing but contempt for both established and emerging professionals.[46] Lawyers are, of course, staple objects of ridicule, but many other emerging professions also were a source of concern for contemporaries. One of the responses to that kind of social threat was to emasculate its representatives: the tropes of the clerk with ink-stained fingers and bad posture, the weaselly but cowardly lawyer, and even the fastidious doctor are a powerful staples in a cultural repertoire of emasculation. These people might be necessary, the implication goes, but they should not be mistaken for real men.

But these figures simultaneously represent a change in social values about respect-worthiness. They are not only necessary but *increasingly* necessary given the demands for specialization brought by the complex modern world, and they therefore are also increasingly powerful. Even the social mobility they provide can be beneficial, not only to us, who view the developments from a great historical distance, but even to contemporaries. In 1897, looking back on the century in his native England, T. H. S. Escott offered a warm assessment.

> The fusion of classes not less than the organisation of professions or enterprise is the keynote of our epoch. The process has, without an exception, been one of levelling up, not down. The classes called indifferently higher, or older, have proved to possess an unexpected aptitude for communicating the tastes,

the pursuits, the habits, the very instincts, which have descended to them from their forefathers, to the newcomers that the distribution of wealth, the opportunities of industry, the innumerable vicissitudes of life, have incorporated gradually into themselves. Thus it has come to pass that society in England, in itself the most miscellaneous of all conceivable composites, is saturated through and cemented as to its different parts by a real homogeneity.[47]

I don't wish to adjudicate between Hobsbawm's verdict of proletarianization and contemporary gentleman's observation of upward leveling. Rather, I suggest, both are right. At work are two different dimensions of respect-worthiness.

Here is why. As the preceding discussion suggests, in one dimension at play here, at one end lies highly specialized and focused competence and at the other a leisurely dilettantism. Because of the increasing importance of specialized competence, the first end is becoming increasingly socially valuable, but not easily or immediately, as we have seen. And as I have suggested, the enduring social value of amateurism suggests that the transformation might not be complete even now. The other dimension involves physical and intellectual competence, with the professional athlete and the lawyer marking the two ends of the spectrum. As this chapter shows, one prevailing ideology in the nineteenth century connected rather than separated these two. But the social leveling it brought about as well as the increasing social cachet of intellectual competence also helped pry them apart. These two dimensions come into nice tension in the case of amateur and professional sports and finally help us return to the question of gender.

On both dimensions, effeminacy lurks as the end everyone—since we are in a man's world—wants to avoid. One way of describing embourgeoisement is to say that it makes involvement in business, both literal and metaphorical, the way of being a respectable man. By the late nineteenth century, more and more people seemed convinced by what Rousseau had suggested a hundred years earlier in his cultural critiques of civilization: constant leisure is unmanly; not to have to have business of some sort is to fail at being a man. (The familiar irony is that women's actual roles, even for the upper classes, were not at all about constant leisure and idleness.) So a real man will want to be a professional of some sort.

Along the physical/intellectual dimension, of course, the effeminate end of the scale is even more palpable. And so there is a way in which the professional athlete is most firmly secure in his manliness. At the same time, as I have just shown, that is not the prevailing attitude at all: there are contempt and resistance and yet also worries about the professional athlete. He is actually not privileged; he is, as Hobsbawm suggests, "proletarianized," put in his place in a class system. But Escott is also right: professionalism on the one hand and athleticism on the other offer a way of social leveling. The mechanism is the same I identified in chapter 2: the dilemma can be politically exploited by clever actors. I now turn to those attempts.

::: *four* :::

Physical Culture for the Masses

This chapter takes us into the twentieth century, but it begins in the world of the previous one. The puzzle here is why newly emerging working-class political organizations seemed so interested in sports. The answer is that they saw sports as thoroughly political and something they might be able to use for their political goals.

Mass sports and mass politics developed roughly simultaneously in the second half of the nineteenth century. That simultaneity wasn't a coincidence. As with the Victorians, here, too, the phenomenon we call physical culture reflected broader social and political culture: Mass sports were first a consequence of some of the same forces that helped generate mass politics. They were also an important part of the mass politics, and they offered political movements an opportunity to debate what those politics ought to look like. I take up some of the debates in this chapter.

The background includes the developments and debates we explored in the previous chapter. For example, the Victorians' idea of moralized physical prowess enabled working classes and other representatives of the former "lower orders" to make claims for standing, even dignity. The mechanism is the same as in bourgeois dueling: a contingent understanding about the meaning of a practice can make it into a political tool that can be used even against precisely the ideas and values it is supposed to uphold. But this isn't the only way in which mass sports are political, and that points to another fact we have encountered before: the use of such political weapons contains inherent tensions. The weapons might be duds, they might backfire, and they might be blanks, offering satisfying bangs but ultimately no more than a political distraction. We encounter all of these positions in the debates about mass sports.

In a related but broader sense, we might see the development of mass sports as one way to bridge some of the political gaps we saw emerging in the previous chapter. One was between elite and ordinary practitioners, the other between sports as a kind of spectacle and sports as something that is participatory. In the nineteenth century, these two dimensions began to merge: elite practitioners were worth watching and even paying money to see. One way of understanding mass sports against that background is to see them as an attempt to develop a "democratic" conception of a practice. Here, the practice in question is sports, but the analogy to a broadly democratic citizenship is obvious to many of the people who write about these issues: getting the right to participate in and receiving political recognition for working-class sports organizations are akin to being recognized as a citizen. Related to this democratization is the almost Rousseauian desire evinced by some working-class sports organizations to bring spectacle and participation together: toward the end of his "Letter to M. d'Alembert on the Theatre," Rousseau envisions a kind of participatory spectacle in which citizens engage in activities that express social as well as individual virtue—the former because of the latter.[1] Although I don't want to make too much of a theorist's influence on the ideals of the practices, the Rousseauian connection isn't entirely a coincidence.

I look at this world through a wider lens. The previous chapter focused mainly on Victorian England. Now I move more freely. In the case of mass sports, the national varieties and international connections afford us a richer picture of both the phenomenon and the debates surrounding it. There is also an important political element: late-nineteenth- and early-twentieth-century Europe (and to some extent North America) had an emerging, even vibrant, civil society existing alongside a state apparatus that was relatively weak in some cases and strong in others but barely democratic in most. Questions about the mechanisms with which one might or might not do politics and affect the state are up in the air.

Leisure, Paternalism, and Social Control

In this section, I consider some of the ways in which modern leisure reflected attempts at paternalistic social control and how the nature of those attempts helped shape one feature in politicized class sports.

To engage in an amateur sport or other recreation requires two things: time and money. Higher social classes generally had enough of both, but in the nineteenth century, leisure became more broadly available. It is not that people necessarily had more time than had earlier been the case; rather, the whole concept of "free time" as different from work emerged only with the "time disciplines" of modern economy.[2] In other words, broadly accessible leisure is a product of the Industrial Revolution because "being at work" and "being off" became much more separable than, say, in the rural agricultural world. They are usually separated by time and place. Other infrastructural changes were also necessary for working classes to take advantage of leisure. Many of these, too, involved the Industrial Revolution: mass production of bicycle tires, balls, and other equipment made varied leisure much more widely available and affordable.[3] Also important, large institutional efforts were necessary: only state institutions and to some extent large corporations could create parks and build stadiums.[4]

Some of the reforms were closely connected to paternalistic worries about lower orders' and particularly urban working classes' capacities and probable tendencies if left unchecked. What later scholars have called a social control thesis suggests that the kinds of leisure opportunities made available for lower social classes reflected elite concerns about the morally corrupting effects of leisure and idleness, modern urban life, and factory work as well as about the political mischief that leisure might catalyze. The right kind of leisure could control and even shape the lower orders in the right ways and prevent mischief.

There certainly was a lot of paternalism to go around. It wasn't even new, as we saw in chapter 1. But interesting changes occurred in paternalism as a result of the new leisure, as the following examples reflect.

In a 1844 letter to the English *Morning Post,* William Wordsworth argued against a proposal that would have extended the railroad to the Lake District so that urban lower orders would have access to natural beauty.

But as a more susceptible taste is undoubtedly a great acquisition, and has been spreading among us for some years, the question is, what means are most likely to be beneficial in extending its operation? Surely that good is not to be obtained by transferring at once uneducated persons in large bodies to particular spots, where the combinations of natural objects are such as would afford the greatest pleasure to those who have been in the habit of observing and studying the peculiar character of such scenes, and how they differ one from another. Instead of tempting artisans and labourers, and the humbler classes of shopkeepers, to ramble to a distance, let us rather look with lively sympathy upon persons in that condition, when, upon a holiday, or on the Sunday, after having attended divine worship, they make little excursions with their wives and children among neighbouring fields, whither the whole of each family might stroll, or be conveyed at much less cost than would be required to take a single individual of the number to the shores of Windermere by the cheapest conveyance. It is in some such way as this only, that persons who must labour daily with their hands for bread in large towns, or are subject to confinement through the week, can be trained to a profitable intercourse with nature where she is the most distinguished by the majesty and sublimity of her forms.[5]

This sentiment is relevant here for two reasons. First, it echoes the recognizably conservative view that human capabilities track social hierarchies and that class status is a perfectly reasonable criterion for deciding who gets what: status is a marker of desert. Second, it illustrates a kind of social control approach to the provision of public goods: because the laboring classes cannot appreciate the Lake District's beauty, they needn't be provided access to it; they *should*, however, be cultivated in ways appropriate to them. Although Wordsworth doesn't mention it here, there is a corollary worry, often expressed, about the kinds of mischief in which the lower orders are wont to engage if they are not suitably cultivated.[6] It is not surprising that Wordsworth had argued in 1836, in terms recognizable to us from chapter 1, that the purpose of education for the lower orders was to ensure that people had "hands full of employment, and a head not above it."[7]

But elite attitudes soon began to change. A mere two decades later, across the Atlantic, Frederick Law Olmsted articulated a much more democratic sentiment about access to natural beauty. In a report to

Congress on Yosemite Valley, he criticized British exclusiveness and defended the accessible-to-all idea of national parks.[8] But his argument was also paternalistic and had Wordsworthian echoes: access to natural beauty would help combat the morally destructive effects of industrial work, urban life, and the other threats that competed for the souls of the nineteenth-century laboring classes.

According to those who subscribe to the social control thesis about this kind of paternalism, its purposes are insidious and the apparent change in attitudes politically meaningless. As late-twentieth-century historians Alan Ingham and Stephen Hardy understand the true motives behind reforms encouraging the lower classes to enjoy their new leisure,

> [T]hese reformers conspiratorially designed programmes which, while providing the illusion of social progress, were actually perpetuating closed class relationships by convincing the children of subordinate groups that they should be happy with their lot.[9]

Although few actors on the ground shared these later commentators' belief that paternalistic social control was *the* reason for their newly gained leisure, it wasn't unreasonable for them to connect the two, benignly or not.

And it can be argued that they were indeed connected. Employer-provided sports opportunities, for example, were often motivated by the desire for a fitter and better-conditioned workforce. Along with temperance policies, physical recreation helped reduce absenteeism and confined potentially destructive social tendencies to safer venues. Of prerevolutionary Russia, Peter Frykholm has written, "Factory owners wished to raise the level of health—and thereby productivity—of their workers by encouraging exercise and by offering an alternative to the heavy drinking that characterized worker life."[10]

One of the most important (perceived) attempts at social control against which the working-class sports organizations would eventually react was nationalism. The connection between nationalism and sports was undeniable. The fact that the modern Olympic movement was based on a competition—however friendly and peaceful—between nations was not lost on anyone at the end of a century that had seen the emergence of nationalism and wars fought in its name. Although the movement may have been an attempt to channel nationalist sentiments into less destructive means than war, it still rode on the fact of nationalist sentiment.[11]

Moreover, the Olympic movement was just one of the better-known examples of the relationship between nationalism and sports. In many countries, sports organizations emerged around some nationalist campaign. For example, Germany's important *Turnen* movement—the word denotes a kind of gymnastics—arose around the 1848 revolution partly to train democratic and republican guerillas, and the movement remained an important expression of German nationalism.[12] In Finland, popular sports emerged alongside male conscription in the late nineteenth century, and although the military was ostensibly part of the Imperial Russian Army, raising the general health and fitness of the Finnish population was an important part of Finnish nationalism, a counter to both the Russians and the Swedish-speaking elites.[13] After the First World War, a high level of popular fitness became increasingly important in many European countries, both serving a symbolic nationalist purpose in the Olympic Games and helping to ensure a fit conscript army.[14]

Despite paternalistic attempts to prevent the emergence of working-class politics, it did of course emerge. Alongside workers' political organizations, sometimes as official parts of them, sometimes independent, arose workers' sports organizations: athletic clubs, teams, associations. By the end of the nineteenth century, internationalism had become one important principle for both types of organizations. Their internationalism was different from the internationalism of the Olympic movement: as Marx and Engels had put it in the *Communist Manifesto*, workers of the world were to unite in international solidarity against their exploiters. As a result, it wasn't surprising that workers wanted to reject the perceived attempt to enlist and deploy practices that supported nationalism and nationalized militarism. The political rhetoric of workers' sports organizations therefore frequently targeted the nationalism in "bourgeois" sports organizations. For example, in a speech at the Third Congress of the International League for Sport and Physical Culture in Leipzig in 1922, Fritz Wildung said,

Proletarians around the world must protect themselves and their youth against this abuse of sport. Your youth must get out of the atmosphere of war, xenophobia [*Volkerhasses*], and murder. The proletarian sport must be put in the service of socialism. It will be a powerful lever for the new culture, and the proletariat will be its bearer. Sport is to break the chains of the proletarian youth, to liberate them from physical and intellectual servitude. It is a fountain of youth for a cultural revival. However, that will not be achievable as long as the workers fraternize with the bourgeoisie in sports. The workers must incorporate their youth in their own ties in the large and increasingly important area of sports to raise them to our ideals in the proletarian spirit.[15]

Following this logic, the well-attended Worker Olympics in the 1920s took place under the explicit guise of "international solidarity" as opposed to international competition.

Finally, the greatest worry about paternalistic social control of leisure was the perception that sport was a new opiate for the masses. Many worried that it was like the Romans' bread and circuses, with the exception that a sufficiently distracted working class wouldn't even be bothered about the lack of bread. The goal of sports and other leisure, exercised through supposedly apolitical national organizations, was, in this view, to depoliticize and distract workers.

Later scholars have found evidence that the worry was at least partly well founded. Many national sports organizations declared loudly that they were apolitical but often did so precisely *because* they were worried about working class, socialist, and communist activism.[16] Channeling support for the ostensibly apolitical state organizations, often at the expense of the working-class organizations if they had already been created, reflected a desire to give the working classes something safe to keep them busy and away from political mischief. This of course made the "neutral" organizations political in themselves.[17] Against all this, then, it made sense that many in the working classes wanted to start or strengthen the workers' own sports organizations: those organizations enabled better control over the political nature and content of the activities than other groups. Julius Deutsch, an influential activist in the Socialist Worker Sports International, argued in his manifesto, *Sport und Politik,* that state and capitalist practices to fund employer-provided sports while excluding workers' organizations because they were "political," as well as general campaigns to recruit workers into "apolitical" organizations, were simply attempts to alienate workers from their class interests.[18]

Even when working-class sports organizations were created or at least significantly strengthened to counter perceived and real social control, their only purpose was not just to protect workers and working-class youth from capitalist and nationalist ideology. The organizations had many different constructive, as opposed to defensive, political purposes, not all of which were compatible.

Exercising Agency

In the worldview reflected in Wordsworth's letter on the railroad and in many other places earlier in this book, society's hierarchical organization is legitimate because it tracks human capabilities, which vary systematically: some people, in such a view, belong to the lower orders, while others belong above. Although ideologies about the total immutability of human capabilities were well on their way out by nineteenth century, as we have seen, such attitudes about the appropriateness of social hierarchies still persisted. If it was true, as George Orwell suggested some decades later, that even Left intellectuals actually despised the *people* who made up working classes while they venerated the *idea* of the working class, it is hardly implausible that broadly paternalistic attitudes about working classes both reflected and expressed beliefs about workers' lesser worth.[19]

Let us think about the competing visions we have been exploring in this book. On the one hand, we have the idea of a hierarchical and undemocratic society; on the other, the vision of a society in which individuals have equal dignity by virtue of their humanity. In chapter 2, I contrasted this equal dignity with positional honor. What is at issue between these visions, we might say, is the general distribution of *positional goods.*

Positional goods are goods both similar to and different from general public goods. Like public goods, they are social: whether one person has them depends on what others have. Unlike public goods, however, my having a positional good requires than there be someone who does *not* have it. So, for example, aristocratic status is a typical positional good: my being noble only makes sense if there are others who aren't.

As the previous chapters began to show, it would be a mistake to think that democratic-egalitarian societies have no place for positional goods. They have—the grounds are simply different. The liberal slogan of "careers open to talents" against aristocratic nepotism and heredity of offices is just one example of a modern distribution principle for positional goods. The distribution of positional goods depends, on this model, on individuals' talents, desire, and effort. This model necessarily makes some grounds for positional goods illegitimate. Birth, particularly in terms of class (but also race and sex), is one that we now consider illegitimate but that was long considered legitimate. That is because birth is supposed to distribute the nonpositional equal dignity we have seen people fighting to realize. Finally, as chapters 1 and 3 have shown, the modern idea is that positional goods may be acceptable if they arise *out* of the acknowledgment of the nonpositional good of dignity: as long as you put any two people on the same starting line, however, the swiftest does win the race and deserve the positional reward, whether it be glory or wealth.

Now, as chapter 2 established, the conceptual priority of dignity doesn't mean it is also a causal one. Or, in more political terms, just because someone believes that people should be regarded as equals, that does not mean that they actually are. Returning to politicized leisure helps us see why. With the emergence of leisure, it remained a sociological fact that people higher up in social hierarchies refused to see those beneath them as bearers of dignity. Rather, they were often thought of as uncouth, unable to appreciate higher cultivation, and, even in the most optimistic readings of positions like Wordsworth's, only *potential* bearers of higher capabilities.

As the bourgeois duelers showed us, one way of challenging such attitudes and thereby the social order that relied on them for ideological justification was to develop social engagements that would show that the attitudes were false. That is one of the reasons leisure was inherently political for the working classes. What that leisure consisted of—that is, what people actually *did* with their leisure—was political.

Among the purposes of working-class sports organizations was to effect such a strategy. Whether they emerged as responses to perceived social control or as responses to actual barriers to working-class participation, they took political advantage of the working-class specificity and became an expression of working-class culture: it mattered that emerging working-class sports organizations carried their working-class pedigree on their sleeves.[20] Doing so allowed them to turn innocuous voluntary participation in physical leisure into a political struggle for emancipation and dignity, even honor.

First, nineteenth- and early-twentieth-century working-class sports organizations made emancipation *physical*. Material needs did, of course, play a great part in working-class political struggles, thanks largely to Marx's materialist idiom in which political complaints were often articulated. But the demand for better material treatment for workers as beings with physical needs is just part of the story. A communiqué at the Socialist Workers Sport International meeting in Helsinki in 1920 declared that "physical improvement is as essential for the international proletariat as its moral rise."[21] The organizations emphasized that how people thought of the body mattered and that exercising the body was exercising autonomy. So, for example, a 1927 German propaganda leaflet stressed,

> Workers! Your body is your only good! But you do not even have liberty over your own body, as your work, your living conditions, public morals, education, etc. are hindering your being yourself. Liberate yourself from these coercions! Liberate yourself from prejudices even towards your nude body! This will help to improve your self-consciousness and you will be able to join the forces of the struggle for liberation.[22]

I will return later to the mobilization of workers but focus now on the liberation of the body. The passage begins with a straightforward Marxist statement: the worker has only her labor power to sell. But the further inferences are interesting. A similar statement from Deutsch's manifesto, *Sport und Politik,* reads,

> For every person who undergoes oppression in the current economic system, sport represents a bit of redemption. When

the worker or employee casts off the chains of the monotonous and boring work which oppresses his body and steps into the sports-field, the human being inside him—that essential person that the capitalist system tried to destroy—awakes. When the woman throws away her rigid fashionable clothes in order to experience joyful movements in a light sport outfit, then she enhances her beauty and pours out the vitality which she earlier had to stifle under the burden of foolish so-called modesty.[23]

To exercise one's body is to exercise agency. This is one way of demonstrating that working-class persons are autonomous agents in themselves and that class therefore is no marker of some intrinsic inferiority. Furthermore, the radical emphasis on nudity makes the point a clever double whammy: by rejecting clothes, one rejects a convention (never mind that wearing clothes isn't just a bourgeois convention) *and* displays the body in its exuberant freedom and dignity. That games and group gymnastics in the nude and in mixed-sex settings were quite popular at worker sporting events suggests that calls for this particular mode of liberation did not go unheeded.[24]

Gender is also relevant in Deutsch's manifesto. Although sympathetic later commentators likely have exaggerated the extent to which working-class sports *really* were feminist, feminist rhetoric did at least play a role, a topic to which I return in the next section.

An earlier example of the connection between physical culture and emancipation puts the point even more enthusiastically. A 1903 poem celebrated the tenth anniversary of the German Arbeiter Turner-Bund, the working-class spin-off from the nationalist Deutsche Turnershaft.

> Stark wuchs der Baum; mit saft'gen Zweigen
> Durchstrebte er das deutsche Land,
> Und unter ihm, in Spiel und Reigen,
> Die Freiheit ihre Stätte fand.

> [The tree grew strongly; with its luscious branches
> It spread through the German land;
> Underneath it, in game and dance,
> Freedom emerged.]

Despite the revolutionary origins of the *Turner* movement, by the end of the century, the poem goes on to claim, freedom had been "forgotten" in the mainstream nationalist movement. Not so in the workers' organization, however, where it went on to "new victories amidst joyous games." Working-class physical culture would also drive away the "pains of existence [*des Daseins Schmerzen*]" and would bring rights to all humankind.[25]

In these and many other examples, the connection between physical culture and freedom is both causal and conceptual: this physical self-cultivation *is* freedom. The last line of the poem reads, "It's freedom, when we seem to be playing."[26] Of course, many of the organizations were *also* tools of mobilization for freedom down the line, as I discuss later, but the distinction is important. In some cases, the different understandings of how sports related to freedom conflicted.

One reason for the conflict is that conceiving of emancipation through physical culture is not a working-class monopoly. The idea is part of a general ideal of personal self-cultivation, whose champions famously come from outside Marxism. Horst Ueberhorst, who quotes the poem, notes that it is hyper-Schillerian and that its ideals come in particular from Schiller's romantic idealist theories of education.[27] We can also hear echoes of J. S. Mill and, more directly, Wilhelm von Humboldt in the sentiments.[28] And as Bernard Yack has argued, in modern radical politics, most roads lead to Rousseau.[29] Here, therefore, it is reasonable to see echoes of Rousseau's celebration of the natural in general and of the virtuous spectacle in particular.[30] Even more directly, there is a close similarity to the Victorian ideology of moralized physical culture we explored in the previous chapter. There are differences, of course: the emphasis here is on liberty, not on moral virtue or moral health (although they mattered, too).

All the same, the main point is that this particular vision of emancipation through sports is not Marxist or even socialist. It is a democratic vision, as it is based on the idea of the general dignity and worth of all people. Being a working-class vision is not arbitrary, but it is contingent: the working classes most recently had gained some leisure; they needed emancipation, and they needed to defend a democratic claim to equal dignity against the hierarchical conceptions according to which the lower orders did not deserve respect.

As a result, it is not surprising to find parallels to later moments of politicized sports, even when this particular class conflict is not on the agenda. For example, many struggles against racism and race-based exclusion are similar. Sometimes there is overlap, as in the socialist Jewish sports organizations in Germany and Poland, for example.[31] Gender works even more starkly, as I argue in the next chapter.

My point is not to take a stand on whether the working-class sports movements and their events—the Workers' Olympiads in the 1920s attracted more participants than ever took part in the "bourgeois" Olympics[32]—are ultimately good politics. I simply want to illustrate the logic on which they were based. A person who believes that an important part of her freedom is realized through participation in physical activities with her fellow workers openly and on the terms she endorses does enjoy real freedom when she does so. It isn't complete liberation, of course, and no one ever proposed that a soccer team or a gymnastics troupe was all freedom meant. But it is a part, and not just because it is something one gets to choose to do. It isn't freedom just because one has a choice—leisure time, say—but that *by* choosing, one shows one is an agent, capable of making choices autonomously and exercising one's agency. To be sure, having a choice is important, and that's why it is no coincidence that these political expressions take place in civil society: they need to be voluntary. (And that's why it doesn't make the same point when "socialist" sports becomes a part of state propaganda apparatus, as happened most notoriously in East Germany and the Soviet Union and as still happens in China and North Korea.)

But many working-class political activists, having read Marx's words on ideological construction, weren't sure that using sports organizations to express working-class agency was enough. Some of them got nervous when they started hearing Schillerian odes to physical self-cultivation and other Enlightenment rhetoric. Those concerns inspired different visions of freedom and of how to use sport as an instrument of working-class collective agency.

Go Reds, Smash State!

If leisure and other practices in civil society were tools *of* capitalist ideology, then they could, one hoped, be tools *against* capitalist ideology. This required that one pay close attention to the content of leisure and not just think that anything workers do is good. Two strategies made sports movements specifically a tool of working-class—particularly anticapitalist—politics. One was a straightforward mobilization strategy, the other a symbolic, revolutionary rejection of "bourgeois" society's ideology. Although the latter resembled the celebration of freedom I discussed earlier, it was, to use the trendy Gramscian term, "counterhegemonic." Capitalist ideology had penetrated civil society so thoroughly that most things people did in it served as an implicit stamp of approval for capitalism. Countering that required an entirely different vision about the meaning of practices in civil society.

Some people regarded *any* focus on leisure as a distraction. After all, orthodox Marxism (and there were orthodox Marxists in working-class organizations) sees the entire civil society as epiphenomenal—that is, causally inert. A thermometer reflects the temperature, but you cannot warm a room, even less the great outdoors, by warming the thermometer. In this view, political engagement in civil society—let alone frivolous leisure!—does nothing to change the fundamental economic relations in society and therefore keeps the proletariat's eyes off the prize. For example, in a turn-of-the-century internal debate in the German socialist movement, Karl Kautsky argued that sports were simply apolitical and would keep those who participated in them from developing class consciousness.[33] Around the same time in Austria, sports seemed to the leaders of the socialist party "as frivolous as a visit to a twilight variety show or the reading of pornographic literature; it would lead the workers up into the hills of fantasy and hedonism rather than into the urban crucible of action against the government."[34] Similarly, in Britain, activists within the Independent Labour Party were troubled by sports, which drew potentially "zealous propagandists" (the desirable thing to be) to frivolity. Party activist Matt Simm was a bit more sanguine but still argued,

> I do not suggest there is anything wrong with football, but there does seem to be something wrong with the majority of people who habitually attend football matches and fill their minds with things that don't matter. . . . Difficult though the task may be to push football out of heads and push Socialism in, the task must be undertaken, for just as surely as football doesn't matter, Socialism matters a very great deal.[35]

It remains an enduring worry for some that the connection between capitalism and liberal democracy on the one hand and modern leisure on the other can make people unwitting and unthinking supporters of an insidious social order. In Ingham and Hardy's 1980s Marxist jargon,

> To view formal subjugation as economic conditioning rather than economic determination, we feel, is important for there are institutionalised games and exercises which can be pursued recreationally (ie, remain in the realm of private labour) but which require the purchasing of the means of participation (eg, equipment and facilities). Such games and exercises are tied to the broader consumption/production relation of capital accumulation and often represent commercially orchestrated ways of spending discretionary income and time, as well as commercially manipulated fashions and tastes.[36]

In other words, as long as leisure remains structured around liberal democratic (and hence, orthodox Marxists say, capitalist) relations, participation in it will be inherently problematic and possibly politically counterproductive. This worry differs from the straightforward social control concern: one doesn't have to tell any kind of conspiracy story about the motives of elite reformers or individual capitalists or even about class interests. A systemic theory about the workings of capitalism suffices.

However, while some working-class activists shared part of this analysis, they believed it was possible to change the *content* of leisure activities to make them counterhegemonic. If capitalist leisure helped to bolster the capitalist state, socialist leisure would help bring about a different social order. In the 1920s, workers' sports organizations, led by the Socialist Workers' Sport International, were urged to convey the message that "[w]orkers should practice sport in a socialist way."[37]

We saw one aspect of this counterhegemonic conception of leisure earlier in the call for worker athletes to shed bourgeois prejudices along with their clothes. But naturalism wasn't a particularly central working-class principle, nor was it unique to Left politics. Even at the other end of the political spectrum, fascist and ultranationalist movements liked to celebrate the noble body of whatever particular nationality they saw as the pinnacle of human race. Much more important for Left sports ideologists was something much more central to sports itself: competition.

Many, though not all, advocates of worker sports saw competition as a direct reflection of capitalist society's key values and thus sought a more egalitarian conception of physical activity. Julius Deutsch, for example, argued that in a capitalist society, sports were getting *increasingly* competitive and individualist.[38] Once Austrian Marxism had gotten over its total hostility toward sports, it still stressed an alternative vision. "Apolitical and neutral sport, which in reality was 'utterly on capitalism's payroll,' was opposed by explicitly political sport in the service of the emancipation of the working class," Reinhard Krammer has written.[39] An Austrian workers' sports magazine declared that "[b]ourgeois sport is without exception geared to individual top performance. Records, records, records! That is the magic word that defines everything in bourgeois sport."[40] When communist leadership took over the British Workers' Sport Federation in 1928, "the main task of working-class sportsmen and women as enshrined in a new constitution was 'an unrelenting struggle against the existing capitalist domination of sport and the introduction of a socialist content into sport and physical recreation.'"[41] Even in the early Soviet Union, where competitive sports quickly became part of a propaganda apparatus to show the supremacy of socialism over capitalism, debates occurred about whether competition was alien to the socialist mind.[42]

Antonio Gramsci shared the view that sport—at least soccer—reflected capitalist values but at the same time encompassed broader commendable ideals. In a short 1918 piece, "Football and *Scopone*," published in the newspaper *Avanti!* Gramsci defended the transparency of "open" societies against the opacity of contemporary Italian politics by contrasting soccer with an Italian card game:

> Observe a game of football: it is a model of individualistic society. It demands initiative, but an initiative which keeps within the framework of the law. Individuals are hierarchically differentiated, but differentiated on the grounds of their particular abilities, rather than their past careers. There is movement, competition, conflict, but they are regulated by an unwritten rule—the rule of fair play, of which the referee's presence is a

constant reminder. The open field—air circulating freely—
healthy lungs—strong muscles, always primed for action.

Here we have what looks almost like a celebration of the values associated with liberalism: rule of law, merit-based competition, and the
ancillary physical benefits, of which Gramsci, with his permanent disability, must have been keenly aware. Later in the piece the apparent
celebration of these values gets even more excited:

> Even in these marginal human activities, we can see a reflec-
> tion of the economic-political structure of different states.
> Sport is a popular activity in those societies in which the capi-
> talist regime's economic individualism has transformed the
> whole way of life, so that economic and political freedom are
> accompanied by a freedom of the spirit and tolerance of the
> opposition.[43]

Of course, this enthusiasm must be put into context: Gramsci's target
here is the political culture that would soon generate the Fascist capture of the state, and we should not forget his other critiques of liberal democratic polities.[44] And his view notwithstanding, the key from
the counterhegemonic perspective is the close connection he, too,
sees between the political values of a capitalist society and its forms of
leisure.

The alternatives to competition varied. For turn-of-the-century
Britain's socialist Clarion Cycling Club, "recreation and socialism
seemed to have been closely connected. In the first place, cycling was
to be a non-competitive socialist sport, as indicated by the decision of
the Birmingham section to protest 'against the large amount of attention paid by (the National Cyclists' Union) to racing matters against
purely road matters.'"[45] Mass and performing gymnastics, often in
mixed-sex settings, were particularly popular and in many cases included most group members. Hiking and noncompetitive cross-country skiing as well as ice skating were the popular Scandinavian counterparts to cycling and mountaineering further south.[46]

Even in cases where the organizations included competitive
sports, they tried to downplay competitiveness. Competitions in the
Workers' Olympics had no qualifying standards; everyone was wel-

come to try. Records were sometimes noted, but they weren't generally celebrated or part of the official purpose of the practice. The noncompetitive logic extended even to the internal philosophies of competitive sports. For example, a 1929 editorial in a German workers' sports magazine offered a socialist understanding of European handball.

> We socialists . . . know that only common life and effort can advance us in our quest to realize socialism. Now competition has a very particular role in this communal effort. . . . A team consists of individual players. . . . However, they can only succeed within the framework of the team, in which all are committed to one another. That leads to a close-knit communal life, which is the foundation of the organic structure and building of the type of society which we seek.[47]

In one debate at an international meeting of workers sports organizations, some participants proposed revising the rules of soccer.

> [D]elegates also proposed that new rules be set for the game of football . . . to diminish the escalating violence and competitiveness in this game. The proposal (presented together with the representatives of Austria and Switzerland) was that in football competitions, the winning team would be decided not only on the basis of goals scored but also through a system of points rewarding "aesthetic and fair play" and "nice combinations." In this way, workers' football would avoid the increasing brutality of bourgeois football, and would be played according to humanist and socialist principles. The idea was to transform football into "a truly collective and wholesome popular game in accordance with our socialist and collectivist *Weltanschauung*."[48]

In this attempt to subvert dominant understandings of sport, gender equality also became important. Although some later partisan commentators exaggerate the extent to which workers' sports were feminist or antiracist, it is true that many did at least make gender equity and to some extent racial and ethnic solidarity pillars of their political programs. While the reality of gender relations may often have been far less rosy than the rhetoric, it did matter that the rhetoric emphasized gender equity. In 1903, the German *Arbeiter-Turnzeitung* had editorialized (with a somewhat less-than-sophisticated view of gender) that sports would help women gain the willpower, initiative, and energy they lacked.[49] Campaigns against corsets and other physically damaging clothes were part of the same effort. The Norwegian workers' sports organization, Arbetarnas idrottførening, instituted a quota in 1937, giving its women's committee the right to participate in the governance of any individual sport in which women were involved.[50] Of course, this change alone did little since it depended on how much women participated in particular sports and on what terms. But women nevertheless got to do more sports and do them earlier than was the case in "bourgeois" sports organizations and could do so on greater terms of equality. For example, women wore more functional athletic clothing. Furthermore, given the contemporary worries in bourgeois society about how sports would make women masculine or simply be unhealthy for them, even the simplistic feminist rhetoric helped frame working-class sports as counterhegemonic.[51]

The main strategic use of working-class sports was, however, as a means of straightforward mobilization. Sports might or might not be political, but the point was to get workers involved in *workers'* organizations and thus expose them to Left information (or propaganda), recruitment, and deployment in properly political activities (and ultimately, in some visions, in the revolution). Even this purely instrumental approach, however, could have a theoretical grounding. German pamphleteer Helmut Wagner saw sports as an instrument of "class hygiene": fighting capitalism would simply need strong bodies.[52] The way sports organizations pursued this strategy reflected larger-scale left-wing politics. In the early twentieth century, umbrella organizations—socialist and communist parties—insisted on a strict separation from bourgeois sports organizations, particularly if communists had a greater say in the matter. This was part of a larger "class against class" strategy, where social boundaries even in civil society had to be stark and follow class lines.[53] With the rise of fascism, a "popular front" thinking replaced the separationist strategy: the goal was to mobilize the less radical Left, the unaffiliated, and even the moderate Right against the extreme Right.[54] In this context, the apolitical and depoliticizing aspects of leisure seemed an advantage because they would initially attract people out of interest in sports, not because of politics. With a boycott of Hitler's 1936 Berlin Olympics as a concrete target, the supporters of the popular front strategy were optimistic. When the large-scale boycott of the Olympics failed, however, and when many workers simply preferred their apolitical, integrated leisure activities, the workers' sports organizations generally came to the end of their politically significant lives.

Capitalism—1, Socialism—0?

So the history of workers' sports is one of the many stories of the decline of the Left. The causes of this particular decline are numerous, and many of them are straightforwardly historical. Few people in Europe had time to think about leisure at the end of the 1930s and during the Second World War. The rise of fascism, particularly Nazism, destroyed many workers' organizations, especially the Jewish socialist sports organizations that had been significant players in, for example, Germany and Poland as late as the mid-1930s.[55] I am not writing history, though, but am thinking about the theoretical implications of politicized leisure in civil society. There are interesting lessons to be drawn.

As in so much Left politics, internal debates, this time about the relationship between sports and politics, were a key feature of the decades of significant workers' sports. Although historians don't think the internal debates were the central cause of the organizations' demise, it is not a coincidence that only where some particular political approach ended up dominant did the movement remain a significant social factor. For example, with the Finnish workers' sports organization, Työväen Urheiluliitto (Workers' Sports Federation), choosing cooperation and even partial integration with the state organization, Suomen Valtakunnan Urheiluliitto (Finnish State's Sports Federation), and downplaying politics beyond a minimal symbolic component, it survived even beyond the end of the Cold War and retains a sizable membership. In 2001, it still had 337,000 members, or more than 5 percent of the Finnish population.[56] In the Soviet Union and, after the Second World War, in other Soviet satellites, the competitive conception of sports won the day. Sports became one way to demonstrate the supposed superiority of the socialist person over decadent, bourgeois people. Of course, in this role, sports became an important instrument of the state propaganda apparatus and represented the original working-class aspirations as little as the states they served. *Leisure* sports ended up as apolitical and, in one of those ironic turns of history, distractions for people to escape the oppressive state.

Elsewhere, the organizations lost their most important element, mass participation; some never attracted it. Sometimes workers were bribed into the "bourgeois" organizations by greater funding, better access to competitions, and the like; sometimes they were even blackmailed into joining.[57] Most working-class athletes who had hopes and aspirations of elite-level competition or professional sports gave up on the workers' organizations, even if they were politically congenial. For example, Finnish running legend Paavo Nurmi preferred the opportunity to run in the Olympics to class solidarity.[58] Many workers had also been displeased with the anticompetitive rhetoric. Soccer might have reflected the competitive spirit of the capitalist society, but they wanted to play it anyway. In general, many simply wanted to use their leisure for the things they enjoyed and resisted more ideological activists' attempt to have politics dictate leisure content.

Conclusion

How are we to read what happened to workers' sports? Does it show that capitalist hegemony won out against Left resistance? Did the opiate work, after all, before counterhegemonic antidotes kicked in? Some took and others still take this position, not just about working-class sports but about contemporary civil society, which the market has permeated even more effectively than in the early twentieth century and where an ideology of self-fashioning allegedly dominates.[59] In this view, people are simply suckered into thinking that having leisure and the ability to engage in it *is* freedom.

Or is it the other way round? Is having leisure, in and of itself and regardless of other, some yet unrealized social opportunities, *really* part of what it means to be free? Melissa Orlie suggests that even today, worries about the late-capitalist penetration of our lives notwithstanding, self-fashioning in seemingly nonpolitical contexts can be a way of expressing or even enacting our citizenship.[60] Whether such an analysis is appealing depends in part on whether people's own beliefs about their leisure activities matter. In the crudest Marxist stories of false consciousness, individuals' beliefs don't much matter; they are inevitably fooled. But the Marxist understanding needn't be the only game in town. These days, we tend to worry about facile claims of false consciousness. It's not that the crude Marxists, however naive we now think they were, are *always* wrong when they say someone doesn't understand his real interests. People do have false beliefs and beliefs that go against their interests and principles. But my point is, rather, that some straightforward fact of the matter or a principle seldom settles the question. Is my choice of which basketball shoes to buy innocuous and purely apolitical, or a political wrong, or even an exercise of democratic citizenship? The different answers and controversies about them are in themselves political, and there is no a priori principle that rules some options out.[61]

We might gesture toward a stronger claim yet: Gramsci made the point that a connection exists between the norms and values of soccer, on the one hand, and the norms and values of a liberal democratic society: fairness rules as an ideal in both. Broad historical covariance isn't an argument in itself, and even less is the survival of competitive sports in the Soviet world an early sign of the regime's inevitable demise. But there is something intriguing—we'll it leave it at "intriguing" until the conclusion of this book—about the parallels between sport and liberal democracy: Both have a set of constitutive norms that aim at a baseline of equal opportunity but that allow for and even celebrate excellence. And in both, the ideals come into regular and crashing tension with the venality of everyday practice.

Before we get to those questions, there is an entirely different dimension on which we might think about the decline of working-class sports organizations. It has to do with social categories: Why, we might ask, should social class be salient for dividing sports categories? We now tend to think that it shouldn't and that, as we have seen in this and the previous chapter, such divisions are in themselves insidious: they emerged in attempts to prevent some people from having opportunities that others enjoyed. In other words, it is a familiar story of discrimination. But we also saw that those attempts made the divisions political and politically meaningful: they could be contested and rejected exactly because they made little sense by the internal criteria of (ordinary bourgeois) sport.

I am suggesting, therefore, that a set of practices and a set of debates we have seen in the context of early-twentieth-century working-class sports is much like the now more familiar, more recent debates about identity politics. We have seen that a contingent distinction (between the working class and the bourgeois, say) can be politicized in part to undermine that very distinction. And we have seen—pace critics of identity politics—that such politicization needn't reify (make permanent) the categories that are being contested. They may—if the view of an alternative, noncompetitive "socialist" sport had prevailed, the differences would have persisted longer. It's a matter of idle conjecture, of course: the first half of the twentieth century is politically so complex that questions of what might have produced alternative outcomes in a slice of society are almost anyone's guess. But, I insist, it is now unsustainable to say that athletic merit correlates with social class. Moreover, debates we have explored in this and the previous chapter are what made such claims unsustainable.

None of this is to claim that there should not be sports categories that track and map onto other recognizable social distinctions. To say so would be absurd in the light of all the evidence we arguably take for granted: athletic competition divided into age groups, sex groups, and various other categories. However intuitive that might seem, it gets counterintuitive quickly. And as it gets counterintuitive, the questions get interestingly political. In the next chapter, I move ahead to the last fin de siècle we have known and take up related debates from the end of the twentieth century.

::: *part three* :::

::: *five* :::

Being a Woman and Other Disabilities

"We're not going for a hug, we're going for a fucking gold medal."
—SCOTT HOGSETT, *a member of the U.S. Paralympic quadriplegic*
rugby team, on his motives for participating in the Paralympics

In figure 3, a photo from a University of Michigan basketball game in around 1910, you don't see any spectators. Perhaps it's no surprise: even today, a good many intramural college games take place with no spectators. In fact, even women's varsity sports tend to get very few spectators. But that absence of spectators isn't just a coincidence: there were supposed to be no spectators in women's sporting events in the early twentieth century, despite what strikes us as excessively modest—and probably uncomfortable—clothing.[1] This is worth keeping in mind when we think about political controversies of our own era: critics of the gender-equity policies enacted under Title IX often cite women's lack of interest in competitive sports as a reason why strictly proportional equity in college sports is a silly policy.[2] Surely, one might think, it matters for a person's interest in a pursuit what sort of incentives are associated—and have historically been associated—with it. Social appreciation from admiring spectators is one such incentive, and it is an incentive whose absence for a long time was an explicit policy.

The lack of publicity was only a small part of the cluster of policies that limited and shaped women's opportunities to participate in sports for much of the twentieth century. In U.S. education, this changed significantly in 1972 with the enactment of Title IX of the Federal Education Amendments,[3] which required the commitment of equal resources to boys' and girls' sports in educational institutions. In fact, it required gender equity in the provision of and access to educational opportunities in general, but both the campaigning that led to its enactment and the continuing controversies of the past three

Fig. 3. Women's basketball game, Barbour Gym, University of Michigan, ca. 1910. (Reproduced by permission of the Bentley Historical Library, University of Michigan, Ann Arbor.)

decades have kept things focused on sports. Although Title IX changed things significantly, there has also been much continuity. For example, no women's sport is what universities call a "revenue" sport—that is, a sport so popular that its paying spectators make it a major business. And, anyway, if we look past universities, the history of women's participation in elite sports has been a slow and bumpy road to more inclusion. (Pop quiz: When did women's pole vault become an Olympic event? Answer: 2000.)

The history of the politics of women's sports has been written competently by others.[4] Here, I am interested in trying to understand the difference difference makes: how ideas about status and standing, equality and excellence, voluntary choices and justice get sorted out when the perceived differences between *groups* of people, not just individuals, aren't so obviously contingent as the class differences we explored in the previous chapter. I don't want to suggest that, say, gender differences are somehow permanently real—in other words, I am not an essentialist about gender—but I do show that in some cases equality requires the acknowledgment of differences. That isn't news to anyone who has a passing familiarity either with civil rights arguments or the theorizing behind such arguments. But there are new things to be said: ideals of personhood and norms that attach to different types of personhood matter when we try to understand questions of equality of opportunity. Here I explore whether there can be a *right* to meaningful competition, and if so, on what terms, *given* that there are differences that make a difference in terms of excellence.

The provocative title of this chapter serves two purposes. First, it points to one conception of women that is, fortunately, almost gone at the beginning of the twenty-first century but that has affected women's opportunities particularly in terms of physical culture. Second, I want us think about the idea of disability itself: in addition to disentangling *women* from *disability,* we might also try to disentangle *disability* from something that, almost by definition, can't be understood as excellence. These two aspects, women and disability, disability and its association with whatever is the opposite of excellence, are connected. So perhaps provocatively, I focus in this chapter on people who still are unequivocally understood to have disabilities (as much as there can be clarity on who counts as having a disability). In analyzing the contemporary politics of disability sports, I shed light on the logics and the political mechanisms that help us understand the contingent relationships between the norms and ideals of personhood, equality, excellence, and justice. The point is not that women's participation in sports has had only to do with beliefs about their weakness and physical vulnerability. Those beliefs mattered much and informed debates about the nature and terms of women's participation for a long time and arguably still do so to some extent today.[5] And they were tangled up with other beliefs and attitudes about what was proper for women (for example, chastity).[6]

Let's think about "real" disabilities, then. In summer 1999, nine wheelchair users filed a suit against the organizers of the New York City Marathon (NYCM), alleging discrimination that violated the Americans with Disabilities Act (ADA), which was enacted in 1990. Wheelchair athletes had been allowed to participate in the NYCM, one of the world's largest marathon races, for twenty years, but not on the same terms as able-bodied runners. The plaintiffs alleged that police routinely but randomly stopped wheelchair participants—sometimes for up to forty minutes—so that elite runners could pass; that no competitive wheelchair division existed; and that they received no prizes, award ceremonies, or media exposure.[7] The general theme of these practices was that people with disabilities didn't really count as athletes. For example, that they could be stopped implied that improving the times in which they finished the 26.2-mile race wasn't significant, even though it could be a goal for even the most recreational, five-hour, able-bodied marathoner. The lack of a *competitive* wheelchair division implied the same, since it lumped together hand-pushed racing wheelchairs and chairs using bicycle gears. The implications were made explicit by the absence of prizes or even finishers' medals for these athletes.

This particular dispute has been settled, more or less happily and, given recent progress in disability sport, might seem like only an ugly reminder of a bygone era, much like earlier stories of women's exclusion from sports. In fact, evidence suggests that disability sport has followed women's sports in getting significantly mainstreamed and in getting people with disabilities recognized as athletes. Since 1988, the Paralympic Games—the Olympics for athletes with disabilities—have been held in the same venues as the Olympic Games, and there has been increasing cooperation between the International Paralympic Committee and the International Olympic Committee.[8] Golfer Casey Martin's 2001 U.S. Supreme Court victory that enabled him to use a cart on the PGA Tour also was seen as a major victory for disability sport.[9] And, in running, the NYCM had been a bit of an outlier, anyway: most of the world's other major marathons had had competitive wheelchair divisions at least since the 1980s.

But things aren't quite that simple. How mainstream disability sport has become remains an open question, and the political and legal victories haven't been forgone conclusions. Tenacious opposition persists. Disability litigation is one of the many areas in which some Americans believe the country has become "overlawyered."[10] In general, the NYCM case points to still tricky questions about the participation of people with disabilities in sports and similar social practices. On what terms may people with disabilities participate in competitive sports? *What* particular sports can they participate in, and why? How can we tell who should be allowed to participate? These issues ultimately raise questions about social justice: Do voluntary civil-societal pursuits of excellence—where distinguishing between better and worse is the whole point—fall within the scope of social justice? If so, how do we determine when justice has been done and when an injustice of some kind exists? Although significant differences exist between different kinds of groups—people with disabilities, women, people from different racial groups, for example—some of the broad questions are the same.

The easy but mistaken answer is that questions of justice don't even arise in cases like the NYCM challenge. That is because, on such a view, social justice is about the equal distribution of what Alasdair Macintyre calls *external* goods and not about goods *internal* to a practice: a liberal democratic state ensures that you have a *right to pursue* a job (external good) but no *entitlement to one* (internal good); a right to education (external) but not to become the valedictorian at your school (internal).[11] Similarly, the view goes, the ADA or Title IX and other such institutionalized rights at most ensure an eligible person a right to participate in a pursuit of excellence but no entitlement to anything that would count as excellence.

The easy answer is mistaken because it confuses participation with *meaningful* participation. A person's mere presence at a pursuit does not mean she actually participates in it; it depends on the terms on which she does it. The simplest and often the most innocuous example is one with which I began this chapter: whether others show up to watch you makes a difference. This observation does not obviate the bigger questions, just refocuses them: Can there be a right to a meaningful participation in a pursuit of excellence, and on what terms? I will not argue for absurdities: justice can't demand that field hockey be made as popular and lucrative as football. (How could one do it, anyway?) But for that reason, the terms of what counts as meaningful participation are important and are not at all obvious.

The answer is that it depends on the interplay among three factors: the politicization of a practice (someone needs to make a demand), institutionalized principles of justice (e.g., the ADA), and sometimes inchoate, often controversial ideas of what the practices in question are all about. In what follows, I explore the relationship between the factors in disability sport, focusing on the latter two. First, there are many ways to interpret the spirit of the ADA, and a successful argument for a right to a pursuit of excellence requires that the ADA be understood as an anticaste principle. That interpretation allows me to show how even voluntary, ostensibly apolitical social practices can stigmatize groups of people—people with disabilities, for example—and how such practices may be refigured to bring about social justice.

The ADA as an Anticaste Principle

In her 1984 book, *The Disabled State,* Deborah Stone argues that the key to understanding disability politically is to think of the state as attempting to maintain the uneasy boundary between two distributive systems, work and need.[12] At least in the West, the historical thread in disability policies had been to make sure that those "genuinely" unable to work got whatever help they deserved without those able to work receiving perverse incentives not to do so. If we accept Stone's analysis, then the ADA looks truly groundbreaking: the U.S. Congress explicitly framed the law as a corrective to unjust *discrimination* against people with disabilities. There is much to be said for reading the ADA as a good-faith piece of civil rights legislation, the kind of legislation that shows the state's commitment, however grudging at times, to the fact that distributive justice isn't only about the just distribution of material goods: it can be about the just distribution of rights, opportunities, capabilities, and even recognition and respect.[13] The ADA is premised on the idea that disability policy shouldn't only involve taking care of needs while discouraging shirking; it tries to correct the world so that having a disability does not mean that someone is entitled to fewer opportunities and respect than nondisabled persons. The ADA enshrines that social value into law and says that the value is important enough for the state to use its coercive apparatus to enforce it.

The precise nature of that social value is open to some interpretation. Samuel Bagenstos has argued that the injustice in the case of disability is the creation of *stigma* and that the best interpretation of the ADA is to read it as an institutionalized piece of what Cass Sunstein calls the "anticaste principle."[14] In that view, the state wants to ensure that people with disabilities not become a group seen as less worthy than people without disabilities. Insofar as people with disabilities *have* been treated as less worthy than others, the state must try to eradicate such practices.

Sports, Civil Society, and Justice

This book has focused on the social sphere we call civil society, and I have argued that the need for this focus hasn't been a coincidence: many political issues must be negotiated in civil society. But when we begin talking about questions of justice in a context where a well-established (safely consolidated, political scientists like to say) democratic state is responsible for maintaining the justice of institutions, complications arise. On the one hand, a safely consolidated, stable state that citizens for the most part trust and can influence is preferable to a capricious, unreliable, or explicitly oppressive state. The wheelchair athletes can turn to the ADA, an *institutionalized* principle of justice, making their situation much better than those of the workers we saw in the previous chapter. But on the other hand, the role of civil society in a liberal democratic society makes this political resource a double-edged sword. Civil society is the social sphere for voluntary activity, and part of the point of its existence in a well-organized liberal democratic society is that the state keeps its distance from it: the state has the potential to become an intrusive busybody, and its reach into civil society therefore should be minimal, the conventional liberal intuitions go. The intuitions are well founded, but still: that practices in civil society are voluntary does not mean that they cannot fall within the purview of justice. Civil rights struggles over the past century have convincingly established that questions of justice arise in civil society. That is, for example, what the ADA's public accommodations clause addresses: public accommodations, which are parts of civil society, must be accessible to people with disabilities. But what remains open is the way and extent to which *specific* practices are to be open to all comers—or what "all comers" actually means. The legitimately discriminatory nature of sports—discriminating between better and worse by internal standards—makes them a particularly good case to puzzle through the relationship between legitimate and illegitimate discrimination. It makes them political and politically interesting.

I focus only on the question of whether sports themselves can continue to become instances of justice and injustice to people with disabilities and, by extension, to other ascriptive groups in a liberal democratic state. In effect, I am asking whether Harlan Hahn's observation on disability and work can be more than a metaphor: "The right of disabled citizens to have an equal chance to compete with the nondisabled in a race rigged against them by factors unrelated to their individual talents may be incompatible with the standards of a democratic society."[15]

So the question is: In an actual race—tournament, game, match— are the standards of success "unrelated to the individual talents" of people with disabilities? The intuitive answer of people sympathetic to disability rights is likely yes, as is my final answer in the chapter: "disability" in one dimension does not preclude talent and excellence in others; neither does gender. More strikingly, this can be true even if the "achievements" are by some conventional yardstick different from those in a relevant reference group. But intuitions notwithstanding, the answer isn't obvious. First, people disagree: commenting on the Achilles Track Club lawsuit against the NYCM, an anonymous participant in an online runners' forum wrote in 1999, "I sympathize with the handicapped, but racing isn't something they should try to do." To be sure, the view reflects precisely the attitudes that help generate the stigma the ADA tries to counter. But it also accurately reflects the view that sports are a pursuit in which difference makes a difference and in that way reflects a more general position specifically critical of disability rights: "Even if one concedes a role for government in eliminating private discrimination, one must also acknowledge that discrimination against disabled individuals is different in kind from discrimination by reason of race, national origin, religion, or sex."[16] The theoretical and political challenge for those who think that Hahn's point applies in sports is to show why and how the difference of a disability isn't the same as comparatively less valuable talent.

To anticipate my conclusion: we can meet the challenge, at least part of the way, by rethinking the meaning of excellence in sport. Doing so shows us that this meaning indeed admits different kinds of talents without requiring any fundamental change in the meaning of excellence. My argument, in other words, isn't about dumbing down excellence in sport but simply about showing that disability can be perfectly compatible with that excellence.

I deliberately bring up the conservative worry about general equality: the next step of the argument requires that we turn to questions of the equality of opportunity.

Equal Opportunity to What?

Let's return to the New York City Marathon and the lawsuit brought by the nine members of the Achilles Track Club, an international organization for wheelchair athletes.

In their defense, the New York Road Runners Club (NYRRC), which conducts the marathon, cited concern for wheelchair users' safety as one of the reasons their progress was often delayed and why they weren't always allowed to start at the official starting line.[17] The plaintiffs considered these arguments both patronizing and disingenuous, and soon enough the NYRRC began to make real concessions, which led to a general out-of-court settlement. For the November 1999 marathon, the club promised that wheelchairs would not be delayed on the course, and organizers agreed to introduce a special wheelchair division for the 2000 race and prize money by 2001. (In the nondisabled divisions, the prize money runs into tens of thousands of dollars.)

So although the problem has gone away and although the NYCM was, as I said earlier, a political laggard in the world of distance running, it is useful for our exploration to begin with the philosopher's usual move and call into question something no longer in dispute. Why should wheelchair athletes participate in a *footrace?* Wheelchairs have wheels; footraces, by definition, are events where people run or walk. First, why should wheelchair users get to participate at all, and, second, why should they participate in footraces? Let's begin with the second, more specific question: Why footraces? The answer is a pragmatic one, although no less robust for that: although a wheelchair user can, on the average, move faster than a person on foot (which is why wheelchair athletes usually begin their race a few minutes before runners), the speed is closest to that of a person on foot. Notably, push-rim wheelchairs are significantly slower than racing bicycles, the other possible reference group. Furthermore, a wheelchair is the most quotidian mode of movement for a person with a mobility disability, just as feet are for able-bodied persons. Part of the appeal of organized running and walking for people who enjoy it is that it is so easy to do; one can, in theory, jump into a footrace just as one is. The more general idea is that disability is not the same as *inability.* As Karen DePauw and Susan Gavron have observed, the recent tendency in disability sport classification has been to focus on functional *abilities,* not on disability—that is, on what a person can do instead of what she cannot do.[18]

This gets us to the question of why athletes with disabilities should get to participate in an able-bodied persons' race in the first place. Here is a rough first cut for an answer: Wheelchair athletes should get to participate (1) because some wheelchair users *can* engage in a competition that is in most essentials the same as the competition by people not in wheelchairs, (2) because some of them also *want* to engage in such competitions, and (3) because our intuitions about the norms of a liberal society say that if someone wants to do something she can do without burdening others, she should get to. That was the logic on which people with disabilities argued for their admittance into footraces in the late 1970s; earlier, it was one of the Title IX arguments. With disability, things weren't quite as simple at that time because before the passage of the ADA, a gap existed between the political intuitions and a *specific* institutionalized principle that would apply. To some extent, the Civil Rights Act of 1964 as well as later disability-specific statutes such as the Architectural Barriers Act or the Rehabilitation Act enacted to help people with disabilities in other contexts afforded enough legal and political comparisons for a legitimate case by analogy.[19] But still, one could argue that people with disabilities were until very recently much in the same extralegal boat as the workers and bourgeois duelers of my earlier chapters.

In the case of the NYCM, again a visible landmark in these matters, much turned on how the wheelchair users' ability to participate was interpreted and on whether the ideals of equal opportunity applied in the case. Interest in participation wasn't the issue, or the legal case would not have arisen. The organizers of the race did not deny that people with disabilities can participate in *some* athletic activities but argued that they could not participate in a footrace aimed primarily at able-bodied runners without seriously endangering everyone. Fred Lebow and James Fixx, the race directors, argued in a hearing in front of the New York Human Rights Commission that the speed of the wheelchairs made them so dangerous to biped runners that they should not be allowed to participate.[20] The argument didn't fly, however, and by October 1980, the Human Rights Appeal Board issued a final ruling that wheelchair athletes had to be allowed to participate.

More theoretically, in any loosely liberal polity, one central notion of equality is the idea that opportunities should be equalized. As I suggested earlier, by the end of the twentieth century, this idea was firmly established as a norm directing the state; such wasn't the case in the controversies we saw in the previous chapters. But the difficulty still is to figure out what it means: people differ in needs, inclinations, and talents. Differential needs may mean that equal opportunity requires differential resources: wheelchair ramps in buildings are a familiar example. Differential inclinations and talents mean that it can be difficult to tell whether someone lacks or has lacked equal opportunities: maybe my relative poverty reflects an earlier choice not to pursue the American Dream, or maybe I did pursue it but invested my time and money badly. In neither case is it obvious that I lacked opportunities comparably equal to others.

For these two reasons—that different needs require different resources and that inequality of achievement does not prove inequality of opportunity—Amartya Sen has argued that the best interpretation of equality is an *equal capability* to function as a human being.[21] People are equal when they enjoy the capability—utilized or not—to pursue the variety of things that society considers worthy of a full human life. People are unequal when they are denied any such capability, whether as a result of intentional discrimination (explicitly racist, sexist, or ableist beliefs, say) or structures that produce a discriminatory effect (e.g., people with disabilities systematically lacking access to educational resources).

The implications for disability are important. Unlike in the periods that parts 1 and 2 of this book covered, the assumption of equal human dignity is now more or less a given. So if we think that any human being is prima facie eligible for a full human life, then we have to be attentive, from the word *go,* to people's widely diverse opportunities and abilities to reach it. This requires that even severe "natural" physiological limitations be rendered as costless as possible. "Natural" limitations include human-dependent actions such as accidents, but the idea is the same: if my capability is or gets limited, justice demands that the limitation be as costless as possible. The ideal, even if it is not fully realizable, is that neither nature nor accident denies anyone the capability to function.

Among the familiar implications of this view is the argument for why the state is not only justified but required to use extra resources for people with disabilities when renovating buildings to make them accessible, for example. The logic was also applicable in the context of the wheelchair marathon controversy in the late 1970s. *Washington Post* columnist Colman McCarthy, for example, argued,

> I side with the handicapped. If the wheelchair is what they have been forced to use for transportation, then the wheels of their vehicle are actually their feet and legs. Why should either an accident of birth, or an accident on the highway or a war zone, disbar someone from sharing the roadway with the able during a marathon?[22]

The language might already grate our ears, but the point is clear. To deny wheelchair users participation would be to deny them an equal opportunity to engage in a meaningful human activity; that the actual mode of their activity—wheelchairs instead of feet—is different is by itself no argument. They can have recognizably comparable activity even in the same event. Where genuine logistical differences arise because of the physical aspects of the wheelchairs, providers of the services must try to accommodate them instead of using the difference as grounds for denying the right to participate. In practice, that has been done quite successfully through measures like letting the wheelchairs begin their race a little before the runners or by letting blind athletes use guides.

All this should be familiar and uncontroversial in principle if not in practice. It still makes a difference, however, to what extent we take the "reasonable accommodations" now explicitly required by the ADA to imply something like "compensation for misfortunes." Many people have tended to think of them on those terms: like the anonymous commentator in the runners' online forum, they may "feel for the handicapped." This can help foster the idea that equalization is somehow equivalent to remedial education, itself an idea laden with a patronizing attitude and so a source of a stigma. When someone is stigmatized, her identity is "spoiled," as Erving Goffman has put it.[23] This isn't, in the first instance, about the goings-on in her head: the "spoiled identity" is the person's social identity, how others see her. One of the things people don't expect of "defectives" is excellence.

This is why the argument requires our interpreting the ADA as an anticaste principle: in that interpretation, to think that a person cannot or should not hope for an excellence is to stigmatize and is thus inconsistent with the demands of justice. For this reason as well, the demands of justice are not met when wheelchair athletes just get to wheel through the course of the NYCM: they are, in some way, obviously participating in the event, but they are not participating in what makes the event what it is. They are specifically denied the richer opportunity.

But I have not yet offered an argument for why justice requires that wheelchair users be allowed to participate in this pursuit of excellence on these particular terms. We also don't know how the argument so far applies to disability sport in general. For example, does the current arrangement for Paralympic Games—same venues as the Olympic Games, different time—satisfy or violate the demands of justice? To say that these issues are purely logistical is to sidestep the question: the equality-as-capability model explicitly denies the primacy of logistical considerations: there are no "purely logistical" considerations.

Despite the legitimately bad rap from which the notion of "separate but equal" suffers, it may sometimes be legitimate. That depends on why the separation exists, and that in turn depends on the internal meaning and logic of the practice in question. I now turn to the meaning and logic of competition.

Meaningful Competitions

One of the reasons I focus on sports is that they constitute a social practice where the notion of excellence is relatively straightforward. In sports, there are reasonably clear measures of excellence, of ranking participants, of measuring relative success. Competitors aim to do as well as possible and ultimately to win.

Of course, especially in recreational sports, many people don't aim to win; increasingly, people don't aim at excellence at all, as in the alternative conceptions of sports—"socialist sport"—discussed in the previous chapter. In our contemporary world, people engage in sports for health, to raise funds for a charity, to have fun with friends—in short, for recreation. Even so, the notion of competition is still partly constitutive of most such events: people do get ranked, whether or not they care about that ranking, and winners do get awards. Given the nature of the practice, opportunity to participate in it on fully equal terms would mean an equal opportunity to meaningful competition.

Consider what "meaningful competition" means. "The hope of winning" might be one interpretation. The Olympic slogan, "Citius, altius, fortius" (Faster, higher, stronger), captures this idea: there are straightforward objective measures of achievement, and excellence is ascribed to people comparatively by how they line up in displaying their prowess. The greatest praiseworthiness is due the person who outperforms everyone else because he or she has reached the goal everyone seeks. It seems to follow, then, that for competition to be meaningful, everyone must have a realistic hope of being the winner. But this is impossible: people's talents and abilities vary widely, both because of agent-independent reasons ("natural" and "normal" distribution of talents, available resources, and so forth) and reasons that depend on the person's own efforts (e.g., practice). Especially in recreational sports, the majority of people have zero hope of winning, regardless of how much they might practice. Most of the forty thousand runners in the NYCM don't even dream of winning the race.

Another interpretation of "meaningful competition" might be to eliminate the effects of the luck of birth and other factors that don't depend on a person's individual efforts. That way, the argument might go, competition would indeed be fair: the person who applied herself most diligently to practice would come out as the winner: A for effort. The insurmountable difficulty with this approach, however, is that it is impossible to separate the factors clearly enough. While there is some agreement of what, say, genetic factors contribute to particular kinds of athletic prowess, these factors tend to vary greatly: I might be a good distance runner thanks to my natural motor efficiency (itself likely an genetic interaction effect); you might be good because of your congenitally high number of red blood cells. Second, there are agent-independent causes for those mental dispositions that motivate persons in pursuits of excellence. Attention deficit hyperactivity disorder (ADHD), for example, can impair a person's ability to excel academically or in an athletic pursuit.[24] Some of these are "natural" (that is, something with which the person is born); others may depend on forms of "nurture."[25] And, finally, for better or for worse, social conceptions of excellence do, as a matter of sociological fact, incorporate both appreciation for individual effort *and* relationships among people. A figure skater's quadruple jump is praiseworthy precisely because it is so difficult for anyone to accomplish, and no matter how much I train, I will not merit similar appreciation if I can't even get off the ice. Sometimes "A for effort" makes no sense. In fact, while university students who receive Bs on assignments frequently lament, "I worked so hard on it," instructors generally and reasonably think "A for effort" was really abandoned as a principle sometime in elementary school. This is all the more true for sports: *just* working hard is not enough for excellence.

But then we have another problem. Let us zoom out from disability and consider excellence along the lines of gender divisions. Our intuitions now (if not in 1910) are supposed to be pretty clear about gender as meaningful demarcation line in sports. It turns out that the intuitions aren't so clear: theoretically messy social practices abound. For example, Title IX is still controversial and in fact is coming under increasing criticism from some directions. One of the arguments is that since women's athletic performance "simply" is less impressive than men's, this demand for equality amounts to dumbing down of sports and to the inflation of "excellence." The argument is not the most important one critics of Title IX have marshaled, but it has been significant. In September 2000, tennis star John McEnroe went on record disparaging the women's tennis phenomenon the Williams sisters as being merely equal to mediocre male players, to "good college athletes."[26] The claim is, to be sure, at best arguable factually, and McEnroe hardly has a reputation as a tireless feminist. But his point raises a question: *if* athletic achievements aren't appreciated on a unitary, objective scale, then what separates a scale?

One might think that these McEnroe-style arguments represent some relics of a fortunately disappearing era, and in a way, they likely do. But the arguments are often couched in a rhetoric of equality: since the principles of equality and antidiscrimination ask us not to make social differences salient, the argument goes, Title IX requirements, different athletic divisions and awards for women, say, are discrimination.[27] Whether the equality rhetoric is sincere is not central. Similarly, it doesn't settle the issue to remember that at least according to the capability-based understanding of equality differences in fact must be closely focused on. The question is why *these* differences ought to matter. When one argues that women or people with disabilities ought to have a chance to dream of winning and not be victims of circumstance, the critic could say that a healthy male who lacks the natural endowment to make it to the top is in no different position in that he also can't conceivably dream of being a winner. Sure, in many sports, women on average have somewhat "lesser" performances than men, but there are many women who are better than I, the author of this book, am. I know this: they have beaten me. Some women can outperform men: marathoner Paula Radcliffe can easily outperform Mika LaVaque-Manty and thousands of other men, too. So why should we have gender divisions in sports? Why should I be satisfied with a tenth place in my division when a woman who is actually slower than I am might be the winner in some particular sporting event? And if I am to put up with the fact that I can't dream of winning the NYCM, why can't a person with a disability put up with that fact?

Mightn't we just admit that talents are normally distributed? That is, there is a bell curve where on the right-hand tail are the truly talented, on the left-hand side the talentless, and in the middle large mass of mediocrity? Norman Daniels points out in his discussion of mental disability the seemingly benign fact that talents are normally distributed actually raises rather than obviates questions of disability justice.[28] One might argue, as people used to, that disability in any given dimension simply represents the left tail of a bell curve of that particular dimension: they are weak end of the normal distribution of that talent; too bad for them, but that's how the dice got thrown. But for better or for worse—for better, as far as I'm concerned—we no longer think quite that, as we saw: disability is almost never such a total condition that there are no dimensions on which a person might count as talented. This applies not only to Stephen Hawking but to many athletes with disabilities: as soon as you find the right measure, you'll realize that talents of many different kinds are also normally distributed *among* people with disabilities. Moreover, this distribution difference isn't just a result of our zooming in on the tail end of a larger population's distribution. In the case of a couple of athletic values— courage and dexterity, say—the athletes involved in quadriplegic rugby (popularly known as murderball) land in the talent distribution curve of a population that involves people with and without disabilities.[29] Not, I would surmise, somewhere on the left tail.

But then we have a problem. On the one hand, we can find courageous and talented individuals in the groups that one might have thought as deficient, whether they be women or people with disabilities. On the other hand, there are also irreducible differences in the way the talent gets displayed. One familiar solution to this tension between two sets of considerations is that "excellence" gets relativized to some particular reference group. For a female figure skater, it is excellent to achieve a triple jump, for example. These groups are "ascriptive proxies": the groups are carved out in a way that makes competition meaningful. The idea is that two randomly selected individuals from a given reference group should have an equal hope of beating one another in a head-to-head effort.

These classifications are contingent. All of this applies directly to disability sport, and thinking about disability sport shows us in spades what has been true about women's sport. In disability sport, the divisions and categories are more numerous than in other sport, but the logic isn't. "Classification is simply a structure for competition. Not unlike wrestling, boxing and weightlifting, where athletes are categorized by weight classes, athletes with disabilities are grouped in classes defined by the degree of function presented by the disability."[30]

Similarly on the one hand and very differently on the other, the logic of "open competition"—the "freedom to enter an event in which one meets eligibility requirements with respect to times and distances, with no consideration given to functional or medical classification"—gets us into considering the question of meaningful competition.[31] In disability sport, the idea of open competition is that anyone who can compete can join in. It is not only true in disability sport. If visually impaired runner Marla Runyan prefers to compete in the Olympics instead of Paralympics, she can do it. One problem is that it may seem to imply that the level of excellence in the Olympics is greater. On the flip side of this tricky coin is South African sprinter Oscar Pistorius, who was born without fibulae in his lower legs and who therefore uses prosthetic lower legs known as the Cheetahs.[32] Pistorius made a bid to move from the Paralympics to able-bodied sport, but the International Amateur Athletics Federation resisted on the grounds that his prostheses gave him an unfair advantage. Unlike in the case of wheelchairs, where the speed advantage is obvious, Pistorius's case required complicated adjudication on whether he had an obvious advantage or simply lots of talent and hard work. After a long and complicated process, he was cleared to participate in the 2008 Olympics but failed to qualify for the South African team—so much for his "obvious" advantage. (He ended up participating in the 2008 Paralympics, winning multiple gold medals there.)[33] The case nicely illustrates the several ambiguities of disability sports.

So while the issues are quite complicated, these considerations suggest that "meaningful competition" for wheelchair athletes would be competition among other, similarly *situated* even if not similarly *talented* wheelchair users. Wheelchairs affect athletic performance: on average, in the aggregate, they make the athletes faster than biped runners. A separate competitive division for wheelchair users is a way of making sure competition also remains meaningful for runners. And since the type of wheelchair a person uses reflects her functionality, the logic also suggests that there should be many wheelchair categories, not just one: the average differences caused by the mechanical differences both change the nature of the endeavor and make an average difference in the outcomes.[34]

Still, the functional understanding of meaningful competition can seem to come into tension with ideas of excellence, however contingent the latter. There are many ways of carving out groups so that their aggregate and average performances vary. Why are some ways chosen over others? Why are some mandated by considerations of justice and others not? The concern—historically attributed, as I have suggested in this book, to conservatives—is that a proliferation of categories will dumb down notions of excellence. "If everybody is special," a character puts it in the popular film *The Incredibles*, "then nobody is."[35]

Although this may be true in the abstract and although the concern is real, there is no obvious reason to believe that proliferation of categories *by itself* creates a slippery slope to mediocrity. Let's consider the issue with another recent category controversy. The newest addition in many endurance sports has been the creation of weight categories. In many footraces, for example, heavier runners now get to compete in "Clydesdale" divisions on the undeniable logic that in running, weight is functional: carrying more puts one at a disadvantage relative to lighter persons. While commonplace in many other sports—wrestling, boxing—these divisions are highly controversial in endurance sports.

The controversy has several causes.[36] The most obvious one is that the demand for such categories is explicitly political, just as in (other) disability sports: activists in organizations such as Team Clydesdale make a political demand for inclusion.[37] This can generate opposition for many reasons; the most important is based on the widely held but most likely false belief that a person's weight is more or less up to her and that *she,* therefore, can make competition meaningful for herself simply by losing weight. This is analogous to the argument that if I fail my examination because I haven't studied, I have no cause for complaint. The background principle is what some philosophers call "luck egalitarianism": equality requires eliminating the "arbitrary" effects of agent-independent factors for how a person's life turns out, but it doesn't require compensation for the opportunities she herself has squandered.[38] This argument depends on the extent to which weight really is within a person's voluntary control—there are good reasons to think the voluntarists exaggerate it—and the outcome of the weight category debate in that respect will partly depend on the outcome of the larger empirical and political controversy.[39]

But the general point is that a weight category in these endurance sports is wholly contingent, the justifiability of which depends on social conventions and *on political agreement among participants,* not on any obviously undeniable facts. Facts matter, of course, as the controversy about the causes of a person's weight suggests, but equally significant is the interpretation of the facts and the decision about which facts are salient and which aren't. The key open question for society to settle is whether heavy endurance athletes' performances count as excellence. It's contingent but not arbitrary: it depends on what kinds of reasons end up winning the day. At the moment, there is no agreement on weight. Issues are significantly more settled but nevertheless analogous in the case of disability, sex, and race: society's contingent—if in some quarters grudging—view is that category separation on the basis of disability and sex is legitimate, whereas race-based categories would now indeed seem insidious (even if race might make a functional difference in terms of achievement).[40]

Meaningful competition is thus determined by social conventions, which, in turn, reflect social values. There is no reliable decision principle that would settle the case of which differences ought to be regarded as salient and which shouldn't, even when antidiscrimination law tells us to be careful with some particular ones. First, sometimes we can't even agree on how we should conceive some social practice. (Is education about producing a skilled workforce or informed citizenry?) Second, even when we agree on the point of a practice—say, sports—we may disagree on what it means. But, again, the disagreements needn't be irreconcilable. I have tried to suggest why wheelchair athletes have a compelling logic for their inclusion: long-distance endurance sports are about endurance, and it would be unfair to ban people with disabilities who nevertheless can test their endurance. At the same time, it would not make sense to allow someone with an electric wheelchair to participate. But although I find the U.S. Supreme Court's decision to allow Casey Martin to use an electric cart on the PGA Tour compelling, it strikes me as less *obviously* correct. There are difficult open questions: should it be a constitutive rule of golf that competitors walk between holes, as the PGA argued against Martin? And even if it not, might the PGA Tour or similar institution unilaterally change its conception of measuring golf excellence to include such a rule? There are better and worse reasons, and sometimes we come to agreements. But the questions aren't settled by anything other than the contingent reasons we all can try to marshal.

Conclusion

I have argued that even in a stable liberal democracy, voluntary civil-societal practices such as sports can come within the purview of justice and that we can argue—on the basis of contingent reasons and against the backdrop of antidiscrimination laws such as Title IX or the ADA—that people can have a defensible a right to meaningful competition. What meaningful competition is within a given set of practices and how that right is interpreted can vary widely. Moreover, it depends, as I have argued, on how the practices in question are understood. Competition in sports is about excellence, and the political arguments therefore concern the nature and meaning of excellence. I have suggested some of the ways in which supporters of disability sport have shown disability to be perfectly compatible with athletic excellence, but I have also pointed to the ways in which these questions are unavoidably contingent. For that reason, they often remain—appropriately—political. The same goes for gender.

What, then, about cases where disability sport appears organized on a "separate but equal" principle? Or what about cases where performing takes place outside public view, as in the 1910 women's basketball game mentioned at the beginning of this chapter? Insofar as the anticaste principle against the stigmatization of people with disabilities is compelling, the Achilles Track Club athletes' demand that they be allowed to participate *as* athletes in the NYCM and not in some parallel event is significant: Stigmatization and its opposite, respect, are social expressions. In this case, for example, the millions who line the streets of New York to watch the event are, intentionally or not, part of a collective expression of respect for the participants. In a slightly different case, the opening ceremonies of the 2000 Sydney Olympics, one of the final torchbearers was Betty Cuthbert, a wheelchair user, and the final one an Australian Aboriginal athlete, Cathy Freeman; both (obviously) were women. We could interpret this as distasteful tokenism that attempts to hide Australia's enduring stigmatization of people with disabilities and its indigenous population. Or, worse, we might interpret it as a lamentably politically correct concession to people who have no place being appreciated alongside "real" athletes. But we can also interpret Cuthbert's and Freeman's inclusion as a genuine expression of equal respect for people with disabilities, racial minorities, and women.[41] One thing about sport—high-visibility Olympic sport in particular—is that it *says* something in addition to what it *does:* whether it changes people's attitudes and beliefs, whether it hides existing practices of discrimination and oppression, its symbolic message matters as a kind of political recognition.[42]

I conclude with two different sets of considerations. First, this chapter began with an early-twentieth-century image of sporting women and has ended with a very different one. Whereas the University of Michigan basketball players engaged in their sport without spectators, Cuthbert and Freeman paraded—and, in Freeman's case, competed spectacularly—in front of potentially billions. Does this mean that the prior stigmas, be it being a woman or having a disability, are all gone? Not quite yet seems like a reasonable answer. In addition, there remains something potentially gendered in the conception of the kind of excellence that athletes exemplify. The stereotypes about excessively masculine female athletes aren't anywhere as prevalent as they used to be, but they can still cast a shadow over women's engagement in sports.[43] Male athletes with disabilities, too, can perceive their stigma of disability as an emasculation: for many of the quad rugby athletes depicted in the documentary *Murderball,* display of their masculinity on the one hand and concern about others' perception of them as lacking sexual prowess on the other are clearly important preoccupations.[44]

Second is a related but different sort of issue: There is the question of whether the separation of Paralympics and Olympics poses a problem of equality. Is it a benign or problematic form of "separate but equal?" On the one hand, we may point to a trajectory of greater recognition of Paralympics by important institutional players such as the International Olympic Committee: the events may be separate, but the message surely is that they are more comparable than they used to be.[45] And we may join Simon Darcy in sounding a cautious note of optimism about the actual arrangements in the 2000 Sydney Paralympics, even if they were far from perfect and even if their long-term effects on social attitudes toward disability may be uncertain.[46] That may suggest that the separateness of the events is not a problem. But on the other hand, precisely the separateness may cause the wide disparity in spectatorship and attendance: in Sydney, for example, spectators at the Olympics outnumbered the spectators at the Paralympics by five to one.[47] And whatever official recognition athletes with disabilities received as equals, Darcy's evaluation suggests, came through political pressure from disability activists.[48] It is, in short, not yet clear yet that a separate event really recognizes a comparable excellence.

As I have suggested, all this depends largely on broader social attitudes—*l'opinion publique,* as Rousseau called it. The state cannot make up a new ethos about disability sport any better than it can make such an ethos about dueling. In the final chapter of the book, I turn to a contemporary (and enduring) controversy in sports in which *l'opinion publique* about questions of fairness, achievement, and human flourishing are being debated if not (yet) sorted out.

six

The Political Theory of Doping

Doping scandals are something you might encounter on tabloid covers in the grocery store checkout line: they are melodramatic, delightfully sordid stories about the moral foibles of people whom society worships a bit too much for its own good. There is the melodrama about sprinters Tim Montgomery and Marion Jones, the former royal couple of American track and field now disgraced by doping suspension (Montgomery) and a criminal conviction for lying about doping (Jones). There are home run kings Mark McGwire, Sammy Sosa, and—primus inter pares—Barry Bonds, with their various surprisingly slow falls from grace.[1]

As of this writing, an asterisk next to Barry Bonds's lifetime home run record is the only sanction that is even being considered, although the aftermath of the December 2007 Mitchell Report on doping in baseball may still produce the sort of disgrace many people think Bonds deserves.[2] Still, all this makes things seem more tantalizingly scandalous and exciting than a matter for sober political theorizing. It gets worse: there are also the cloak-and-dagger stories of black medical bags full of used syringes and bloody rags (the Finnish Nordic team in the 2001 Nordic World Championships, the Austrian biathletes at the 2006 Winter Olympics, or professional cyclists in pretty much every setting where there has been a publicized doping raid). But politically, one might think, doping scandals are not particularly interesting. Insofar as someone claims they are—say, U.S. president George W. Bush in his 2004 State of the Union address or U.S. senator John McCain—critics see them at best as slightly pathetic reflections of a generally right-wing obsession about individual ethics and drug use; at worst, they are distractions from what really should matter politically: the Iraq War or the economy.

I disagree: they do matter politically. The West's contemporary cultural obsession with athletic doping reflects and illustrates deep tensions in conceptions of fairness, achievement, and human cultivation and flourishing. The objectively trivial stakes in what are forms of entertainment and recreation become important as a moral laboratory. Here, I offer an interpretation of the phenomenon of doping in sports based on that idea. This chapter connects the seedy side of sports to what A. Bartlett Giamatti celebrated in his normative interpretation of sports as a reflection of humankind's highest aspirations.[3] The specific aspiration on which I focus here is the value of *fairness* (Is it a constitutive norm in sports? Does a commitment to fairness entail a ban on doping, or does it suggest that doping should be permitted?) and the concept of *achievement* (Is achievement necessarily connected to fairness? And if not, how do we understand it?). Each of these questions suggests that we can ultimately see sports as reflecting our great cultural hopes about human *flourishing* and about the means to pursue such flourishing.[4]

The concepts of fairness, achievement, and human flourishing are connected to the central concepts of this book, equality and excellence, as the previous chapter suggested. A large part of fairness in sports, as in life in general, is the guarantee of meaningfully equal opportunities for people to pursue excellence. And what counts as excellence depends on how we think of achievements and flourishing.

I will not argue what fairness and achievement should mean in some abstract way; I only show how doping illustrates tensions in our various ways of thinking about these concepts and how those tensions, in turn, help shape what those ideas mean for *us*. I say slightly more conclusive things about human flourishing, though. The most interesting tension that doping highlights about human flourishing is that the highest form of autonomous activity necessarily butts against a complete abdication of autonomy: the limit at which you are your most truly autonomous self-made man is also the point at which you border on the nonhuman, an artifact, an instrument, a biological machine, a cyborg. Where that limit lies is contingent, depending as it does on the development of technologies, but it is not arbitrary. There are two ways of taking this idea, I further argue. We can think of it as a tragedy of sorts, a tragedy about modernity. Or we can be less dramatic and argue that we can identify, however contingently and imperfectly, a meaningful and separable boundary. In slightly more prosaic terms, there are good reasons to think that our concerns about doping in sports track a real problem about what it means to be a person and what we want to call a human life.

The deliberately pretentious title of this chapter has three purposes. One is to take an issue that doesn't seem politically very significant and to show that it actually is quite significant. We remain in civil society, as we have for most of this book, but even the narrowly political and the state figure in here. The second reason is to ask how one goes about *theorizing* such questions. One approach might be to take the doping phenomenon in morally neutral terms and simply to explain it. I sketch what such an explanation might look like, but I also argue that it doesn't get at many of the politically interesting questions. Another approach would take the perspective of ideology critique of some kind. Taking "ideology" in the Marxist sense, as obfuscation, at best partially true beliefs, this approach would show how and why the politically interesting questions are obscured by the popular rhetoric about doping. In that critique, the idea is that the contemporary obsession itself distorts what is really at stake: the doping obsession is an overkill response meant to whitewash the corrupt past of international sports organizations, say, or part of the Republican red herring "war on drugs."[5] This is akin to the kinds of worries we saw left-wing activists express about bread and circuses back in chapter 4. Yet another approach would be conventionally normative, trying to come to at least a strong normative conclusion about how or what might be acceptable.

All of these approaches have their values; none of them are what I have been doing in this book or what I continue to do in this chapter. Political philosophers from Aristotle to John Rawls have argued that we should take ordinary moral conceptions as our point of departure and retain them as an important if not unchangeable benchmark. They need not—indeed, should not—be decisive, but it is not helpful to dismiss them or even explain them away: if people who care about sports find doping morally problematic, then those sentiments should be taken seriously as moral sentiments.

And so the third way in which political theory is important here is the way in which theorists are often taken to be naive about political realities. An understanding of doping as a widespread, systematic practice of hypocrisy, a cynical collusion of organizations, athletes, doctors, coaches, business, and spectators, might lead one either to despair or to the conclusion that people are self-interest maximizers, no matter what they say. But such a conclusion is not, I insist, the only one: our inchoate intuition that something about doping is wrong is worth preserving. Some athletes and spectators are sincere, not merely naive, when they say that there is something noble about their pursuit. And some of those values are, I argue, conceptually necessary: They fundamentally shape the practices that sports are.

The different dimensions on which I focus—fairness, achievement, human flourishing—are in tension with one another. For example, insofar as we think of doping as a matter of cheating, it presupposes not only a reasonable degree of clarity on the moral rules governing the practice but also the existence of moral agents whom we can reasonably hold accountable. Conversely, when we think of athletes as borderline Frankenstein monsters, as John Hoberman's "mortal engines" or Ellis Cashmore's "performance machines," they begin to lose their moral agency.[6] It isn't only because their means of pursuing flourishing are "nonnatural" but because they are often pawns in the hands of their coaches, managers, and medical advisers, who themselves are responding to and taking advantage of the biopolitical incentives of the age. These different perspectives on the problem may ultimately be compatible—indeed, I argue that they are—but they do seem in the first instance inconsistent.

Alasdair Macintyre famously argued in the 1980s that the problem with modernity is that its conceptions of ethical life and meaning are so fragmented that any practice can generate several mutually incompatible and even mutually incoherent understandings.[7] He lamented this (supposed) fact. My background assumption is the opposite: the conflicts and incompatibilities force us to take stock of our values, aspirations, practices, and logics, no less so here than in the earlier episodes we've explored in this book. I return to this theme in the conclusion.

Many important and interesting questions go beyond the scope of what I can do here. One of them is the question of specific institutions. Modern sports in particular afford us a rich, complicated case study of institutional design, bureaucracy, and regulation in a globalized world. The regulation of doping is a particularly tricky test case for those institutions: involved are states and state institutions, international organizations at various levels—the umbrella International Olympic Committee (IOC), sports-specific organizations such as the international soccer governing body (FIFA), the International Amateur Athletic Federation, and so forth, and their national member organizations (USA Track and Field and the like). Created at the turn of the millennium, the World Anti-Doping Agency (WADA) has variously fraught relationships with national antidoping organizations (e.g., the U.S. Anti-Doping Agency), the IOC, and sports-specific organizations and even states. Furthermore, the highly political history of doping enforcement adds an important dimension that would likely be necessary for a complete analysis of contemporary doping policies: the argument is that doping became so rampant in part because more or less corrupt officials in governing organizations—corrupt all the way to the top, to longtime IOC president Juan Antonio Samaranch—benefited from it.[8] All of this is politically interesting but goes beyond the civil-societal focus of this book.

Quid Rides? Athletes as Representatives

What are the problems with doping? There are many ways to carve them out; the most general way would be division into two: One, doping is a bad idea; it is dangerous. Two, doping is wrong; it is a form of cheating. As President Bush put it in his 2004 State of the Union address, "The use of performance-enhancing drugs like steroids in baseball, football, and other sports is dangerous, and it sends the wrong message—that there are shortcuts to accomplishment, and that performance is more important than character."[9] We can quickly add corollaries. Because it is done by cultural icons and people whom many—particularly the young, whether for good reasons or not—regard as role models, it can set a bad example. Steroid use, for example, can be dangerous for adult athletes; it can be far more dangerous to young athletes who mimic their idols. Add to that the supposed wrongness of the practice, and doping athletes not only encourage dangerous behavior but also erode morals.[10] As a matter of fact, most experts agree that doping is not quite as dangerous as its most hysterical critics say it is, but the idea of our idols—or worse, our children's idols—glorifying it can still seem appalling.[11]

Now, every generation in history has found some reason to lament trends in current culture: we've always been going to hell in a hand-basket in some way or another. (I will return to this theme in the conclusion.) So there are reasons to take the warnings about these trends with a grain of salt. It is true that there is a reported erosion in, for example, the American sports-spectating public's concern with some forms of cheating: some surveys suggest that people are not as troubled as they used to be about rule-breaking in sports. It is not clear whether the attitude change is caused by doping or whether it betokens some deeper and more deleterious moral erosion.[12] Maybe; maybe not.

Still, the idea that doping is cheating makes sense. Given the ideals associated with sports, it seems particularly disappointing. We have long since given up the hope that chapter 3's Victorians retained about a person's physical prowess reflecting his moral probity, but claims about "sportsmanship" and "Olympic ideals" and "fair competition" are not empty: they are to some extent constitutive of the practice of sports, and they do matter for the moral psychology of athletes themselves. In other words, although we might acknowledge that many athletes are at best morally as imperfect as any of us, *as* athletes in the game, on the track, or in the pool, their dishonesty is deeply upsetting.

That is because athletes are, in a way, our representatives. They don't act in our name as politicians do, but they are our surrogates.

> The spectator invests his surrogate out there with all his carefree hopes, his aspirations for freedom, his yearning for transmutation of business into leisure, war into peace, effort into grace. To take the acts of physical toil—lifting, throwing, bending, jumping, pushing, grasping, stretching, running, hoisting, the constantly repeated acts that for millennia have meant work—and to bound them in time or by rules or boundaries in a green enclosure surrounded by an amphitheater or at least a gallery (thus combining garden and city, a place removed from care but in this real world) is to replicate the arena of humankind's highest aspiration.[13]

Should we so invest our athletes? That question is mainly moot as long as it's a matter of fact that we do. "Shame!" screamed the 150-

point banner headline in a Finnish tabloid in 2001 after virtually the country's entire cross-country ski team had been caught doping in the Nordic World Championships. (The shame was exacerbated by the fact that Finland hosted the event, placing the crime as well as the shame almost literally on the team's own doorstep.) Similarly, "Baseball's Shame," declared a *New York Times* editorial when doping revelations and the sport's inability to police itself became widely known in 2004.[14] If America's pastime tolerates wrongdoing, then it reflects on America itself, the idea went.

That gets us to the final corollary: doping is both a bad idea and wrong because it is a perverse way to pursue human flourishing. It violates, critics say, what is natural about the pursuit of human excellence: it takes advantage of means of which humans should not take advantage and so pushes humanity to a scary twilight in which human agency renders us borderline nonhuman—"mortal engines," as Hoberman calls the athletic ideal.[15]

Giamatti *is* right, I want to claim, when he says that sports reflect, in part, humankind's highest aspirations. He isn't so naive as to think that they realize those aspirations—he made the claim around the time he, as the commissioner of Major League Baseball, had to deal with the infamous Pete Rose gambling scandal. Sports are ideological in the positive, non-Marxist sense of the term: the values they exemplify reflect what society values. But just because sports and its practitioners are imperfect doesn't mean that there is not something profoundly problematic about moral failures in it.

Part of the bigger reason is that sports, like many other not constitutively instrumental human practices, is an arena where society gets to (or at least tries to) sort out its values, as I pointed out in the introduction. By "not constitutively instrumental," I mean human pursuits that others more elegantly call leisure, in contrast to work.[16] Allen Guttmann calls such a practice "autotelic": it is a practice whose telos, its end, comes from itself.[17] In reflecting our highest aspirations, sports, like other arenas of leisure, notably art, are playgrounds for our broader value conversations. One way to understand the playground metaphor in this instance is to say that sports allow us to test, question, refine, and reform many of our political and moral conceptions—What does it mean to "play fair?" for example—without those questions necessarily becoming questions of social justice, as was the case in the previous chapter. To be sure, questions of social justice might even arise in connection to doping: it is not difficult to argue that what the East German doping machine, for example, did to many individuals was a straightforward state-perpetrated injustice: it involved children, it sidestepped questions of consent, and in general it turned individuals into tools of the state.[18] But the specific ways in which I address the question here are at some distance from immediate questions of social justice, even though they very much are about questions of fairness, achievement, and human flourishing.

What Is Doping?

The second reported use of the word *doping* in the *Oxford English Dictionary* pointed to the use of performance-enhancing drugs, as opposed to recreational or malicious drug use. The quotation in the dictionary is from 1900 and refers to racehorses. By 1913, there is a reference to human athletes' doping. Although the practice of trying to enhance athletic performance in various pharmaceutical ways has existed for a long time, it is significantly a twentieth-century problem. Since the 1930s, when testosterone was first synthesized, the possibilities of pharmaceutical enhancement of athletic—and other kinds of—human performance became increasingly appealing.[19] It became an acknowledged problem in sports in the late 1950s and early 1960s; the IOC passed its first antidoping resolution in 1962, and several 1962 articles in the *Bulletin du Comité International Olympique* addressed the question.[20] Even earlier, the term *doping* (*le doping* in the IOC's official French) was always associated with *illicit* drug-based performance enhancement.

Quickly—and obviously—the question of what counted as doping arose. All athletes try to enhance their performance in various ways—through training as well as through better equipment and better nutrition—and clear intuitions notwithstanding, there had to be some good reasons for understanding why pharmaceutical enhancement was inappropriate and what counted as pharmaceutical or otherwise inappropriate enhancement. The former question has always been harder, although the argument right from the start was more or less what I introduced earlier: Doping is a bad idea, and it is a form of cheating. The definitional issues were somewhat more manageable, although not immediately.

In 1962, Giuseppe La Cava, the secretary-general of the International Federation of Sports Medicine, defined *doping* as "the use of energy-providing substances other than food, aiming to increase the competitive output in advance."[21] One of the obvious problems with this definition is that it is too vague; it also ignores the ways in which performance can be enhanced by things that don't provide energy: beta-blockers, which slow a person's heart rate and which can therefore enhance the performance of, say, target shooters and race car drivers, don't provide energy but do now count as doping. In 1968, A. F. Creff, a Paris-based doctor, was even more general in the *Olympic Review Newsletter:* he defined doping as "the use of any non-physiological means (it being understood that physiology is the science dealing with the organic functions characteristic of life), i.e., any means that are not fundamentally natural."[22] Apart from generality, this obviously begged the important question of what counts as "fundamentally natural."

There was a another way of going about the definitional problem. By 1965, an anonymous editorial in the *Bulletin du Comité International Olympique* had taken the Potter Stewart "I know it when I see it" line on doping: "It is said that, to define doping is, if not impossible, at least extremely difficult, and yet every one who takes part in competitive sport or who administers it knows exactly what it means. The definition lies not in words but in integrity of character."[23] This may have been a noble sentiment, but it was even more problematic than La Cava's for the purposes of policymaking. It had something going for it, however: although there were difficulties about boundary drawing, one could make empirical observations about what athletes did, especially in the shadows, where you presumably do things you think are wrong. And so, since the 1960s, the definitions of doping have generally been based on observations about what athletes in a given sport are doing in secrecy to enhance their performance in comparison to the competition. More recently, doping codes have also paid attention to what athletes do *to hide* what they have done to enhance their performance. The key insight there, reflected in some other early definitions surveyed in mid-1970s by Marie-José Mimiague, is that they are substances that an athlete assumes will give him an edge over the competition exactly *because* they are either little known or banned.[24] The most recent official understanding of doping is purely nominalist and helpful exactly for that reason. WADA's *World Anti-Doping Code* defines doping simply as "the occurrence of one or more of the anti-doping rule violations set forth in Article 2.1 through Article 2.8 of the *Code*."[25] The violations are then defined, most importantly, as the "presence of *Prohibited Substance* or its *Metabolites* or *Markers* in an *Athlete's* bodily *Specimen*" (sec. 2.1) or as "*Use* or *Attempted Use* of a *Prohibited Substance* or a *Prohibited Method*" (sec. 2.2). The "Prohibited List's" principle is that the substance satisfies any two of the three following conditions: it might enhance sport performance (sec. 4.3.1.1) or be dangerous to the athlete (sec. 4.3.1.2) or that the WADA determines that the substance or the method violates the "spirit of sport" (sec. 4.3.1.3).

The things that athletes do to enhance their performance depend on the nature of the sport. Many use various kinds of stimulants: the use of amphetamines in the 1950s was one of the first causes for alarm. Stimulants such as amphetamines are helpful where the overall demands of the sport are grueling: baseball's long season and frequent games are the best example. There are also more specific stimulants that give—or are supposed to give—energy for a given event. In addition to amphetamines, there are ephedrine and pseudoephedrine, alcohol, and even caffeine. Steroids represent another kind of doping. They are so strongly associated with doping that in everyday talk, "steroids" often stand in for any kind of doping. The purpose of steroid use is usually to strengthen the body over the long term by building muscle tissue (*anabolic* means "tissue-building"). That is why the manufacture of synthetic testosterone was such an important event for the possibility of doping. Steroids are also so popular because athletes in many sports obviously benefit from greater muscle mass (and generally subsequent strength): weight lifting, hitting home runs in baseball, rowing, sprinting, and so forth. More recently, the use of human growth hormone—currently undetectable by doping tests—has become popular.

Not all athletes benefit from greater strength or muscle mass. In endurance sports in particular, blood's oxygen carrying capacity (VO_2max) is the single-most-important variable for performance. VO_2max depends on a person's hemoglobin count (the number of red blood cells per unit of blood), and that number can be manipulated. The most obvious way to manipulate it is by training; it can also be increased by exposing the body to low-oxygen air for sustained periods (ergo training in high altitudes and the use of hypobaric chambers) or by using a substance called erythropoietin (EPO). EPO use counts as doping, but this type of performance enhancement also has led to the development—probably in the late 1970s—of "blood doping": giving an athlete transfusions of hemoglobin-rich blood that might in fact be her own, withdrawn and stored after, say, a long period of training at altitude. For this reason, the WADA code specifies *methods* in addition to substances: in blood doping, all substances involved may be perfectly "natural" and even the athlete's own.

Third, as I mentioned previously, performance can be enhanced by slowing down or calming the body with substances such as beta-blockers. Beta-blockers, like many doping substances, have legitimate therapeutic uses.

Finally, the WADA code regards masking agents as a form of doping. The idea with masking agents is to cover the use of performance-enhancing substances. For example, plasma expanders can cover the use of EPO because hemoglobin counts are given as numbers of red blood cells per unit of blood volume, and that number goes down when you increase the volume of plasma.[26]

Actually, "finally" is not quite right. Those categories roughly cover the existing types of doping, but a real specter haunts sports: gene manipulation. It is probably only a matter of time until genes relevant for athletic performance get identified and methods for manipulating them in an individual are developed. That possibility places entirely new challenges on doping enforcement, on the concrete side of things. It is also an instance of the general worries we tend to have about the brave new world of gene manipulation. It is not clear to me that it really is the kind of watershed that many people think it is: all of the problems about the scientific, technological, and biological manipulation of human beings that it captures are already on the table with any other form of doping. The irreversible changes that gene manipulation can bring about in an individual differ fundamentally only on the assumption that genotype determines what we are, and there are good reasons to resist such a view. The sex change that the East German hormone doping forced Andreas—formerly Heidi—Krieger to undergo feels, from his perspective, just as profound and real as the gene manipulations might.[27] At the same time, *that* it looms so large as a problem is significant and reflects what I say here.

Cold Wars and Rational Fools:
The Political Economy of Doping

> It is easy for most of us to keep our hands from picking and steal-
> ing when picking and stealing plainly lead to prison diet and prison
> garments. But when silks and satins come of it, and with the silks
> and satins general respect, the net result of honesty does not seem
> to be so secure.
>
> —ANTHONY TROLLOPE

"It's human nature to obtain an edge, whether in combat, in business or in sports," says Charles Yesalis, a Penn State health scientist and famous opponent of doping.[28] This is a familiar line in contexts where someone wants to explain a ubiquitous human behavior: it is just the way we are. As an opponent of doping, Yesalis doesn't, of course, want to draw the inference that just because this tendency is—or might be—natural, it is good. Our natural tendencies can be checked in all sorts of ways, depending on what we consider appropriate. Restrictions on doping are, in Yesalis's and other doping opponents' view, a way of preventing our natural "edge-seeking" tendency from turning to doping.

Claims of human nature are as controversial as they are common. Such claims are conceptually messy: it is hard to figure out what they might mean, in the first instance, and it is hard to separate natural from nonnatural effects. There is no immediate reason to think that "trying to obtain an edge" is natural, universal, or unavoidable. But Yesalis's point is worth taking seriously in a slightly weaker form: sports are, by definition, a pursuit in which obtaining an edge matters, and it might indeed be true that for anyone involved in sports, there is a temptation and maybe even tendency to seek such edges beyond what's legitimate. In fact, to explain the prevalence of doping, Yesalis's point might be a good place to start; the rest is textbook social science. First, we need an account of structural forces that shape the world in certain ways (thus creating "incentives"), and we need "microfoundations" (a story of how individual actors negotiate those structures). On the whole, for doping these accounts are about as straightforward as they come.

First, on the structural side, nationalism, the Cold War, and global capitalism in its various forms have all played a role in creating the structures that foster doping. In all cases, sports have been harnessed into those political-economic competitions, both symbolically and concretely. In a context of nationalism, a victory associated with a country is merit to the country and, as is often the case, demerit to its rivals and opponents. The Cold War represented, in a way, a hypertrophied version of nationalism: at stake was not only the symbolic glory of one bloc over the other but competing theories of communist and capitalist countries' moral and physical prowess and their abilities to create and foster human capital. Nationalism has remained an important structural incentive in the post–Cold War world, but perhaps the most important one is capitalism—or, more specifically, market forces. First, since the 1970s and 1980s, changes in the international rules about athletic professionalism have made sports literally a job for far more people than legitimately was previously the case. The related financial stakes in sports as a product for consumption—as entertainment for spectators and as a lifestyle (where acquiring the lifestyle correctly doesn't only mean engaging in a sport but engaging in it with the right gear)—have simply increased the money available both for athletes and particularly for those who benefit from the athletes. So there has been much at stake for elite-level athletes. And so the microfoundations: given the stakes and given the nature of elite-level sport, doping becomes a rational choice.

Elite athletes are remarkably even. This is in part a consequence of decades of competition and development of training methods: they have brought most sports to the boundary where elite-level progress is infinitesimal. In some speed sports, winners and losers are separated by thousandths of a second. (It is convenient that measurement technologies have also developed: no one would bother to watch a luging competition, say, where every Olympic participant ties with the others because stopwatches show only tenths of a second.) At the same time, the variables that affect performances have remained numerous and in fact have increased. So any small edge over one's competitors may well redound to one's benefit. And then it seems that as long as the odds of getting caught for any rule violation can be kept low—and clearly much effort in the illicit drug business goes exactly to reducing the odds by developing masking agents—it makes sense for an athlete or her coach to resort to doping. In simple terms, here is the calculus of a rational elite athlete: "The potential benefit of any small edge, including doping (great) minus the chance of getting caught for doping (small), is significantly greater than zero." Bring on the steroids.

This microfoundations story also points to a familiar tragedy connected with this logic. Not only does the set of incentives encourage cheating, but it can make cheating nearly universal. Because any athlete is in the circumstances of uncertainty about whether her competitors are doping, the rational response is to assume that they are.[29]

This general story has important nuances. For example, the microfoundations look somewhat different in a context such as the former Soviet bloc, where individual freedoms and rights were restricted and the state therefore was able to use force and generally not worry about informed consent. The incentive structures and thus the range of meaningful responses also vary in terms of other opportunities: for example, where athletic success represents one of the only ways out of poverty, as it can do both in the North American inner city and the Third World, the stakes can be significantly higher. Another way of putting this point is that structural differences make doping the rational incentive for different people in different contexts: it may be the director of a national or subnational sports program, it may be a coach, or it may be the athlete herself. It may be all of them, of course, or some of them to various degrees, but the idea remains the same: someone has a rational incentive to take the risk of doping.

But good as this story is, it isn't quite enough. To explain the phenomenon is not, in this case, to understand it fully. One of the reasons is that this explanation points to one obvious answer that in most cases at least so far has been rejected. If doping is a form of cheating (an unfair advantage) but its use is ubiquitous (so it's more of a leveler than an advantage), it seems obvious that one solution would be to legalize it. That way, the question of uncertainty disappears. Legalization would also make possible better research on what kinds of doping actually work: when it can be done out in the open—or as much as the pharmaceutical industry can keep things open—better research will point to efficacious and safer performance-enhancing drugs. Hoberman argues that this logic was one of the reasons behind the de facto permissibility of doping until 1999, when the IOC finally cracked down—or was forced to crack down—on the practices.[30] But it matters that doping hasn't gone the way of amateurism in sports: for years, elite athletes were "shamateurs," supported by shady but lucrative deals or, in the case of communist countries, fully by the state. To bring order to the practice, the IOC and other organizations got rid of the rules banning professionals and began a regulated professionalism in sports. For doping, this solution has so far been, for the most part, rejected, even though the suggestion has been made. We need to understand why.

Fairness

If you ask the proverbial person on the street what is wrong with doping, she will likely say that doping is bad because it is wrong: it is a form of cheating. Even many athletes feel this way, which is in part why proposals to legalize and so regulate doping have failed.[31] Since sports organizations started taking official positions against doping, doping has counted as an explicit violation of the rules of individual sports and, over the last few years, as a violation of the *World Anti-Doping Code*. But above the letter of sports law, many people see doping as a violation of the principle of fair competition. Some people even think that principle is one constitutive norm for sports—that is, it is a norm that makes a sport what it is, so its violation actually makes the athlete something other than a participant in sport. In the same way that someone confused about the constitutive rules of soccer is not playing soccer if he runs across the field carrying the ball in his hands, a doper, one might say, is no longer an athlete. Whether fair competition is in fact a constitutive norm for sport is an open question; I will return to it later. First, though, there is one particular difficulty with the violations of just the letter of the law.

The purpose of rules of any kind is to regulate practice in a way that the practice is orderly, sensible, possible, sustainable, meaningful: rules provide a kind of furniture of the social world in which lives are better. So also in sports—so, perhaps, particularly in sports.[32] But not all rules are constitutive: you can violate some rules without ceasing to engage in the practice that the rules regulate. Many traffic laws are like that. Sometimes violating such laws is not only common but in fact strategically and perhaps even morally reasonable: a modest amount of jaywalking, for example, can make traffic flow more smoothly. The same can be true of sports: some degree of rule violation as a general practice can be a de facto accepted way of the ordinary business of a game or an event. This is not the same logic as the one used by the sporting *Homo economicus* I discussed in the previous section; his doping presupposes that the rules deter *others* and so is only meaningful on the assumption that others don't dope. Here, instead, the idea is that the principle is fine but that its letter is too strict and can be violated within reason. But it doesn't follow from its frequent breach that the rule should not exist: traffic flows faster if everybody knows that "fifty-five miles per hour" really means anything under sixty-five miles per hour, but things get disastrous quickly if people—even just a few people—think that the rule is utterly meaningless because few follow it to the letter.

The first difficulty, then, is to show that doping isn't like slightly—but only slightly—excessive roughness in ice hockey. Some people suggest that is exactly what it was prior to the real crackdown around the millennium; some also argue that *some* forms of doping should continue to be like that, even if all forms shouldn't. Michael Sokolove has recently suggested that baseball will lose its character if its ubiquitous amphetamine use ends.[33] Conceptually, the issue is relatively simple: although the purely strategic use of doping—getting an edge over the competition—may result in everyone becoming a rational doping fool, it does presuppose that it is not something everyone does.[34] But once the practice becomes so widespread as to seem ubiquitous, the strategic use isn't to get an edge *over* one's competition but to get to a level playing field. The unofficial rhetoric of many athletes in sports rife with doping is that "Everyone does it," and they therefore must do it, too. It's likely an excuse or at least an exercise in some bad faith, but it is not a crazy position from a rational perspective, as we saw in the previous section.

What follows? First, the obvious: some violations of explicit rules aren't really cheating. Second: explicit rules themselves don't cash out the intuition that doping is wrong. Third, most importantly: this seems to be so exactly because there is some broader background notion of fairness to which the rules loosely attach. Where there is wiggle room, it is exactly because the explicit rules don't precisely capture the principle of fairness. One possible response is to consider the "Everyone's doing it, so why shouldn't I?" protest. One doesn't frequently encounter this protest in public—which should suggest something on its own—but it is part of the folklore around elite sports.[35] Let's do a counterfactual evaluation: Would everyone dope if it were legal? If not, then its use may well reflect assumptions that indeed not everyone is doing it. We might even assume that even now, not everyone is doing it. The empirics about doping being what they are, we can't be sure, but some athletes have taken such public positions against doping that even a minimal principle of charity ought to lead us to assume that they are indeed clean.[36] We don't quite need to take their word for it, either. For example, British distance runner Paula Radcliffe's campaign for drug-free sport includes a personal commitment to submit to frequent drug testing.[37] Some athletes have also endorsed volunteer programs in which a longitudinal health profile is used to track sudden changes, thereby potentially revealing the use of even undetectable performance enhancers.[38]

So if we assume, for now, that the simple fact of a continued controversy over whether doping is wrong suggests that the practice, at least in some of its forms, is an attempt to cheat and to cheat not only some overeager bureaucracy or naive audiences but one's competitors. In other words, doping is an attempt to affect outcomes in ways that are not fair.

Is fairness a constitutive norm of sport? If it is, it wasn't always so: the ancient Olympics had no use for such a concept.[39] If we consider boxing in the ancient Olympics a sport, fairness is not a constitutive norm. (It matters, of course, whether we *know* what ancient boxing was like. If we know that it had no controls for equal skill or size and that deaths were frequent, we might actually say it is not a sport. My sense is that our intuitions are conflicted on this, but that needn't concern us here.) So fairness is certainly *contingent* as a norm. It emerged with recognizably modern forms of sport in the eighteenth century as a way of facilitating gambling but also in reflection of the moral value of equal chance.[40] Its contingency notwithstanding, it's perfectly possible to say that fairness is *now* a constitutive norm of sport.

Possible doesn't yet make it so. But our current—though contingent—understanding of sport is that fairness is a constitutive norm. I want to suggest that it is less the "fact" of doping (whatever that fact is) than the presumption that it is an *attempt* to violate and take advantage of the principle of fairness that bothers us about doping and makes us regard it as wrong. Another way of understanding fairness as a constitutive norm of sports is to say that it helps secure meaningful competition, the kind of competition that makes any given sport what it is as a practice and makes it worth pursuing. The idea is that for you to commit yourself to be a football player or a skater or a gymnast is to make a contingent, voluntary commitment that *that* pursuit is a source of meaning for you. As Robert Butcher and Angela Schneider put it, fair play is a sign of "respect for the game."[41]

We can make the point in ethical terms. If fairness is a constitutive norm of sports, then doping, inasmuch as it reflects an attempt to get around the principle of fairness, is a moral contradiction. It is in relatively straightforward way a violation of Kant's categorical imperative: one cannot consistently will the maxim—roughly, the principle of the end and its related conduct—without undermining the meaning of the practice. Maxims of unregulated competition, Kantian ethicist Barbara Herman has argued, fail the moral tests that make competition possible as a *joint* project.[42] One constitutive norm of sport is that not everyone can win, but winning in *a* sport, in *a* game, presupposes a community whose joint project the sport or the game is. To want to cheat is, then, a form of disrespect toward the joint project. This disrespect is less a matter of individual psychology—although arguably part of our disappointment with cheaters is that they fail to have the right attitude—than a matter of *understanding* the practice.

Does this reflect the reality of how athletes think about sports? Certainly not fully: some pursue a sport because it is a way out of poverty or a way to honor and glory, a way to get the girl or the boy. But as an empirical matter, it does reflect reality to at least some extent: there are many athletes who affirm fairness both in word and deed. Even the word matters: it helps shape one important aspect of cultural understanding of sports. How frequently does the phrase *fair play* occur when we talk about sports? We often talk about fair play because we don't agree whether something counts as fair or not, but the whole point is that the value is there in the background. And, again, the principle of charity requires that we give at least some athletes the benefit of the doubt.

But what if fairness actually *isn't* a constitutive norm for sports? What if the rhetoric of fair play and noble competition was never more than ideological prattling, not even wishful thinking as much as window dressing for other interests: entertainment, gambling, communal loyalty?[43] What if we think that a healthy sense of roguish cunning is just the way to go? We admire—or some of us do, anyway—the sly Odysseus, for example, exactly for his willingness to snub his nose at notions of fair play.[44] Maybe the point about sports is that we are actually uneasy about how much fairness should regulate it. All sports require some degree of strategic thinking, and part of being strategic is to take advantage where advantage can be taken. I have assumed with Giamatti that sports reflect humans' highest aspirations, but there is a very different way of thinking about sports: they can be seen as "civilized" version of human tendencies toward and even desires for violence and warfare. This is historian Norbert Elias's understanding. And if this is the case, then a very different set of intuitions comes to play: all is fair in love and war, we like to think, and a victory by any means necessary might indeed be perfectly respectable, even commendable.

This alternative understanding of sports doesn't imply a total lack of rules. Rather, it is simply the position that Thomas Hobbes's Fool famously articulates in chapter 15 of *Leviathan*. Of course there are going to be rules and regulations, but a smart actor will break them when doing so is in his interest: "[E]very man's conservation, and contentment, being committed to his own care, there could be no reason, why every man might not do what he thought conduced thereunto: and therefore also to make, or not make; keep, or not keep covenants, was not against reason, when it conduced to one's benefit."[45] As a result, the two understandings of sports also aren't as inconsistent as they might seem. To be sure, the two *moralities*—insofar as the Fool's is a morality—cannot coexist as the moral foundations of sports, but we can have good reason to understand or interpret sports as reflecting both. This "multivocality" of our understanding of sports, in part, lies at the heart of the questions about fairness. If this rings some bells familiar from the earlier chapters, my point is partly made.

So far, this discussion of fairness has hovered over the specific question of doping; I have presupposed simply that if an athlete uses performance-enhancing drugs or methods to cheat, it presents a problem. But there is another question of fairness about doping. Ellis Cashmore, a critic of antidoping policies, has argued that antidoping rules themselves are unfair because they are arbitrary.

> "Let's say four teams of long distance skiers want a competitive edge," Cashmore explained. "Austria opts for blood doping to pump up the desired oxygen-carrying blood cells. Finland achieves much the same result, but by training at altitude. Germany also trains at altitude in, say, Kenya, last year, extracts the enriched blood from its athletes then transfuses their own blood back prior to the games. Denmark instructs its athletes to sleep in hypobaric chambers. All achieve the same results via different methods. Under current rules, Austria and Germany are cheating. How come? This is not logically consistent; it is arbitrary and hypocritical."[46]

Cashmore is right to think that there are great difficulties in drawing boundaries between what should and should not be acceptable ways of enhancing one's performance. But it doesn't follow from the difficulties of boundary drawing that they are either arbitrary or hypocritical. It may be, but it's not obvious. A large part of the answer has to do with our ideas about what counts as "natural," as I will discuss shortly. But we can begin to make our way to that discussion by remaining in a more recognizably political and ethical terrain. At issue is a familiar distinction between "procedural" and "substantive" norms and values. Fairness is procedural; it is connected, in uneasy and interesting ways, to the substantive question of merit and achievement.

Achievement

"Shortcuts to accomplishment" is how President Bush described steroid use. What's wrong with shortcuts? For Bush and many others, it's the idea of fairness I just discussed: achievement isn't really achievement if you get there via a shortcut. So, strictly speaking, there can be no shortcuts to achievement because the shortcut makes the outcome something other than an achievement. Another way of understanding it would be to say that a person deserves the merit connected to achievement only when she gets there fairly, without taking shortcuts. There are, in other words, two slightly different ways of understanding "achievement": In the first sense, the achievement is defined in part procedurally; it depends on how one gets there. In the second, achievement is independent of the process, even if the merit connected to it might depend on how one gets there.

Only the first understanding might seem really to be at work in sports. Sports are, after all, thoroughly constructed and "not constitutively instrumental," as I suggested earlier. And as we saw in the previous chapter, its measures of achievement—the Olympic ideals of "Citius, altius, fortius," for example—are almost wholly contingent. So it is hard to imagine achievement in sports meaningfully separable from the process of achieving it. The world-record holder in the men's one-hundred-meter dash is called the world's fastest man, but there is a way in which that is quite arbitrary: to be sure, the actual velocity a hundred-meter sprinter achieves is greater than the velocity of the runners in the two-hundred-meter dash, but why one hundred meters? There may well be a distance short of a hundred meters where one could temporarily achieve an even greater velocity (ten meters? fifteen? forty-three?). Even more importantly, if velocity is what we care about, why don't we call a bicyclist, or motorcyclist, or a jet pilot faster? The point is that 9.79 seconds as the time it takes you to travel one hundred meters counts as an achievement if you run it, but not if you bike it or drive it or fly it.

Behind this value is the idea that achievement takes work. "She makes it seem so easy" is a form of admiration that reflects our thinking it actually *isn't* easy, whether we are talking about a triple axel in figure skating or a 2:22 marathon or a ten-second hundred meters. Here, sports indeed reflect the broader value of hard work and effort as a means to merit, and the contingency of achievement in it drives the point home well.

One reflection of this logic is the proposal that in some sports, all existing world and other records should be expunged or at least "asterisked"—that is, marked as questionable. The suggestion has been made recently after the realization that in the 1970s and 1980s, many if not most record-breaking achievements were likely the result of doping.[47] It also arose in 2007 when suspected doper Barry Bonds broke Hank Aaron's home run record in baseball: given the suspicions, a large number of baseball fans considered the record tainted and thought it should be flagged as suspicious.[48] Part of the point is that inasmuch as attempts to break records form an important motivation for athletes, "tainted" records are a perverse benchmark: they are not meaningful in themselves, and they foster more doping because they may well be unreachable cleanly.

But the other understanding of achievement is also at play in sports. We all know, even when our students try to claim otherwise, that the "A for effort" principle as a standard of merit went out the window sometime by second grade. Although it is true that a triple axel or a 2:22 marathon isn't easy, both are far easier for some than for others. No amount of effort and hard work would get me running a 2:22 marathon, and a triple jump is even more impossible a dream. I'm just not lucky enough to have the potential that I might train to achieve such results. That lack of luck has to do with my natural limits, which may or may not be genetic but certainly are outside my control. (A joke among athletes is that the best way to increase your likelihood of success is to choose your parents well.)

In other words, we don't just appreciate effort; we appreciate talent, elegance, beauty, strength, speed. Here, there is a divergence in the question of for whom a competition is meaningful. If two athletes are competing, all they need is a roughly equal chance of beating each other to have the competition be meaningful for them, and it doesn't matter objectively how fast or how strong or how talented they are in comparison to anyone else. But for spectators of sports—a crucial feature of modern sports, particularly at the elite level—it makes a difference whether the competition achieves something worthwhile. "Worthwhile," too, is contingent, as we saw in the previous chapter, but it can be contingent on different factors from what makes the competition meaningful to its participants. If, for example, spectators really care about record breaking, then they may well have an interest in doped competition. Some surveys of attitudes toward sports seem to suggest this indeed is happening: for example, audiences loved baseball's turn-of-the-millennium home run competitions among McGuire, Sosa, and Bonds, and later revelations that the three athletes' abilities resulted partly from doping have not made attitudes more strongly antidoping.[49] And as I mentioned earlier, Sokolove argued recently that if baseball really gets rid of amphetamines, it may change the nature of the play so much that audiences will not care for it anymore.[50]

To say, then, that doping is wrong because it tries to sidestep all the hard work and effort achievement requires simply begs the question: there is no obvious answer to why or when doping is a "shortcut" to achievement. Furthermore, no elite athlete relies on doping alone: EPO allows you to perform better in part because it allows you to train harder. Thus there is a set of conflicting intuitions when it comes to achievement. The intuitions aren't only about sports, but sports capture the conflict in helpful ways. Connected to these procedural and substantive questions is the question of what it means for humans to flourish. That may be the conceptually gnarliest and politically most significant question.

Flourishing

Better Sporting through Chemistry

Athletes dope because they believe it gives them an edge over others, but it is remarkable that they often don't have any clue about whether that actually happens.

This might, of course, be just another way in which athletes are rational fools: they think they are doing something smart, but they are doing something stupid. That's probably part of the story. But another part, possibly a little more painful to us, is that they are just like the rest of us. Their understanding of science can be quite misguided. For example, in the 2001 Nordic World Championships in Finland, the substance the Finnish skiers were found to have used was a plasma expander called Hemohes.[51] Athletes had previously used Hemohes as a masking agent for EPO use; some also thought that it might help on its own, without the (detectable) EPO.

Does a plasma expander enhance an endurance athlete's performance? It may, but we don't know: the actual scientific research isn't available, and the athletes—or, actually, their coaches—relied on a priori reasoning, not research. It is not obvious that any specific research results are forthcoming anytime soon, and that's not only because plasma expanders are now a prohibited substance. Although exercise physiology lives closer to "rigorous" natural sciences than, say, to the notoriously fuzzy social sciences, it is fiendishly difficult to arrive at convincing—or even significant—results. Say you want to study elite performance? Good luck finding enough volunteers to get statistically significant results. You want to recruit the masses? Fine, but don't make inferences about rare traits. You want to understand the specific causal mechanisms of a performance? Good luck relying on relatively crude correlational data for your causal inferences.[52]

Why do athletes persist? One might simply defend the rationality, if not the ethics, of doping by saying that under conditions of uncertainty, you might as well assume that doping *might* give you an edge. That argument gets stronger when we admit that although doping may be dangerous, its absolute and relative dangers have been largely exaggerated.[53] That argument is completely consistent with the rational-choice explanation I offered previously. But more is going on: part of the story is a kind of science ideology. Athletes, like most of us, believe in the power of science to help solve our problems. Those beliefs are often particularly strong among the scientifically uninformed: we believe in the power of science but lack the inferential skills—or discipline—to evaluate not only scientific literature but our own experiences. (How many perfectly intelligent people insist on the power of, say, echinacea on the grounds that "it works for me"?)

Science has played an important dual role in human attempts at a kind of species self-understanding. On the one hand, we have been trying to understand the extent to which the "starry heavens above" (the natural world of physical cause and effect) constrain the "moral law within" (our freedom as autonomous, self-willing agents).[54] On the other hand, as we saw in chapter 3, since the nineteenth century in particular, we have thought that science, as a profoundly human practice itself, can help us achieve higher forms of flourishing and even help us push against and break some of nature's constraints. Although this is arguably a long-term trend since the nineteenth century, fluctuations have occurred. At the moment, we are in a moment of one particular kind of enthusiasm about the possibilities of science: we are undergoing a boom time specifically for life sciences, and it is not surprising or even a coincidence that there is both an enthusiasm and simultaneous deep cultural worry about what we can do and be as biological beings. So although I agree with Hoberman's argument about why sports so exercise our worries about human possibilities, I find his metaphor of "mortal engines" for athletes somewhat misleading: athletes are, to be sure, mortal, but what worries us is that they are products of science without being *mechanical*. They are not engines; they are something else, something possibly new.

Nature versus Nurture

In addition to considering doping cheating, the proverbial person on the street might find it bad because it is "unnatural." That was the way to demarcate doping from legitimate means of performance enhancement in the early days of doping monitoring, and that is the way many people still like to think about it. Doping is an "unnatural" or "abnormal" way of enhancing one's performance, as opposed to the natural means.[55] But as the definition debates show, the claim of "naturalness" doesn't do very much, and most people who think about the matter quickly realize that the label "natural" is problematic. What makes doping interesting is in part the trouble it makes for our thinking about the boundary between natural and nonnatural, whatever that might mean.

In concrete terms, there are two related ways in which talk of the natural informs and alas confuses the discussion of doping. The first one lurks in the background: it is the idea that what is natural is good. One does not have to agree completely with David Hume and his followers about the fact/value gap to acknowledge that something's being natural doesn't have to mean it is good. Just consider the question the next time you get a prescription of (unnatural?) synthetic antibiotics against the (natural?) common cold. The second one follows from what I have said and those involved in doping regulation have acknowledged: it is fiendishly difficult to draw any meaningful boundary between what nature provides and what nurture supplements. Are hypobaric chambers, which simulate high-altitude conditions, a natural way to improve your body?[56] If not, why is taking an airplane to the Rockies more natural? None of this is to say that we should try to eliminate the nature talk from the doping debate, at least when trying to understand it in a political context. The debates about doping are, in an important way, contributions to the nature/nurture debates; at the same time, that distinction is entirely unhelpful in sorting things out.

Part of the problem is, as some of the definition attempts suggest, that when we use *natural,* we really mean *normal,* as in "normally distributed in a population" or "within one standard deviation of the population mean" or something similar. Athletic ability, especially at the elite level, is by definition not normally distributed. It is, as I suggested in the previous chapter, on the right-hand tail of whatever bell curve we might imagine about a specific talent. People sometimes call supremely talented athletes "freaks of nature," and even if they do so partly tongue-in-cheek, there is something to the idea. The boundary-drawing problem arises in new ways. Consider the controversy over gender categories and biological sex in sports: On the one hand, it makes many kinds of competition meaningful to create gender divisions because on average and in the aggregate, differences exist between men and women, as I argued in the preceding chapter. On the other hand, in some sports, "masculine" traits in women, including nonstandard testosterone/estrogen ratios, are exactly what creates the rare abilities. Putting it more starkly, if the distribution of some particular athletic ability piggybacks on the distribution of biological sex differences in such a way that a particular excellence might map onto a person's being "intersexed," then it is little use to say, "Sure, there really are five sexes, but because of their frequency, it makes sense to talk of two main ones—the male and female sexes—and map social distinctions and divisions on those."[57] What is natural even in this sense doesn't determine where boundaries ought to go.[58]

So there is no neutral, noncontroversial concept with which to describe the supposed boundary between natural and whatever its opposite is. That's no surprise: if there were, doping would be less of a conceptual problem. But to say that there isn't anything noncontroversial doesn't mean we completely lack a perch from which to evaluate the issues, and Cashmore's claim of arbitrariness and hypocrisy might be problematic. I introduce a distinction here that will give us a handle on the problem without presupposing a solution: the distinction between artificial and nonartificial.

The first important point is that the contrast to artificial isn't natural. By *artificial,* I simply mean something that is a result of human contrivance, *in a contingent and context-dependent way.* For example, many East African endurance athletes tend to have high hemoglobin counts. Do they have it naturally? That depends on what we mean by *natural,* and even then we might be not able to answer the question. Perhaps there are important heritable traits in their blood, but it's confounded by an obvious demographic fact: they have lived their entire lives at high altitudes, where the lower oxygen content of the air over time increases a person's red blood cells. So, natural? We don't know. Artificial? No. They haven't had to do anything unusual, given their culture and geographical and social location, to attain that characteristic. So something is nonartificial if a person has not had to do anything that an average person in her culture wouldn't have done. This doesn't mean that the traits or characteristics themselves have to be widely distributed in the person's culture, as my previous discussion suggests. Not all East Africans are equally fast, and some aren't fast at all. Athletic talent, most scientists agree, requires a lot of congenital luck: it requires the happy coincidence of inheriting traits that together amount to the potential of those traits being trained into athletic excellence. (It's that issue of choosing your parents well.) In our vernacular, we call such things natural, but the label does nothing: it makes no meaningful difference that my blood might have a congenitally high oxygen-carrying capacity, and you grew up in Boulder. Both are just nonartificial.

Artificial doesn't mean anything negative or pejorative. Training, deliberate diet, attention to one's equipment, and doping are all artificial.[59] If anything, *artificial,* in the most general sense, means something valuable: it is what makes something human, because we think that deliberate, purposeful, reflective, autonomous, free action is what most clearly distinguishes us from other animals. To create an artifact is to engage in something quintessentially human. This distinction helps us pay attention to the various uses of *natural* in these debates without privileging any one conception. It also points to one of the reasons we are uneasy about doping: to create an artifact is quintessentially human, but to turn humans themselves into artifacts seems to trouble us. It shouldn't—it really is a good thing to be a self-made man—but our worries may indeed reflect the idea that there is a limit beyond which we start thinking of ourselves as something other than human.

There are a couple of ways might try to dispel this apparent paradox. One might simply argue that doping reflects an extreme but not fundamentally different form of what Foucault and Foucauldians have called "biopolitics" and the "technologies of the self": athletes are, in various ways, the effects of forms of modern power. They become who—or, more properly, what—they are not through anything we might call meaningfully agentic action. And because power in the modern world works through discourses of materiality, biology, science, and the body, the idea that there is something profoundly different in the doping kind of artificiality as opposed to training kind of artificiality is just a reflection of one increasingly obsolete discourse about humanity: the modern discourse is a discourse of the "plasticity" of the body.[60]

Those uninitiated to the language of fin de siècle social theory might want this in simpler terms. Roughly, the Foucauldian idea is that there never really was much of an autonomous self to be found anywhere in the modern world: most of what we do and have done is to shape ourselves according to prevailing ideas of what it means to be normal. Those prevailing ideas—about health, education, politics, looks, tastes—are not some conspiracies managed by a man behind the curtain, with ill intentions to boot. Instead, they are often well intentioned. The problem, though, is that their overall effect isn't traceable to any type of actor. We are, in a sense, the effects of a power that is not exercised by anyone or anything but that is a conflation and confusion of multiple different systems of ideas—"discourses." In this view, the futuristic hyperdoped designer athlete who is more a living robot than a person is not a new sort of beast at all but merely the newest version of what we've been for quite a while: an effect of the various forces acting on us. When I refrain from smoking, eat local and organic, dress in this way, drive that sort of car, and follow those kinds of other lifestyle choices, thinking all of them "mine," I'm actually already—always already—in the same boat as the athlete. Neither of us is free to escape the forces acting on us.

The Foucauldian story has its value, but it forces us to explain away—that is, dismiss—the value talk and the related idea of athletes as autonomous agents. But if we think, as I believe we should, that people's on-the-ground understandings, including value talk and ascriptions of agency to athletes, should not just be explained away, then the story remains incomplete.

Another approach might be more recuperative. Instead of the modern athlete being a "mortal engine" or a "plastic product of disciplinary discourses," she might be a "cyborg," to use Donna Haraway's now famous metaphor: an artifact indeed, but one whose transgression of the natural/nonnatural boundary needn't make her nonagentic. Instead, that fact might represent a new form of agency, freedom, autonomy.[61] In this model, doping itself is neither good nor bad, but as a phenomenon it—more than "conventional" artificialities such as training—broadens our horizons about our human possibilities. The Harawayian project isn't an ideological celebration of modern biopolitics and its bionic hopes but is a recognition of what some developments allow us to see and think; it is far more cautious about what those developments really allow us to *be*.

I offer a qualified endorsement of cyborgian conception of doping: thinking about its paradoxes points to possibly new conceptions of our practices and ourselves. Very soon, if not already, we'll be able to manipulate our genes to produce better athletes (and smarter and better-looking and healthier people). Should we? On what terms? With what consequences? But my endorsement is qualified for the same reasons that I resist the Foucauldian line: the on-the-ground ideas of human flourishing against which doping and other modern biopolitics push include the idea of a meaningful boundary between acceptable and unacceptable kinds of artificial practices, and I want to keep the possibility of such a boundary in the picture. In simpler terms, as a political solution to the question of doping, Haraway's cyborg manifesto—Let's see what we can do and what it makes us!—would trouble more of us than just naive Republicans.

Boundaries

By way of conclusion, I consider briefly what the boundary between legitimate and illegitimate means to pursue human flourishing might look like. My argument is a kind of qualified conservatism, and it turns on an analogy from language usage. There are two ideal-typical notions of how usage ought to change: in one camp are people who think usage rules are akin to laws of nature. They are unchanging, dependent on deep structural logics and semantic rigidity, and they should continue to be so. ("Split infinitives are *just* wrong!") This means that any usage change is essentially for the worse: the disappearance of the subjunctive from Americans' grammatical repertoire, the use of the sentence adverb *however* as a conjunction, and the like. At the other extreme is the idea that any way of using the language is legitimate because we know usage does change and who's to say whether you should or should not split an infinitive. Of course, neither position is coherent: language does change, but, at the same time, it relies on conventional rules to be intelligible. Some of those conventions might be universal and permanent—if Noam Chomsky is right—but more important is that *some* rules necessarily structure our usage.

Between those two extremes lie a variety of positions, and here I want to stake a claim to one as a reasonable analogy to the doping debates. My qualified conservatism acknowledges change as unavoidable—even change that one might reasonably argue is for the worse. For example, the increasingly common use of *disconnect* as a noun, one could argue, impoverishes our vocabulary because it seems to opt for a trendy neologism despite the existence of perfectly intelligible alternatives (*disjuncture, disconnection*). One might argue that, at some point, it will become necessary to accept this change, just as we have grown to accept *contact* as a verb without balking or as we are more slowly but grudgingly coming to accept *hopefully* as an idiomatic equivalent to "I hope that . . ." But for *disconnect,* the time hasn't quite yet come (or so I would argue). In other words, one must insist on rules exactly when there is pressure for their abandonment, even if one realizes that change might come about.

To argue against this analogy on the grounds that doping is, in fact, already thoroughly widespread in sports, a necessary part of it, and reflects trends *increasingly* popular among nonathletes—our own "instrumentalization" of ourselves in pursuit of better performances from schools to the bedroom—will not do. Trends aren't necessarily for the better. And trends aren't a full representation of reality: taking doping *more* seriously is also a recent trend and may, as I have suggested, reflect our reasonable misgivings about the artificial manipulation of ourselves and our lives.

The answer remains necessarily contingent, and for good reasons. Not long ago, having a physical or mental disability rendered a person fundamentally unable to flourish as a human being. That wasn't because there was some brute fact of the matter about it, as we saw in the previous chapter, but because the vast majority of people, reasonably or unreasonably but almost always unthinkingly, believed so. Developments in *technologies* (our ability to sustain and improve the lives of people with disabilities) and changes in *attitudes* (in our beliefs about what we can and should wish for people with disabilities) and changes in social and political commitments as a consequence of the other two have changed the world radically. At the same time, politically and morally fraught questions remain open: it isn't a matter just of attitudes or technologies but also of nature's constraints. The life of a person with a disability may differ fundamentally from the lives of those without disabilities, and it is possible, at least in some cases, at the end of the day, that it remains qualitatively worse.

I raise the case of people with disabilities only as a poignant example; the questions are open more broadly. Former Oakland Raiders standout John Matuszak, who had retired from football at thirty-one after a glorious career, died in 1989 at thirty-eight.[62] His death was widely believed to have been caused by his use of steroids during his career. At first glance, one might think this an obvious ground for the antidoping argument: steroids might not be as dangerous as some claim they are, but they *are* dangerous. Perhaps so. But one question that remains open is whether they in fact helped Matuszak flourish more brilliantly than he ever would have without doping. Would he have? Would he have flourished so without football? Does it matter to what extent football and doping are coextensive? What do we think? What do fans think? What would he have thought? A similar question arose in my discussion of dueling in chapter 2: at issue is the question of under what conditions life is worth living.

Perhaps it is better to burn out than it is to rust, live free and die young. Our intuitions and even our considered judgments point in different directions. They don't point in *all* directions, so it is not turtles all the way down. The key dimensions are these: There is the dimension on which we have costly excellence for a few—excellence in part *because* it is costly—and increasingly equal yet diverse opportunities to a sustained life over an increasingly long period. Then there is the dimension on which at one end we have the notion that achievement is an achievement by any means necessary as long as people think so— here Matuszak's and Bonds's supposed doping is immaterial—and at the other end the idea that achievement is intelligible only in reference to procedural rules of fairness. And then we have the dimension on which we don't quite know what those rules should be without understanding how we value human flourishing.

In other words, it is a cycle. But it isn't vicious, even if it isn't fully virtuous, either. As I have suggested, there must be rules for the various kinds of boundary drawing. So far, sufficiently deep intuitions about some "natural" limit to human flourishing and the idea of doping as cheating remain reasonable. These solutions will of course be limited. No one ever expects full compliance on any set of rules that we craft to regulate our social life; that's no news. But the extent and type of noncompliance—that is, *what* the contingent failures in our rules are—are also an important guide for us to understand better our own values and conflicts between our various values. That's where a theorist can play a role; that is what I have tried to do.

Conclusion

"An Old Question Raised Again: Is the Human Race Constantly Progressing?"

This book explores the political tension between equality and excellence in modernity.[1] Its conclusions are necessarily contingent. Despite the historical survey, the book is animated by an interest in contemporary controversies over equality and excellence—by ongoing debates about affirmative action, for example, and more broadly by questions of merit and achievement in the age of "biopolitics"—but my purpose has not been to offer policy proposals to solve our problems or the equality/excellence problem in general. Enduring and irreducible tensions exist between the modern commitments to equality and excellence, and those tensions get solved, in any given situation, only contingently. The general modern approach to these tensions—fair, meritocratic, meaningful competition on terms of equality of opportunity—has only kept raising questions of its own, as we have seen. But these contingent conclusions don't mean that we can't outline specific implications. One contribution of this book is to help us better wrap our minds around such questions: I have tried to put things into a historical and conceptual context in a way that affords us a better handle on how to think about our own debates.

Three narratives of modernity compete for our endorsement. The first one says that modernity has been a story of progress, however halting and however slow. An extreme version of this is a kind of Panglossianism we often call Whig history: history is a story of progress to *this* moment, the very best moment possible. It's a secular theodicy of sorts: ours may not always have been the best of all possible worlds, but it has more less become one, or close to it. The progress narrative doesn't have to come in this extreme Panglossian form, though. For most people who do discern and celebrate patterns and paths of progress, there are still a ways to go, and things might have gone otherwise, anyway. But progress it is.

The second narrative is precisely the opposite: modernity is a story of a trip to hell in a handbasket or, to mix metaphors, a faster and larger snowball down from pleasant summit to a valley of mediocrity. One flavor of this narrative is famously associated with conservatism: such modern inventions as equality and democracy as well as the rights of men and of women all manage to dumb down hopes of excellence. I briefly recounted this version at the beginning of this book. But it's not just a conservative lament. A left-wing variant talks of a "dialectic of Enlightenment": the promise of freedom gives people the freedom to be mindless consumers; the promise of equality gives everyone an equal unfreedom; the promise of reason and the slogan about knowledge being power have brought us gas chambers and nuclear weapons.[2]

Finally, the third version offers a cool Gallic shrug: "Plus ça change, plus c'est la même chose." Or the same in American: It's the same déjà vu all over again. Whether we're good or bad, we've been and will continue to be the same. One way of defending that view would be to say that there is some such thing as a universal and transhistorical human nature. That means nature makes us pursue the same kinds of things, whether we are in the late Pleistocene or late capitalism, and makes us pursue them in recognizably similar ways.

None of these accounts suffices as the comprehensive normative assessment of modernity, even though all of them have something going for them. Let me explain why by beginning with the third version.

A colleague once reported receiving an undergraduate paper that argued,

> Utilitarianism is wrong because it violates the second law of thermodynamics, and *we should not violate the second law of thermodynamics.*

One of the reasons we chuckle at the student is that the argument commits what philosophers used to call a category error. The laws of thermodynamics are not the sorts of things that can be violated, not by us or, insofar as we know, anything else in this universe. They are laws of nature and thus are not subject to human contrivance. On the contrary, we are subject to them: they set the parameters for our physical existence in the world. Whether there is something *in addition* to our subjection to the laws of nature, as varieties of religions insist, or whether they leave room for theories of autonomous human action, as many philosophers have hoped, is a matter of controversy. But everyone concedes that nature sets pretty strict constraints on our physical life. There are some things we can't be or do. Levitation will never solve the problem of overcrowded sidewalks, we won't ever compute the first million decimals of π in our heads, and while the world record in the hundred-meter dash is likely to improve in the years to come, it cannot become zero seconds—probably not even five seconds, but don't quote me on this when future bionic sprinters shatter it. Call this idea the *nature's constraint thesis*.

Almost equally uncontroversial is what the thesis implies for normative theorizing. Kant famously enshrined the idea in the postulate *ought* implies *can,* from which logic tells us that *cannot* entails, loosely, *need not*. Moral or political injunctions that exhort us to the impossible are simply void, and generating them is a waste of ink. The antiutilitarian undergraduate simply did more than was necessary: if one could show that utilitarianism indeed violated the second law of thermodynamics, that would be enough to establish the needed reductio ad absurdum.

Here the agreements end. One set of controversies concerns the scope of nature's constraints: What, *exactly,* are the parameters within which meaningful *oughts* might be issued? One way to think of the question is to go metaphysical and get involved in the centuries-old free will/determinism question. Another way is to sidestep philosophical metaphysics and think about the question in empirical—particularly sociological and political—terms: human political possibilities depend on what kinds of physical beings they are, so knowledge of "human nature," whatever that is, becomes an important political question.

This is not news. The prevailing view has been that whatever nature's constraints, there is plenty of conceptual space for politics. In this book, I have shown that there is indeed a conceptual place for political and moral questions—questions of ought, questions of justice, of dignity and equality and excellence—but that those conclusions are reached not by ignoring the question of nature's constraints but by paying attention to them.

For that reason, too, the third narrative about a transhistorical human nature does not suffice as an account of modernity. This is not because it is false. In fact, it may be true: it is possible that there is a human nature that is not only universal but transhistorical and therefore that overall human motivations as well as the patterns of human thought and action always remain generally the same.[3] But because the *specific* things by which humans are motivated depend on the things humans have made—call them meanings and values—and because those things do change, it isn't interesting, in the face of obvious change, to say that we haven't fundamentally changed. Perhaps we haven't, but because the world has changed, it behooves us to make sense of our responses to it. This is particularly true when, as I have shown, our ideas about what we naturally are have also changed. For better or for worse, our debates about whether there is something called human nature and if so, what it is just get thrown into the bigger debate, at least for now.

In other words, the third option cannot serve as a foundation for our judgments of our age because of gnarly epistemic difficulties (we do not yet know whether there is a transhistorical human nature and if there is, what it is) and because those epistemic difficulties make claims about human nature part of the political debate. At the same time, as I have argued throughout and particularly in part 3, it is uncontroversial that nature sets some constraints on what we can do or be. It simply cannot serve as the fixed constant that would allow us comprehensively to evaluate social and political phenomena. Both the Victorians' notion that a man's physical prowess is a mirror to his character and the antidopers' idea that the distinction between natural and nonnatural means of improvement is easy to find are chimera.

In fact, the problem with the other narratives is the same: all try to fix a value constant that would then give one the possibility to evaluate other values and social and political phenomena in a comprehensive way. As I suggested in the introduction and have shown in the chapters that followed, the values of equality and excellence are fictions. That doesn't make them useless, but it means that they can't be fixed in place.

The Political Value of Indispensable Fictions

The progressive, Left-liberal hope that the tension between equality and excellence gets solved easily through meritocratic equality of opportunity has been a myth from its inception, as we saw beginning in chapter 1 and frequently in what followed. This doesn't mean that the solution is incoherent as an idea but does mean it remains a source of controversy—appropriately.

The progressive vision of modernity has much to show for itself. Most importantly, the modern ideal of the equal dignity of all human beings has, by the early twenty-first century, met with immense success. The value commands at least lip service even from those who deny it in deed. Although we would, of course, want more than lip service, it is a valuable thing in itself and not easily achieved, as I have suggested: even in the countries with the oldest commitments to equal dignity, its realization has been all too recent in many domains. But there it now is, and the enthusiasm of those who celebrate political progress is understandable. In most cases, respect for the equal human dignity and the creation of institutions that make the respect meaningful have stemmed from the development of the democratic state. As part 3 shows, making claims of equal justice in a stable liberal democratic society is an entirely different affair from a situation where the state is either weak or neither liberal nor democratic.

But the state is a blunt instrument, as John Stuart Mill observed in *On Liberty*.[4] Important political questions remain outside its purview even where the state is genuinely interested in respecting everyone's equal dignity and trying to guarantee that others do so, too. That is because the state actually can't provide all that dignity means: part of a person's dignity—her respect-worthiness—continues to come from her autonomy, from what *she* does or can do. The reason, as we have seen, has to do with the way the theoretical ideal of equal dignity and its practical instantiations continue to blur together. A person's ability to demonstrate her autonomy can remain an important reason for whether she enjoys the respect her putative status as a human being warrants.

This blurring of theoretical and practical conceptions of dignity has been politically valuable, as we have seen. It has invited challenges to existing notions of respect-worthiness and of related ideas of what counts as excellence. We saw this in the case of dueling; we saw it in the case of disability sports. There is no reason to think that our existing schemes of understanding equal opportunity and of assigning value to certain kinds of excellence will remain what they are now. That is a feature of this account, not a bug in it: the kind of theoretical account this book has offered has left room for actual politics. I am leery of philosopher-kings for both theoretical and political reasons and would be troubled—not to say a bit megalomaniac—if I thought I had fixed concepts that so clearly have been in a flux at least since the eighteenth century. To outline what those concepts are, how we have argued about them, and, perhaps most importantly, the kinds of path-dependencies that follow from certain kinds of argumentative and political strategies must suffice as this book's contributions.

Honor and Emasculation

None of this is to say that there aren't normative conclusions to be drawn, as I suggested at the beginning. First, as I said, the progressive hope of easy reconciliation between equality and excellence is a myth. They can be reconciled, but only contingently. Second, this doesn't mean that the conservative lament about modernity being a dumbing-down project, a movement toward equality at the expense of excellence, is a sustainable position, either. After all, as I have shown, conceptions of excellence have always presupposed a baseline of equality and a set of constitutive norms that allow us to make our judgments. When we learn that boxing in the ancient Olympics did not care about weight classes, fairness, rough talent equalization, and the like, we tend to think that it did not measure boxing excellence. It's not that it objectively didn't—it likely did for the Greeks—but our notion of excellence presupposes something more than the ability to pummel your opponent into a pulp: we want to know whether there was a meaningful contest in the first place.

So the conservative vision of modernity is conceptually problematic. But conservatives aren't talking only about conceptual relations when they say that modernity has dumbed down our hopes of excellence: they point to actual changes in our understandings and standards. Here, the worries are worth thinking about.

Our egalitarian age has diminished the social value of honor. It is not that honor is completely gone from modern cultures. It has been turned into other kinds of excellence in some contexts—some of the cases this book has canvassed—and it does characterize various subcultures even in democratic societies. But its cachet as a political ideal does seem to have diminished.

Some contemporary political thinkers have lamented the lowered profile of honor talk, some even for modern, democratic, and liberal reasons. Sharon Krause, for example, has tried to recuperate the value, render it compatible, and point to its instantiations in slightly unusual quarters: among early feminists, in the civil rights movement.[5]

I don't deny the possibility or even value of interpreting the political agency of some notable actors such as Martin Luther King Jr. as honorable, but I am less sanguine about the resuscitation of honor talk than Krause is. Where honor subcultures still exist to any significant degree, honor seems to remain gendered in the way we saw in chapter 2. Think of the resurgence of practices such as honor killings, which are all about gender, or the way honor motivates slightly more benign forms of masculine violence in defense of women's supposed virtue. I don't mean that the kind of honor Krause seeks to revalue and the kind of honor that leads brothers to murder their "dishonored" sisters are the same concept, and I don't disagree with the defenders of honor talk that we *could* reinterpret honor in a way that is not gendered. But what worries me is that on the ground, honor seems quite gendered.

It isn't that I condemn all instances where honor of this gendered kind is in place (although I do condemn some). In fact, my argument about the political employment of honor in earlier parts of modernity may help explain some of the persistence of honor cultures: among lower socioeconomic classes, among discriminated-against ethnic and religious minorities, for example. It's not necessarily their supposed primitivity or lack of education or intelligence that makes such groups cling onto honor, but their very powerlessness. Acting on the norms of honor in the face of disrespect can be a form of purchasing a bit of the dignity disrespect, oppression, and disempowerment try to deny.[6] But that is not a reason to celebrate honor; it is a reason to hope for social change in which respect doesn't depend, as it does in the case of masculine honor, on the subordination of a group of people.

One variant of the conservative lament about modern dumbing down is to see modernity as a grand emasculation project. Men were men, now they are sissies, as Leo, the anonymous defender of dueling in chapter 2, claimed; you may still hear it even from your perfectly intelligent colleagues around the water cooler. The claim is partly true, although it is not a reason to lament anything. What we have seen is a slow decoupling of excellence as the monopoly of men. This has come in two forms. On the one hand, as we saw in chapter 3, one modern shift has involved an increasing appreciation of competences that aren't about the physical defense of the weaker. Hence the modern professional over the heroic soldier. On the other hand, we have seen the decoupling of assumptions that certain kinds of excellences are possible only for biological males. Women can be athletes; they can also be soldiers. These phenomena seem to me an obvious reason to celebrate rather than lament modernity: emasculation is not dumbing down, and if we live in an emasculated era, good for us.

But whether we live in an emasculated era is an open question. Full gender equity remains as much an unrealized dream as a partly realized ideal. Further, as my argument about nature's constraints implies, even our enlightened age may want to see some differences as making a difference. That is, there are differences between males and females; the jury appears to be out on what they are and what to make of them. Whatever the outcomes, the questions are political, even when they involve the "natural."

Coda

My last remarks suggest I am inclining to celebrate the progressive vision of modernity. Lest the implications of my argument be misconstrued, I want to return to the qualified conservatism with which I ended chapter 6.

I live in a progressive university town, so perhaps it's no surprise that the local YMCA advertises children's soccer camps by announcing cheerfully, "Every child plays, every child wins!" While the sentiment is well intentioned, it is both incoherent and unfortunate. We do of course know the concept of win-win situations—dueling was one such situation, in a perverse way, as we saw in chapter 2—but strictly speaking, sports aren't win-win. Sports, as competitive pursuits of excellence, are necessarily positional; it is part of their constitutive norms.

But even beyond this conceptual nitpicking, the idea that "Every child wins!" is politically unfortunate. In chapter 1, we saw some naive models of child rearing; the Y's cheeriness represents the naïveté of our own age. In fact, there might be reason to borrow from Johann Bernhard Basedow's book: children should feel good about their pursuits, and they should be on children's terms. A defender of the Y might refer to this idea and say that competitive activities for children set the bar too high: only the victorious find them satisfying. Perhaps. But the idea of competition and other standards of excellence—which means that every child does *not* win—keep the concept of victory meaningful. Even in autotelic pursuits—where the goal of the pursuit comes from its internal norms—it is necessary to retain some standards for separating the wheat from the chaff. This is because of Kant's insight we saw in chapters 1 and 2. The notion of human autonomy requires a sense of efficacy: a person isn't someone who merely is but someone who acts. And for something to count as action, there has to be a standard of evaluation that separates it from mere behavior.

Notes

INTRODUCTION

1. Litsky, "Wheelchair Athletes File a Complaint."

2. Suggs, "Foes of Title IX"; Zimbalist, "Backlash against Title IX"; Gavora, *Tilting the Playing Field;* Boxill, "Title IX and Gender Equity."

3. See under "Achievement" in chapter 6.

4. In analytic political philosophy, this has been one of the major questions in the debates John Rawls's work began in the 1970s, even though Rawls (as well as others) have offered several arguments to show why the tension can be theoretically solved. For his classic early statement, see Rawls, *Theory of Justice;* for an early rejoinder insisting on the tension's difficulty, see Nozick, *Anarchy, State, and Utopia.*

5. My idea echoes Veblen's famous arguments about the demonstration of status, although the context and details are different. See Veblen, *Theory of the Leisure Class.*

6. Coetzee, *Giving Offense,* 14.

7. Darwall, *Impartial Reason.*

8. I am very much in sympathy with Schmidt, "What Enlightenment Project?" and Muthu, *Enlightenment against Empire,* regarding the semantic and substantive ambiguities in our use of the term *Enlightenment.* Here I use the concept freely but specifically: by *Enlightenment,* I mean primarily the German eighteenth-century *Aufklärung*—i.e., the constellation of religiously tolerant and politically reformist ideas in the latter half of the eighteenth century. By *Enlighteners,* I refer to the *Aufklärer*—i.e., people who were taken to be or who took themselves to be champions of the Enlightenment. For the purposes of my argument, even thinkers on the fringes of or in opposition to the *Aufklärung* can count. The early variety of German Romanticism—the *Frühromantik*—is an example. See Beiser, "Early Romanticism and the *Aufklärung*"; Beiser, "Romantic Education."

9. Kant's formulation is the most famous; see WE. (Abbreviations for Kant's works are listed in References.) See also Süstermann, "Ist es eine so gleichgültige Sache, dem großen Haufen Freyheit zu predigen?"

10. Dewey, "Ethics of Democracy," 244.

11. There are important exceptions to this narrowness. The best known is the work of Onora O'Neill. See O'Neill, *Constructions of Reason.*

12. Rawls, "Idea of an Overlapping Consensus"; Rawls, *Political Liberalism;* Rawls, "Law of Peoples"; Rawls, *Justice as Fairness.*

13. This idea is generally attributed to Max Weber. See, e.g., his "Politics as a Vocation." Jürgen Habermas argues that this dual nature characterizes law, one of the central institutions of the modern state. Law has both "normativity" (you obey it because you endorse the idea that you *ought* to obey it) and "facticity" (you obey it because if you don't, you'll be thrown in jail). See his *Between Facts and Norms.*

14. I draw from Herzog, *Happy Slaves,* with this and the following example.

15. See, e.g., Putnam, *Bowling Alone;* Putnam, Leonardi, and Nanetti, *Making Democracy Work;* Tocqueville, *Democracy in America.*

16. These ideas build on my theory of political agency developed in LaVaque-Manty, *Arguments and Fists.*

17. Giamatti, *Take Time for Paradise.*

18. Hume, *Treatise of Human Nature,* bk. 3, pt. 2, sec. ii.

19. See, e.g., Sen, *Inequality Reexamined;* Sen, "Capability and Well-Being."

20. Rousseau also thought along these lines. See his *Discourse on the Origin of Inequality.*

21. Hobbes, *Leviathan,* chap. 13.

22. I also use abbreviations to refer to the titles of Kant's works. Those abbreviations are listed at the beginning of the references section at the end of the volume.

CHAPTER 1

1. Schama makes the same point. See his *Embarrassment of Riches,* chap. 7.

2. I have in mind the debates inspired by the work of Philippe Ariès. See Ariès, *Centuries of Childhood;* Ariès and Duby, *History of Private Life;* and a sample of later contributions in Adrian Wilson, "The Infancy of the History of Childhood"; Cunningham, *Children and Childhood in Western Society;* Fass, *Encyclopedia of Children and Childhood;* Heywood, *History of Childhood.*

3. Mendelssohn, "On the Question: What Is Enlightenment?" 53.

4. On *Bildung* in general, see Brunner, Conze, and Koselleck, *Geschichtliche Grundbegriffe.* On the intrinsic value, see, e.g., Beiser, "Romantic Education"; Schiller, *On the Aesthetic Education of Man.*

5. For a discussion of the difference between the two concepts, see Brunner, Conze, and Koselleck, *Geschichtliche Grundbegriffe,* 1:511.

6. Johann Amos Comenius, *Joh. Amos Commenii Orbis sensualium pictus,* 244.

7. For a fascinating discussion of children and these devices in the context of the seventeenth-century Netherlands, see Schama, *Embarrassment of Riches,* 486–96.

8. See Arendt, *Lectures on Kant's Political Philosophy,* 76, where she thinks Kant's point in the first *Critique* about examples being the *Gängelwagen* of the power of judgment is a positive one.

9. I am uneasy about George Di Giovanni's translation of *Jünglingsalter* as "adolescence" because the concept arguably did not exist until the late nineteenth century. "Youth," while more vague, would be better. The term is gendered: a *Jüngling* is a boy who is no longer a child but not quite yet a young man.

10. I use the impersonal and objectifying *it* to refer to "the child" to capture Kant's gender-neutral language. The German *das Kind* is in the grammatical neuter.

11. The term *Philantropinen* does not have the connotation we most commonly associate with it these days—i.e., the financial support of worthy public causes. It did involve varying degree of paternalism, though far less in Basedow's case than in, say, the slightly later Swiss variants. The key idea, however, is a general concern for humanity, and if a convenient term were available, the best translation would evoke a kind of hybrid between humanists and humanitarians.

12. Basedow, *Vorstellung an Menschenfreunde,* 17. Hereafter, I will refer to the *Vorstellung* with the in-text parenthetical VM. MB will refer to his *Methodenbuch* and EW to *Elementarwerke,* both of which are in Basedow, *Ausgewählte Schriften.*

13. Review of Guthsmuth's *Gymnastik für die Jugend.*

14. Villaume, "Über die Gewalt der Leidenschaften in den Jünglingsjahren," 153.

15. Schapiro, "What Is a Child?" makes a similar argument about Kant's view of children; see esp. 735–36.

16. Pestalozzi, "Ein Gespräch über Volksaufklärung und Volksbildung"; Compayré, *Johann Heinrich Pestalozzi.*

17. Campe, *Abridgement of the New Robinson Crusoe,* 5.

18. Campe, *Robinson the Younger by Mr. Campe,* 2.

19. Ibid., v.

20. Campe, *Abridgement of the New Robinson Crusoe,* 7–9.

21. Neuendorf, "Fragmente über Basedow"; Göring, "Johann Bernhard Basedow," lxxviii.

22. "Einleitung," in Basedow, *Vorstellung an Menschenfreunde,* 11.

23. Epstein, *Genesis of German Conservatism,* 79–81.

24. See Epstein's discussion of the conservative reaction in ibid., 79–81, as well as sec. 3 in the discussion of "Bildung" in Brunner, Conze, and Koselleck, *Geschichtliche Grundbegriffe,* 1:511.

25. See Brunner, Conze, and Koselleck, *Geschichtliche Grundbegriffe,* 1:511. The *Revisionswerk* is available in digital facsimile at the Bibliothek für Bildungsgeschichtliche Forschung, online at http://www.bbf.dipf.de/cgi-opac/catalog.pl?t_digishow=x&zid=ad566 (accessed July 10, 2006).

26. Herzog, *Poisoning the Minds of the Lower Orders,* offers a nuanced reading of such concerns in England; Epstein, *Genesis of German Conservatism,* does so for the German-speaking world.

27. I have benefited from conversations with Claire Rasmussen on this point.

28. See, e.g., P 9:463 for Kant worrying about making children effeminate (*weichlich*).

CHAPTER 2

1. See, e.g., Taylor, *Multiculturalism and the Politics of Recognition;* Taylor, *Sources of the Self,* esp. chaps. 10–11; Berger, "On the Obsolescence of the Concept of Honour." See also the discussion in Krause, *Liberalism with Honor,* chap. 1, which I echo, although our emphases ultimately differ.

2. Contemporary and later commentators have felt comfortable describing dueling as a general Euro-American phenomenon, even when they acknowledged re-

gional, cultural, and temporal variations. See, e.g., Hausner, *Ueber den Zweikampf;* Sabine, *Notes on Duels and Duelling.*

3. Bacon, "Charge Touching Duels," 305.

4. Richelieu, *Political Testament,* 22–23 for the English; Richelieu, *Testament politique,* 154–55 for the original.

5. E.g., Bennett, *Discourse against the Fatal Practice of Duelling,* 18; for the general point, see Peltonen, *Duel in Early Modern England,* 88.

6. Sabine, *Notes on Duels and Duelling,* 41. See also Albert, *Physiologie du duel,* 169.

7. Frevert, "Bürgerlichkeit und Ehre"; Frevert, "Bourgeois Honour"; Frevert, *Men of Honour;* McAleer, *Dueling;* Mosse, "Nobility and Bourgeoisie," 90–91.

8. On the German bourgeois critique of aristocracy, see Epstein, *Genesis of German Conservatism,* 186–88. On the "feudalization" of the German bourgeoisie, see McAleer, *Dueling,* 197; for a critique, see, e.g., Mosse, "Nobility and Bourgeoisie."

9. Frevert, "Bürgerlichkeit und Ehre," 102; Frevert, *Men of Honour,* 4, 182. See also Kiernan, *Duel in European History,* 281. For Weber's views, see esp. Max Weber, "National Character and the Junkers"; see also Max Weber, "Economic Policy and the National Interest," as well as Marianne Weber's account in *Max Weber,* 473, 478 (also quoted by Frevert). I return to this particular case later.

10. Académie des Sciences Morales et Politiques, *Catalogue des Actes de Henri II,* vols. 1, 4; Sabine, *Notes on Duels and Duelling,* 6; Billacois, *Duel,* 95; Monestier, *Duels,* 106.

11. Baldick, *Duel,* 49; Monestier, *Duels,* 106.

12. The brief synthetic history in the following paragraphs relies heavily on Neilson, *Trial by Combat;* Baldick, *Duel;* Kiernan, *Duel in European History;* McAleer, *Dueling;* Frevert, *Men of Honour;* Billacois, *Duel;* Sabine, *Notes on Duels and Duelling;* Hausner, *Ueber den Zweikampf;* Peltonen, *Duel in Early Modern England;* Monestier, *Duels;* Truman, *Field of Honor;* Hey, *Dissertation on Duelling.*

13. Selden, *Duello,* 24 (spelling and punctuation largely modernized). See also Baldick, *Duel;* Billacois, *Duel,* chap. 3; Neilson, *Trial by Combat;* Monestier, *Duels,* 33–48.

14. Truman, *Field of Honor,* 20, quoting sixteenth-century French statesman Duc Maximilien de Sully.

15. An intermediary state of *chivalric dueling* made duels a ritual for display of a knight's Christian probity: "This was a meeting in single combat between two knights, generally on horseback and always with great public ceremonial, to settle the difference of law, possession of honour" (Baldick, *Duel,* 22).

16. Neilson, *Trial by Combat,* 293.

17. Selden, *Duello,* 14.

18. Kiernan, *Duel in European History,* 48. See also Wood, *Radicalism of the American Revolution,* 41.

19. Kiernan, *Duel in European History.*

20. Billacois, *Duel,* 76–82.

21. Ibid., 78.

22. Rousseau, "Letter to M. d'Alembert on the Theatre," 71.

23. Hattenhauer, *Allgemeines Landrecht für die Preußischen Staaten von 1794,* pt. 2, heading 20, sec. 671, p. 693. See also Frevert, *Men of Honour,* 28.

24. On the controversy, see Epstein, *Genesis of German Conservatism,* 372–87. For evidence of Kant's familiarity with the Civil Code controversy, see J. G. C. C. Kiesewetter's June 14, 1791, letter to Kant in *Correspondence,* 11:264–66 (377–78 of the translation). Reinhart Koselleck reads Kant's *Rechtslehre* as a general repudiation of the common law; see his *Preußen zwischen Reform und Revolution,* 153–54.

25. This is most fully developed in the *Rechtslehre,* but it also occurs in various forms in "The Idea for a Universal History with a Cosmopolitan Purpose," "What Is Enlightenment?" "Conjectural Beginning of Human History," *Perpetual Peace,* and *The Conflict of the Faculties.* See LaVaque-Manty, *Arguments and Fists;* Ellis, *Kant's Politics.*

26. Ellis, *Kant's Politics.*

27. See Koselleck, *Preußen zwischen Reform und Revolution,* 80.

28. Kant elaborates women's dependence at sec. 46 of RL, 6:313–15; "That May Be True in Theory, but Is It True in Practice?" 8:294–97; and A 7:192. I discuss this at greater length in LaVaque-Manty, "Kant's Children." For review of other contemporary views on how feminine honor was properly expressed, see "Familie," in Brunner, Conze, and Koselleck, *Geschichtliche Grundbegriffe;* Rebekka Habermas, *Frauen und Männer des Bürgertums.*

29. Chishull, *Against Duelling,* 12.

30. Hobbes, *Leviathan,* chap. 27, para. 35, p. 201.

31. Rousseau, "Letter to M. d'Alembert on the Theatre," 67–75.

32. Ibid., 68.

33. Sabine, *Notes on Duels and Duelling,* 249. Baldick, *Duel,* 97, also quotes the passage, as does Truman, *Field of Honor,* 206.

34. Sabine, *Notes on Duels and Duelling,* 248.

35. Blackstone, *Commentaries,* 2403–4.

36. Sabine, *Notes on Duels and Duelling,* 10. But for Peel's ambivalence, see Escott, *Social Transformations of the Victorian Age,* 291.

37. Hausner, *Ueber den Zweikampf,* 19.

38. Rousseau, "Letter to M. d'Alembert on the Theatre," Sabine, *Notes on Duels and Duelling,* 41–47, and Escott, *Social Transformations of the Victorian Age,* 290–93, make this point. On produeling public opinion in eighteenth-century France, see Monestier, *Duels,* 205–7.

39. See also DV 6:468, where Kant says that "even rank and dignity" are contingent relations that "depend in part on arbitrary arrangements."

40. Consider here Kant's famous distinction between two ways of valuing people: they can have dignity as persons and *price* as people "in the system of nature" (G 4:434; DV 6:434). My discussion suggests that the distinction is less about the changeability of the value than about its fungibility: you can lose your dignity, but you cannot give it *to* someone or get it from someone. That, of course, is exactly consistent with *individualized* points of honor, the prevailing conception of dueling.

41. Frevert, *Men of Honour,* 113.

42. Freeman, *Affairs of Honor,* 166.

43. Montesquieu, *Persian Letters* (1999), letter 90. I also use Montesquieu, *Persian Letters* (1973).

44. Truman, *Field of Honor,* 190. The "expressions" Winchelsea had made against Wellington had to do with their dispute over the Roman Catholic Relief Bill;

Winchelsea had accused Wellington of trying to introduce "Popery into every department of the state." See Baldick, *Duel,* 104; Sabine, *Notes on Duels and Duelling,* 306. On parliamentary attempts to prevent insults from turning into duels, see Herzog, *Poisoning the Minds of the Lower Orders,* 143–44.

45. Kiernan, *Duel in European History,* 143.

46. That the scar was actually mark of a social status of course means that to speak of "harm" is partly misleading.

47. Rousseau, "Letter to M. d'Alembert on the Theatre," 71n.

48. Montesquieu, *Persian Letters* (1999), letter 59. Betts's translation here is both inexact and grammatically awkward. The end of the passage reads in French, "il l'observe si bien, qu'il y a six mois il reçut cent coups de bâton pour ne le pas violer."

49. Frevert, *Men of Honour,* 26; but see Billacois, *Duel,* 73. See also Kiernan, *Duel in European History,* 113.

50. At the same time, as the contemporary and retrospective reaction to that famous duel suggests, public opinion may already have shifted to the extent that people generally saw Hamilton as having behaved honorably in both agreeing to the duel and shooting in the air. There is still no agreed-on consensus on whether Hamilton fired in the air by mistake or deliberately. Burr's behavior with regard to the entire challenge also caused many contemporaries to regard him as the dishonorable party. For a discussion of this matter, see Freeman, *Affairs of Honor.* For two more contemporary accounts, see Sabine, *Notes on Duels and Duelling;* Truman, *Field of Honor.*

51. Kiernan, *Duel in European History,* 49; see also McAleer, *Dueling,* 9.

52. Even Max Weber expresses this; see his "National Character and the Junkers." See also Mommsen, *Max Weber and German Politics,* 100. On the general conservative attitudes about bourgeois and "parvenu" pretensions to aristocratic privileges, see Epstein, *Genesis of German Conservatism,* 188–201.

53. Baldick, *Duel,* 125; Rutledge, "Dueling in Antebellum Mississippi," 185–86. See also Freeman, *Affairs of Honor,* 168–69; Krause, *Liberalism with Honor,* 120–31; Wood, *Radicalism of the American Revolution,* 345.

54. Berger, "On the Obsolescence of the Concept of Honour," 157.

55. Simmel, "Web of Group Affiliations," 163.

56. McAleer, *Dueling,* 3.

57. Kiernan, *Duel in European History,* 15.

58. Tocqueville, *Democracy in America,* vol. 2, bk. 2, chap. 5.

59. LaVaque-Manty, *Arguments and Fists,* 72–74.

60. Frevert, *Men of Honour,* 183.

61. Hattenhauer, *Allgemeines Landrecht für die Preußischen Staaten von 1794,* pt. 2, heading 9, sec. 1, p. 534.

62. See, e.g., Haslanger, "On Being Objective and Being Objectified"; Pateman, *Sexual Contract;* MacKinnon, *Toward a Feminist Theory of the State;* Ortner, *Making Gender;* Haslanger, "Gender and Race."

63. On women's dueling, see Baldick, *Duel,* chap. 11.

64. Leo, "Ueber Zweikämpfe und ihre Schädlichkeit," 20, 22. See also Frevert, *Men of Honour,* 27.

65. See, again, Kant's discussion of women's dependence at sec. 46 of RL

6:313–15; "That May Be True in Theory, but Is It True in Practice?" 8:294–97; A 7:192.

66. Marianne Weber relates the story in *Max Weber*, 472–82, from which this paragraph draws its information. Frevert discusses it in *Men of Honour*, 182.

67. For an interesting contrast on how a state with no interest in protoliberal or protodemocratic solutions managed to convert honor away from private violence, see the case of Tokugawa Japan discussed by Ikegami, *Taming of the Samurai*.

68. For more information on the cartoons, see Forsyth, *Uses of Art*.

69. Conrad, "Duel," 69.

70. Moretti, "Homo Palpitans." But Dostoyevsky brilliantly discusses dueling and the hierarchies of sidewalk honor in *Notes from the Underground/The Double*, 52–58.

71. Brunner, Conze, and Koselleck, *Geschichtliche Grundbegriffe*, 2:20.

72. See Elias, *Civilizing Process*, for the general argument.

73. See Elias, "Genesis of Sport as a Sociological Problem." See also the work by Elias's collaborator, Eric Dunning, esp. Dunning and Sheard, *Barbarians, Gentlemen and Players*.

CHAPTER 3

1. Spencer, *Education*, 189, 190. This is also quoted by Haley, *Healthy Body and Victorian Culture*, 17.

2. See Clifford, "Body and Mind"; Jacyna, "Physiology of Mind."

3. See, e.g., Mangan, *Games Ethic and Imperialism*.

4. Du Bois-Reymond, *Über die Übung*, 46–47.

5. Haley, *Healthy Body and Victorian Culture*, 23. The popularity of the slogan isn't limited to the nineteenth century. As I was growing up, many Finnish saunas had the slogan on the thermometer, usually above a happily bathing and presumably healthy family.

6. "Healthy Body and a Mind at Ease," 142, 146.

7. Porter, *Flesh in the Age of Reason*, chap. 20.

8. Ibid.

9. See Gilman, *Jew's Body*.

10. "Healthy Body and a Mind at Ease."

11. Quoted in Berryman, "Exercise and the Medical Tradition," 44. See also Park, "Physiologists, Physicians, and Physical Educators," 38.

12. "Healthy Body and a Mind at Ease," 144.

13. Du Bois-Reymond, *Über die Übung*.

14. Haley, *Healthy Body and Victorian Culture*, 154, reviews some of the controversy over the extent to which Arnold was an early "muscular Christian." Whether he was—the evidence suggests that he was at most benignly interested in the sports at Rugby (see Stanley, *Life and Correspondence of Thomas Arnold*, 182; Dunning and Sheard, *Barbarians, Gentlemen and Players*, 78)—is beside the point here. What matters is the way he was plugged into an ideology of health. See also McIntosh, *Fair Play*, 27.

15. Trollope, *British Sports and Pastimes*, 322.

16. Spencer, *Education,* 144, 145, 146.

17. Groos, *Die Spiele der Thiere,* iii.

18. Park, "Decade of the Body," 59.

19. Trollope, *British Sports and Pastimes,* 2

20. Hey, *Dissertation on Duelling,* 84.

21. Elias, "Essay on Sport and Violence," 163, 165.

22. When the "accidents" begin to seem systematic, as happened with American football in the first years of the twentieth century, intervention becomes necessary.

23. Stanley, *Life and Correspondence of Thomas Arnold,* 88.

24. Dunning and Sheard, *Barbarians, Gentlemen and Players,* 96.

25. Ibid., 97.

26. We don't need the Stanford prison experiments to know the extent to which uncontrolled power can lead people. Orwell's indictment of the fagging system in "Such, Such Were the Joys . . ." is just one of the many reminders that the system did not work as well as its promoters said it did. It is also not clear even they fully believed in its working.

27. Beckford, *Thoughts upon Hare and Fox Hunting,* 199. Elias, "Essay on Sport and Violence," also quotes this and many other passages from Beckford.

28. Elias, "Essay on Sport and Violence," 163.

29. Beckford, *Thoughts upon Hare and Fox Hunting,* 200.

30. Sassoon, *Memoirs of a Fox-Hunting Man,* 16.

31. Dunning and Sheard, *Barbarians, Gentlemen and Players,* 97.

32. Trollope, *British Sports and Pastimes,* 2–3, 4.

33. Baker, "Leisure Revolution"; Vamplew, "Sport and Industrialization"; Reid, "Beasts and Brutes"; Haley, *Healthy Body and Victorian Culture;* Hobsbawm, "Mass-Producing Traditions"; Mangan, *Athleticism in the Victorian and Edwardian Public School;* Escott, *Social Transformations of the Victorian Age;* Dunning and Sheard, *Barbarians, Gentlemen and Players;* Park, "Decade of the Body."

34. Trollope, *British Sports and Pastimes,* 298–99.

35. See, e.g., Carlyle, *Past and Present;* Ruskin, *Unto This Last.*

36. Guttmann, *Women's Sports;* Haley, *Healthy Body and Victorian Culture;* Hargreaves, *Sporting Females;* Park, "'Embodied Selves'"; Twin, *Out of the Bleachers.*

37. Trollope, *British Sports and Pastimes,* 6–7.

38. Park, "Physiologists, Physicians, and Physical Educators," 30–31.

39. Carlyle, *Past and Present;* Ruskin, *Unto This Last.*

40. Riess, "From Pitch to Putt," 148.

41. Vamplew, *Pay Up and Play the Game,* 8.

42. Jones, *Sport, Politics, and the Working Class;* Ingham and Hardy, "Sport"; Hobsbawm, "Mass-Producing Traditions."

43. Hobsbawm, "Mass-Producing Traditions," 289.

44. Jones, *Sport, Politics, and the Working Class,* 29.

45. "Healthy Body and a Mind at Ease," 142.

46. Herzog, *Poisoning the Minds of the Lower Orders,* discusses contemporary hand-wringing about social mobility in the late eighteenth and early nineteenth centuries. The dynamics I have in mind are similar but occurred later.

47. Escott, *Social Transformations of the Victorian Age,* 201–2.

CHAPTER 4

1. Rousseau, "Letter to M. d'Alembert on the Theatre."

2. Lowerson and Myerscough, *Time to Spare in Victorian England;* Williams, "From Popular Culture to Public Cliché"; Riordan, "Introduction."

3. Baker, "Leisure Revolution," 83; Jones, *Sport, Politics, and the Working Class,* chap. 2.

4. Ehrenberg, "Aimez-vous les stades?"; Baker, "Leisure Revolution."

5. Wordsworth, "Kendal and Windermere Railway," 343–44.

6. Reid, "Beasts and Brutes"; Williams, "From Popular Culture to Public Cliché"; Jones, *Sport, Politics, and the Working Class;* Baker, "Leisure Revolution"; Herzog, *Poisoning the Minds of the Lower Orders;* Lowerson and Myerscough, *Time to Spare in Victorian England.*

7. Wordsworth, "Speech at the Laying of the Foundation Stone," 296.

8. Spirn, "Constructing Nature."

9. Ingham and Hardy, "Sport," 94.

10. Frykholm, "Soccer and Social Identity in Pre-Revolutionary Moscow," 143.

11. Arnaud, *Athlètes de la République;* Callède, *Politiques sportives en France.*

12. Goltermann, *Körper der Nation;* John, *Politik und Turnen;* Riordan, "Worker Sport within a Worker State."

13. Riordan, introduction.

14. von der Lippe, "Landmarks in the History of Norwegian Worker Sport"; Callède, *Politiques sportives en France.*

15. Ueberhorst, *Frisch, frei, stark und treu,* 333.

16. Riordan, "Worker Sport within a Worker State."

17. The national organizations at times served anti-Left politics beyond being just an apolitical distraction. In Norway, for example, members of the national sports organization, NSF, were used as strikebreakers (von der Lippe, "Landmarks in the History of Norwegian Worker Sport").

18. Gechtman, "Socialist Mass Politics through Sport."

19. Orwell, *Road to Wigan Pier.*

20. Jones, *Sport, Politics, and the Working Class.*

21. Ueberhorst, *Frisch, frei, stark und treu,* 112.

22. Krüger, "The German Way of Worker Sport," 14.

23. Gechtman, "Socialist Mass Politics through Sport," 330.

24. Riordan, "Worker Sport within a Worker State."

25. Ueberhorst, *Frisch, frei, stark und treu,* 44; my translation.

26. Ibid., 44.

27. Ibid., 42. See also Schiller, *On the Aesthetic Education of Man.*

28. Humboldt, *Limits of State Action.*

29. Yack, *Longing for Total Revolution.*

30. Rousseau, "Letter to M. d'Alembert on the Theatre."

31. Gechtman, "Socialist Mass Politics through Sport"; Krüger, "'Once the Olympics Are Through.'"

32. Riordan, introduction.

33. Ueberhorst, *Frisch, frei, stark und treu,* 43.

34. Riordan, "Worker Sport within a Worker State," 84.
35. Jones, *Sport, Politics, and the Working Class,* 28.
36. Ingham and Hardy, "Sport," 91.
37. Gechtman, "Socialist Mass Politics through Sport," 336.
38. Ibid., 330.
39. Krammer, "Austria."
40. Riordan, "Worker Sport within a Worker State," 90.
41. Jones, *Sport, Politics, and the Working Class,* 81.
42. Riordan, "Worker Sport within a Worker State," 51.
43. Gramsci, *Pre-Prison Writings,* 73, 74.
44. It is not just the question of the development of Gramsci's thought in a more critical direction in his later writings, either. In the same year, he offered a sharp critique of liberal civil society. See, e.g., ibid., 70–72.
45. Jones, *Sport, Politics, and the Working Class,* 33.
46. Goltermann, *Körper der Nation;* Jones, *Sport, Politics, and the Working Class;* Laine, "TUL"; Ueberhorst, *Frisch, frei, stark und treu;* Vamplew, "Sport and Industrialization"; von der Lippe, "Landmarks in the History of Norwegian Worker Sport."
47. Ueberhorst, *Frisch, frei, stark und treu,* 139; my translation.
48. Gechtman, "Socialist Mass Politics through Sport," 343.
49. Ueberhorst, *Frisch, frei, stark und treu,* 132.
50. von der Lippe, "Landmarks in the History of Norwegian Worker Sport."
51. Arnaud, *Athlètes de la République,* 325.
52. Riordan, "Worker Sport within a Worker State," 17.
53. Jones, *Sport, Politics, and the Working Class;* Krüger, "'Once the Olympics Are Through'"; John, *Politik und Turnen;* Gechtman, "Socialist Mass Politics through Sport."
54. Pålbrant, "Vital Period in Swedish Worker Sport."
55. Gechtman, "Socialist Mass Politics through Sport"; Krüger, "'Once the Olympics Are Through.'"
56. Suomen Työväen Urheiluliitto, "Esittely."
57. Ueberhorst, *Frisch, frei, stark und treu;* Pålbrant, "Vital Period in Swedish Worker Sport"; Gechtman, "Socialist Mass Politics through Sport"; von der Lippe, "Landmarks in the History of Norwegian Worker Sport."
58. Raevuori, *Paavo Nurmi,* 49.
59. Orlie, "Political Capitalism and the Consumption of Democracy."
60. Ibid.
61. LaVaque-Manty, *Arguments and Fists,* chap. 2.

CHAPTER 5

1. Park, "Sport, Gender and Society in a Transatlantic Victorian Perspective," 86–87.
2. See, e.g., Suggs, "Foes of Title IX"; Gavora, *Tilting the Playing Field.*
3. 20 U.S.C. 1681 et seq.

4. See, e.g., Festle, *Playing Nice;* Guttmann, *Whole New Ball Game;* Hargreaves, *Sporting Females;* Guttmann, *Women's Sports.*

5. I touch on some of these issues later in this chapter. For an example of (occasionally overoptimistic) hopes about changes in attitudes, see Twin, *Out of the Bleachers.*

6. See, e.g., Hargreaves, *Sporting Females;* Park, "Sport, Gender and Society in a Transatlantic Victorian Perspective."

7. Litsky, "Wheelchair Athletes File a Complaint."

8. International Paralympic Committee, "Paralympic Games"; DePauw and Gavron, *Disability and Sport.*

9. Greenhouse, "Disabled Golfer May Use a Cart"; Abbott, "Sports Are a Way of Belonging."

10. On the failure of mainstreaming disability sport, see Darcy, "Politics of Disability and Access." For critiques of ADA litigation, see the disability-related commentary at overlawyered.com (accessed May 9, 2005).

11. MacIntyre, *After Virtue.*

12. Stone, *Disabled State,* chap. 1.

13. Fraser, *Justice Interruptus;* Rawls, *Political Liberalism;* Sen, "Capability and Well-Being"; Young, *Justice and the Politics of Difference.*

14. Bagenstos, "Subordination, Stigma, and 'Disability.'" On stigma, see Goffman, *Stigma;* Karst, *Belonging to America.* On the anticaste principle, see Sunstein, "Anticaste Principle"; see also Francis and Silvers, "Achieving the Right to Live in the World."

15. Hahn, "Disability Policy and the Problem of Discrimination," 312.

16. O'Quinn, *Americans with Disabilities Act.*

17. Litsky, "Wheelchair Athletes File a Complaint"; McKinley, "No Stop Signs on the Course."

18. DePauw and Gavron, *Disability and Sport,* 11, 120–27; see also Sherrill, *Adapted Physical Activity, Recreation, and Sport,* 33–35; International Paralympic Committee, "Classification."

19. On making political arguments with analogies, see Sunstein, "On Analogical Reasoning."

20. McCarthy, "Wheelchair Marathoners Deserve a Chance to Compete."

21. Sen, "Rights and Capabilities"; Sen, *Inequality Reexamined;* Sen, "Capability and Well-Being"; see also Nussbaum, "Human Functioning and Social Justice"; Nussbaum, *Women and Human Development.*

22. McCarthy, "Wheelchair Marathoners Deserve a Chance to Compete."

23. Goffman, *Stigma,* chap. 1.

24. Sherrill, *Adapted Physical Activity, Recreation, and Sport,* 515.

25. I return to the (generally unhelpful) distinction between nature and nurture in the next chapter.

26. Tomkins, "Tennis Artist."

27. See, e.g., Suggs, "Foes of Title IX"; Zimbalist, "Backlash against Title IX"; Schuld, "Flawed Interpretation of Title IX"; but see also Suggs, "Poll Finds Strong Public Backing."

28. Daniels, "Mental Disabilities, Equal Opportunity, and the ADA," 282.

29. Quad rugby became popularly known thanks to Shapiro, Mandel, and Rubin's 2005 documentary, *Murderball.*

30. International Paralympic Committee, "Classification."

31. Sherrill, *Adapted Physical Activity, Recreation, and Sport,* 35.

32. Roberts, "Fear of Disability the Same on a Course or a Track"; Longman, "Amputee Sprinter."

33. Robinson, "Study Suggests That Amputee Holds an Unfair Advantage"; Lay, "Olympic Dream over for 'Blade Runner' Pistorius"; Power, "Pistorius Clocks a World Record."

34. DePauw and Gavron, *Disability and Sport,* chap. 7; International Paralympic Committee, "Classification."

35. Bird, *Incredibles.*

36. For a sample set of issues and opinions, consider the discussions in "Clydesdales and the World Championships."

37. See the issues at http://www.teamclydesdale.com; see also Kirkland, "Representations of Fatness and Personhood."

38. Arneson, "Disability, Discrimination and Priority." For a critique, see Anderson, "What Is the Point of Equality?"

39. See, e.g., Crespo and Arbesman, "Obesity in the United States."

40. Littwin, "Now Everyone's Talking about Boulder Bolder."

41. Cahill, "Olympic Flame and Torch."

42. See Austin, "Performative Utterances," for a distinction between saying and doing with expressions.

43. Connell, *Masculinities.* For a few very different examples, see Longman, "Athletes Embrace Size, Rejecting Stereotypes"; Guillet et al., "Understanding Female Sport Attrition"; Helstein, "Seeing Your Sporting Body."

44. See also Zupan and Swanson, *Gimp,* a memoir by the most visible and charismatic of the athletes in the documentary.

45. Dickinson, "Power of the Paralympics 1996 Games in Atlanta"; Leal, "Disabled Athletes in Training"; Pingree, "Development of the Paralympic Games"; Mascagni, "Paola Fantato."

46. Darcy, "Politics of Disability and Access."

47. Australian Bureau of Statistics, "Year Book Australia."

48. Darcy, "Politics of Disability and Access," 753.

CHAPTER 6

1. For one contemporary account, see Fainaru-Wada and Williams, *Game of Shadows.*

2. Mitchell, *Report to the Commissioner of Baseball.*

3. Giamatti, *Take Time for Paradise.*

4. See also Hoberman, *Mortal Engines,* ix.

5. For a recent example, see "Olympics Meets the War on Drugs"; see also Hoberman, *Testosterone Dream;* Cashmore, *Making Sense of Sport.* For examples of the

supposed alarmism and hypocrisy critics attack, see Voy, *Drugs, Sport, and Politics;* Mc-Closkey and Bailes, *When Winning Costs Too Much.*

6. Cashmore, *Making Sense of Sport;* Hoberman, *Mortal Engines.*

7. MacIntyre, *After Virtue.* For an earlier and slightly more moderate version of the lament, see Anscombe, "Modern Moral Philosophy."

8. "Olympics Meets the War on Drugs"; Cashmore, *Making Sense of Sport;* Jost, "Sports and Drugs"; Hoberman, *Mortal Engines.*

9. Available online at http://www.whitehouse.gov/news/releases/2004/01/20040120-7.html (accessed Oct. 22, 2006).

10. McCloskey and Bailes, *When Winning Costs Too Much.*

11. Voy, *Drugs, Sport, and Politics;* Hoberman, *Testosterone Dreams;* Jost, "Sports and Drugs"; Paddick, "Drugs and Sports."

12. Jost, "Sports and Drugs"; Longman and Connelly, "Americans Suspect Steroid Use In Sports Is Common."

13. Giamatti, *Take Time for Paradise,* 34.

14. "Baseball's Shame."

15. Hoberman, *Mortal Engines.*

16. For a political theorist making an argument about leisure as the highest form of human autonomy, see Booth, "Gone Fishing."

17. Guttmann, *Whole New Ball Game.*

18. Ungerleider, *Faust's Gold;* Longman, "East German Steroids' Toll."

19. Donohoe and Johnson, *Foul Play;* Hoberman, *Testosterone Dreams;* Jost, "Sports and Drugs."

20. "War on Doping in Switzerland"; "Doping" (1962); La Cava, "Use of Drugs in Competitive Sport."

21. La Cava, "Use of Drugs in Competitive Sport," 53.

22. Creff, "Thoughts on Doping."

23. "Doping" (1965), 47.

24. Mimiague, "Doping Problem in Comparative Penal Law." An early statement by Porritt, "Doping and the Use of Chemical Agents," reflects a pretty sophisticated way of thinking about doping: he defines doping as a healthy individual's use of a substance not normally occurring in the body. The definition has its vague elements, but they are contingent in the way that are more consistent with my conception of *artificial* described later in the chapter.

25. *World Anti-Doping Code,* sec. 1.

26. There is a bizarre case of doping where athletes used a masking agent—a plasma expander called Hemohes—*on the assumption that it was performance-enhancing.* I will briefly discuss this case later in the chapter.

27. Longman, "East German Steroids' Toll."

28. Quoted in Jost, "Sports and Drugs," 615.

29. This is the familiar tragic lesson of situations that can be interpreted as the so-called prisoner's dilemma games.

30. Hoberman, *Mortal Engines,* 108.

31. Ibid.

32. John Wilson, *Playing by the Rules.*

33. Sokolove, "From Pastime to Naptime."

34. I'm alluding here to Sen's famous argument about why consistently rational action turns people into fools ("Rational Fools").

35. See, though, the admissions by promoter Jos Hermens about his drug use in Denison, *Greatest,* or, more famously, the "revelations" in Canseco, *Juiced.*

36. I don't mean the vehement denials when accused, which is quite common, but proactive steps in the absence of suspicion to help clean the sport.

37. Hart, "Radcliffe Attacks Cheats."

38. Alexander, "Awful Truth about Drugs in Sports."

39. Elias, "Essay on Sport and Violence."

40. Butcher and Schneider, "Fair Play as Respect for the Game"; Elias, "Genesis of Sport as a Sociological Problem"; McIntosh, *Fair Play.*

41. Butcher and Schneider, "Fair Play as Respect for the Game."

42. Herman, "Cosmopolitan Kingdom of Ends."

43. At the University of Michigan, for example, fans commonly prefer completely lopsided games in the Michigan football team's favor.

44. Herzog, *Cunning.*

45. Hobbes, *Leviathan,* chap. 15, para. 4.

46. "Olympics Meets the War on Drugs."

47. Hoberman, *Testosterone Dreams.*

48. In an ESPN/ABC poll among baseball fans in May 2007—before he broke the record—37 percent of respondents thought Bonds's record should not even be recognized as such even if he passed Aaron's mark. See "Americans Conflicted about Bonds' Home Run Chase." After Bonds broke the record later in the summer, the person who bought the ball that Bonds hit for his 756th home run ran a Web-based survey on what should happen to the ball. According to the Web site, more than ten million people responded, the plurality of whom, 47 percent, thought it should be "branded" with an asterisk and placed in the Baseball Hall of Fame. See http://www .vote756.com.

49. McCloskey and Bailes, *When Winning Costs Too Much;* Jost, "Sports and Drugs"; Longman and Connelly, "Americans Suspect Steroid Use Is Common."

50. Sokolove, "From Pastime to Naptime."

51. George, "Doping Scandals Push Finland's Skiing Icons off Their Podium"; Andrews, "Finland Reels over Skiers' Drug Scandal."

52. For a popularly accessible account of the difficulties of exercise physiology, see Kolata, *Ultimate Fitness.*

53. Jost, "Sports and Drugs"; Paddick, "Drugs and Sports"; Alexander, "Awful Truth about Drugs in Sports."

54. The quoted phrases come from Kant's famous statement in the conclusion to the *Critique of Practical Reason,* CPrR 5:161.

55. "War on Doping in Switzerland," 62.

56. In September 2006, WADA decided against banning hypobaric and hypoxic chambers and other forms of altitude simulation. See Langley, "WADA Decides against Hypoxic Chamber Ban."

57. See Kessler, *Lessons from the Intersexed.*

58. See also Cole, "Resisting the Canon."

59. One of the early IOC positions uses *artificial* to refer only to doping, but that obviously begs the question. See "War on Doping in Switzerland."

60. For analyses of how these discourses work in terms of gender, see Bordo, "Reading the Slender Body"; Cole, "Resisting the Canon."

61. Haraway, "Cyborg Manifesto."

62. I am grateful to Steve Johnston for this example.

CONCLUSION

1. The title of this conclusion comes from Kant, CF 4:79.

2. The concept of the "dialectic of enlightenment" comes from Frankfurt School thinkers Max Horkheimer and Theodor Adorno.

3. See, e.g., Pinker, *Blank Slate;* Dennett, *Freedom Evolves.*

4. Mill, *On Liberty,* chap. 4.

5. Krause, *Liberalism with Honor.*

6. I have addressed this briefly in a very different context in LaVaque-Manty and Mickey, "Ring of Truth."

References

REFERENCES TO IMMANUEL KANT'S WORKS

The volume and page numbers always refer to the standard Akademie Ausgabe of Kant's works (Immanuel Kant, *Gesammelte Schriften,* 29 vols. [Berlin: Preußische Akademie der Wissenchaften, 1902–]). In in-text parentheticals, I have used the following abbreviations. Where I have used translations, they come from *The Cambridge Edition of the Works of Immanuel Kant* (Paul Guyer and Allen Wood, series editors); for the German texts, I have used the PastMasters database of the Akademie Ausgabe.

A   *Anthropologies aus der pragmatischen Hinsicht* (Anthropology from a Pragmatic Point of View)
APB   "Aufsätze, das Philantropin betreffend" (Essays on the Philantropinum)
C   *Correspondence*
CBH   "Mutmaßlicher Anfang der Menschengeschichte" (Conjectural Beginning of Human History)
CF   *Conflict of the Faculties*
CPR   *Critique of Pure Reason*
DV   *Doctrine of Virtue* (part 2 of the *Metaphysics of Morals*)
G   *Groundwork of the Metaphysics of Morals*
LE   *Lectures on Ethics*
P   *Pädagogik* (Education)
R   *Reflexionen über Anthropologie*
Rel   *Religion within the Limits of Mere Reason*
RL   *Rechtslehre* (part 1 of the *Metaphysics of Morals*)
WE   "What Is Enlightenment?"

Abbott, Jim. "Sports Are a Way of Belonging." *New York Times,* February 5, 2001, A21.

Académie des Sciences Morales et Politiques, ed. *Catalogue des Actes de Henri II, Collection des ordonnances des rois de France.* Paris: Impremerie Nationale, 1979.

Albert, Alfred d'. *Physiologie du duel.* Brussels: Meline, Cans, 1853.

Alexander, Brian. "The Awful Truth about Drugs in Sports." *Outside,* July 2005, 100–108.

"Americans Conflicted about Bonds' Home Run Chase." Available online at http://sports.espn.go.com/mlb/news/story?id=2861930 (accessed February 27, 2008).

Anderson, Elizabeth. "What Is the Point of Equality?" *Ethics* 109, no. 2 (1999): 287–337.

Andrews, Edmund L. "Finland Reels over Skiers' Drug Scandal." *New York Times,* March 13, 2001, D1.

Anscombe, G. E. M. "Modern Moral Philosophy." *Philosophy* 33, no. 124 (1958): 1–19.

Arendt, Hannah. *Lectures on Kant's Political Philosophy.* Edited by Ronald Beiner. Chicago: University of Chicago Press, 1992.

Ariès, Philippe. *Centuries of Childhood: A Social History of Family Life.* London: Cape, 1962.

Ariès, Philippe, and Georges Duby. *A History of Private Life.* Cambridge: Harvard University Press, 1987.

Arnaud, Pierre. *Les Athlètes de la République: Gymnastique, sport et idéologie républicaine, 1870–1914.* Paris: L'Harmattan, 1997.

Arneson, Richard J. "Disability, Discrimination and Priority." In *Americans with Disabilities: Exploring Implications of the Law for Individuals and Institutions,* edited by Leslie Pickering Francis and Anita Silvers, 18–33. New York: Routledge, 2000.

Austin, J. L. "Performative Utterances." In *Philosophical Papers,* 3rd ed., edited by J. O. Urmson and G. J. Warnock, 233–52. Oxford: Oxford University Press, 1979.

Australian Bureau of Statistics. "Year Book Australia: A Look Back at the Sydney Olympics and Paralympics." 2002. Available online at http://www.abs.gov.au/Ausstats (accessed May 5, 2005).

Bacon, Francis. "The Charge Touching Duels." In *Francis Bacon: The Major Works,* edited by Brian Vickers, 304–13. Oxford: Oxford University Press, 2002.

Bagenstos, Samuel R. "Subordination, Stigma, and 'Disability.'" *Virginia Law Review* 86, no. 3 (2000): 397–534.

Baker, William J. "The Leisure Revolution in Victorian England: A Review of Recent Literature." *Journal of Sport History* 6, no. 3 (1979): 76–88.

Baldick, Robert. *The Duel: A History of Duelling.* London: Chapman and Hall, 1965.

"Baseball's Shame." *New York Times,* March 6, 2004, A14.

Basedow, Johann Bernhard. *Ausgewählte Schriften.* Langenfalza: Beyer, 1880.

Basedow, Johann Bernhard. *Vorstellung an Menschenfreunde.* Edited by Theodor Fritzsch. Leipzig: Reclam, 1906.

Beckford, Peter. *Thoughts upon Hare and Fox Hunting.* London: Vernor and Hood, 1796.

Beiser, Frederick C. "A Romantic Education: The Concept of *Bildung* in Early German Romanticism." In *Philosophers on Education,* edited by Amélie Oksenberg Rorty, 284–99. London: Routledge, 1998.

Beiser, Frederick C. "Early Romanticism and the *Aufklärung*." In *What Is Enlightenment? Eighteenth-Century Answers and Twentieth-Century Questions,* edited by James Schmidt, 317–29. Berkeley: University of California Press, 1996.

Bennett, John. *A Discourse against the Fatal Practice of Duelling; Occasioned by a Late Melancholy Event, and Preached at St. Mary's Church, in Manchester, on Sunday the 23d of March, 1783.* Manchester: Wheeler, 1783.

Berger, Peter. "On the Obsolescence of the Concept of Honour." In *Liberalism and Its Critics,* edited by Michael Sandel, 149–58. New York: New York University Press, 1984.

Berryman, Jack W. "Exercise and the Medical Tradition from Hippocrates through Antebellum America: A Review Essay." In *Sport and Exercise Science: Essays in the History of Sports Medicine,* edited by Jack W. Berryman and Roberta J. Park, 1–56. Urbana: University of Illinois Press, 1992.

Billacois, François. *The Duel: Its Rise and Fall in Early Modern France.* Translated by Trista Selous. New Haven: Yale University Press, 1990.

Bird, Brad. *The Incredibles.* Walt Disney Pictures, 2004.

Blackstone, Sir William. *Commentaries on the Laws of England.* Edited by William Carey Jones. Vol. 2. Baton Rouge, La.: Claitor's, 1976.

Booth, William James. "Gone Fishing: Making Sense of Marx's Concept of Communism." *Political Theory* 17, no. 2 (1989): 205–22.

Bordo, Susan. "Reading the Slender Body." In *Body/Politics,* edited by Mary Jacobus, Evelyn Fox Keller, and Sally Shuttleworth, 83–112. New York: Routledge, 1990.

Boxill, Jan. "Title IX and Gender Equity." In *Sports Ethics,* edited by Jan Boxill, 254–61. Malden, Mass.: Blackwell, 2003.

Brunner, Otto, Werner Conze, and Reinhart Koselleck, eds. *Geschichtliche Grundbegriffe: Historisches Lexikon zur politish-sozialen Sprache in Deutschland.* Stuttgart: Klett, 1972.

Butcher, Robert, and Angela Schneider. "Fair Play as Respect for the Game." In *Sports Ethics,* edited by Jan Boxill, 153–71. Malden, Mass.: Blackwell, 2003.

Cahill, Janet. "The Olympic Flame and Torch: Running towards Sydney 2000." In *Global and Cultural Critique: Problematizing the Olympic Games: Proceedings of the Fourth International Symposium for Olympic Research,* edited by R. K. Barney, K. B. Wamsley, S. G. Martyn, and G. H. MacDonald, 181–90. London, Ontario: International Centre for Olympic Studies, 1998.

Cahill, Janet. "Political Influence and the Olympic Flame." *Journal of Olympic History* 7, no. 1 (1999): 29–32.

Callède, Jean-Paul. *Les Politiques sportives en France: Eléments de sociologie historique.* Paris: Economica, 2000.

Campe, Joachim Heinrich. *An Abridgement of the New Robinson Crusoe; An Instructive and Entertaining History, for the Use of Children of Both Sexes: Translated from the French: Embellished with Thirty-two Beautiful Cuts.* London: Stockdale, 1789.

Campe, Joachim Heinrich. *Robinson der jungere, zur angenehmen und nutzlichen unterhaltung fur kinder.* Frankfurt, 1781.

Campe, Joachim Heinrich. *Robinson the Younger by Mr. Campe: Illustrated by German Notes for the Use of Those, Which Are Learning English.* Vol. 1. Frankfurt: Kefsler, 1789.

Canseco, Jose. *Juiced: Wild Times, Rampant 'Roids, Smash Hits, and How Baseball Got Big.* New York: Regan, 2005.

Carlyle, Thomas. *Past and Present.* Boston: Houghton Mifflin, 1965.

Cashmore, Ellis. *Making Sense of Sport.* London: Routledge, 1990.

Chishull, Edmund. *Against Duelling: A Sermon Preach'd before the Queen in the Royal Chapel at Windsor-Castle, on November the 23d, 1712.* London: Round, 1712.

Clifford, William Kingdon. "Body and Mind." In *Lectures and Essays by the Late*

William Kingdon Clifford, edited by Leslie Stephen and Frederick Pollock, 1–51. London: Macmillan, 1901.

"Clydesdales and the World Championships." 2002. Available online at *duathlon.com* (accessed April 5, 2005).

Coetzee, J. M. *Giving Offense.* Chicago: University of Chicago Press, 1996.

Cole, Cheryl L. "Resisting the Canon: Feminist Cultural Studies, Sport, and Technologies of the Body." In *Women, Sport, and Culture,* edited by Susan Birrell and Cheryl L. Cole, 5–29. Champaign, Ill.: Human Kinetics, 1994.

Comenius, Johann Amos. *Joh. Amos Commenii Orbis sensualium pictus: Hoc est, Omnium fundamentalium in mundo rerum, & in vitá actionum, pictura & nomenclatura. = Joh. Amos Commenius's Visible World; or, A Picture and Nomenclature of All the Chief Things That Are in the World; and of Mens Employments Therein.* Edited by Charles Hoole. London: Kirton, 1659.

Compayré, Gabriel. *Johann Heinrich Pestalozzi.* New York: Crowell, 1907.

Connell, R. W. *Masculinities.* Berkeley: University of California Press, 1995.

Conrad, Joseph. "The Duel." In *The Complete Short Fiction of Joseph Conrad: Tales,* 4:69–142. Hopewell, N.J.: Ecco, 1992.

Creff, A. F. "Thoughts on Doping." *Olympic Review Newsletter,* no. 12 (September 1968): 447–49.

Crespo, Carlos J., and Joshua Arbesman. "Obesity in the United States." *Physician and Sportsmedicine* 31, no. 11 (2003): 23.

Cunningham, Hugh. *Children and Childhood in Western Society since 1500.* 2nd ed. Harlow: Pearson Longman, 2005.

Daniels, Norman. "Mental Disabilities, Equal Opportunity, and the ADA." In *Mental Disorder, Work Disability, and the Law,* edited by Richard J. Bonnie and John Monahan, 281–97. Chicago: University of Chicago Press, 1997.

Darcy, Simon. "The Politics of Disability and Access: The Sydney 2000 Games Experience." *Disability and Society* 18, no. 6 (2003): 737–57.

Darwall, Stephen L. *Impartial Reason.* Ithaca: Cornell University Press, 1983.

Denison, Jim. *The Greatest: The Haile Gebrselassie Story.* Halcottsville, N.Y.: Breakaway, 2004.

Dennett, Daniel C. *Freedom Evolves.* New York: Viking, 2003.

DePauw, Karen P., and Susan J. Gavron. *Disability and Sport.* Champaign, Ill.: Human Kinetics, 1995.

Dewey, John. "The Ethics of Democracy." In *The Early Works, 1882–1889,* 227–46. Carbondale: Southern Illinois University Press, 1969.

Dickinson, Rachel J. "The Power of the Paralympics 1996 Games in Atlanta." *American Demographics* 18 (May 1, 1996): 15.

Donohoe, Tom, and Neil Johnson. *Foul Play: Drug Abuse in Sports.* Oxford: Blackwell, 1986.

"The Doping." *Bulletin du Comité International Olympique,* no. 78 (1962): 51.

"Doping." *Bulletin du Comité International Olympique,* no. 90 (1965): 47–49.

Dostoyevsky, Fyodor. *Notes from the Underground/The Double.* Translated by Jessie Coulson. Harmondsworth: Penguin, 1972.

Du Bois-Reymond, Emil. *Über die Übung.* Berlin: Hirschwald, 1881.

Dunning, Eric, and Kenneth Sheard. *Barbarians, Gentlemen and Players: A Sociological*

Study of the Development of Rugby Football. New York: New York University Press, 1979.

Ehrenberg, Alain. "Aimez-vous les stades? Architecture de masse et mobilisation." In *Aimez-vous les stades? Les origines des politiques sportives en France 1970–1930,* edited by Alain Ehrenberg, 25–54. Paris: Recherches, 1980.

Elias, Norbert. *The Civilizing Process.* Oxford: Blackwell, 1994.

Elias, Norbert. "An Essay on Sport and Violence." In *Quest for Excitement: Sport and Leisure in the Civilizing Process,* edited by Norbert Elias and Eric Dunning, 150–74. Oxford: Blackwell, 1986.

Elias, Norbert. "The Genesis of Sport as a Sociological Problem." In *Quest for Excitement: Sport and Leisure in the Civilizing Process,* edited by Norbert Elias and Eric Dunning, 126–49. Oxford: Blackwell, 1986.

Ellis, Elisabeth. *Kant's Politics: A Provisional Theory for an Uncertain World.* New Haven: Yale University Press, 2005.

Epstein, Klaus. *The Genesis of German Conservatism.* Princeton: Princeton University Press, 1966.

Escott, Thomas Hay Sweet. *Social Transformations of the Victorian Age.* London: Seeley, 1897.

Fainaru-Wada, Mark, and Lance Williams. *Game of Shadows: Barry Bonds, BALCO, and the Steroids Scandal That Rocked Professional Sports.* New York: Gotham, 2006.

Fass, Paula S. *Encyclopedia of Children and Childhood: In History and Society.* New York: Macmillan, 2004.

Festle, Mary Jo. *Playing Nice: Politics and Apologies in Women's Sports.* New York: Columbia University Press, 1996.

Forsyth, Ilene H. *The Uses of Art: Medieval Metaphor in the Michigan Law Quadrangle.* Ann Arbor: University of Michigan Press, 1993.

Francis, Leslie Pickering, and Anita Silvers. "Achieving the Right to Live in the World: Americans with Disabilities and the Civil Rights Tradition." In *Americans with Disabilities: Exploring Implications of the Law for Individuals and Institutions,* edited by Leslie Pickering Francis and Anita Silvers, xiii–xxx. New York: Routledge, 2000.

Fraser, Nancy. *Justice Interruptus: Critical Reflections on the "Postsocialist" Condition.* New York: Routledge, 1997.

Freeman, Joanne B. *Affairs of Honor: National Politics in the New Republic.* New Haven: Yale University Press, 2001.

Frevert, Ute. "Bourgeois Honour: Middle-Class Duellists in Germany from the Late Eighteenth to the Early Twentieth Century." In *The German Bourgeoisie,* edited by David Blackbourn and Richard J. Evans, 252–92. London: Routledge, 1991.

Frevert, Ute. "Bürgerlichkeit und Ehre: Zur Geschichte des Duells in England und Deutschland." In *Bürgertum im 19. Jahrhundert: Deutschland im europäischen Vergleich,* edited by Jürgen Kocka and Ute Frevert, 101–40. Munich: Deutsche Taschenbuch, 1988.

Frevert, Ute. *Men of Honour: A Social and Cultural History of the Duel.* Translated by Anthony Williams. Cambridge: Polity, 1995.

Frykholm, Peter A. "Soccer and Social Identity in Pre-Revolutionary Moscow." *Journal of Sport History* 24, no. 2 (1997): 143–55.

Gavora, Jessica. *Tilting the Playing Field: Schools, Sports, Sex, and Title IX.* 1st ed. San Francisco: Encounter, 2002.

Gechtman, Roni. "Socialist Mass Politics through Sport: The Bund's Morgnshtern in Poland, 1926–1939." *Journal of Sport History* 26, no. 2 (1999): 326–52.

George, Nicholas. "Doping Scandals Push Finland's Skiing Icons off Their Podium." *Financial Times,* March 3, 2001, 6.

Giamatti, A. Bartlett. *Take Time for Paradise: Americans and Their Games.* New York: Summit, 1989.

Gilman, Sander L. *The Jew's Body.* New York: Routledge, 1991.

Goffman, Erving. *Stigma: Notes on the Management of Spoiled Identity.* New York: Simon and Schuster, 1963.

Goltermann, Svenja. *Körper der Nation: Habitusformierung und die Politik des Turnens 1860–1890.* Göttingen: Vandenhoeck und Ruprecht, 1998.

Göring, Hugo. "Johann Bernhard Basedow: Ein Lebensbild." In *J. B. Basedow's Ausgewählte Schriften,* i–cxii. Langenfalza: Beyer, 1880.

Gramsci, Antonio. *Pre-Prison Writings.* Translated by Virginia Cox. Edited by Richard Bellamy. Cambridge: Cambridge University Press, 1994.

Greenhouse, Linda. "Disabled Golfer May Use a Cart on the PGA Tour, Justices Affirm." *New York Times,* May 30, 2001, A1.

Grisier, Augustin E. F. *Les Armes et le duel.* Paris: Garnier, 1847.

Groos, Karl. *Die Spiele der Thiere.* Jena: Fischer, 1896.

Guillet, Emma, Philippe Sarrazin, Paul Fontayne, and Robert J. Brustad. "Understanding Female Sport Attrition in a Stereotypical Male Sport within the Framework of Eccles's Expectancy-Value Model." *Psychology of Women Quarterly* 30, no. 4 (2006): 358–68.

Guttmann, Allen. *A Whole New Ball Game: An Interpretation of American Sports.* Chapel Hill: University of North Carolina Press, 1988.

Guttmann, Allen. *Women's Sports: A History.* New York: Columbia University Press, 1991.

Habermas, Jürgen. *Between Facts and Norms: Contributions to a Discourse Theory of Law and Democracy.* Cambridge: MIT Press, 1998.

Habermas, Rebekka. *Frauen und Männer des Bürgertums.* Göttingen: Vandenhoeck und Ruprecht, 2000.

Hahn, Harlan. "Disability Policy and the Problem of Discrimination." *American Behavioral Scientist* 28, no. 3 (1985): 293–318.

Haley, Bruce. *The Healthy Body and Victorian Culture.* Cambridge: Harvard University Press, 1978.

Haraway, Donna J. "A Cyborg Manifesto: Science, Technology, and Socialist-Feminism in the Late Twentieth Century." In *Simians, Cyborgs and Women: The Reinvention of Nature,* 149–81. New York: Routledge, 1990.

Hargreaves, Jennifer. *Sporting Females: Critical Issues in the History and Sociology of Women's Sports.* London: Routledge, 1994.

Hart, Simon. "Radcliffe Attacks Cheats." *London Sunday Telegraph,* February 29, 2004, 13.

Haslanger, Sally. "Gender and Race: (What) Are They? (What) Do We Want Them to Be?" *Noûs* 34, no. 1 (2000): 31–55.

Haslanger, Sally. "On Being Objective and Being Objectified." In *A Mind of One's*

Own: Feminist Essays on Reason and Objectivity, edited by Louise M. Antony and Charlotte Witt, 85–125. Boulder, Colo.: Westview, 1993.

Hattenhauer, Hans, ed. *Allgemeines Landrecht für die Preußischen Staaten von 1794.* Frankfurt: Metzner, 1970.

Hausner, Otto. *Ueber den Zweikampf: Geschichte, Gesetzgebung und Lösung.* Vienna: Alma Mater, 1880.

"A Healthy Body and a Mind at Ease." *The Spectator* 2, no. 115 (1776): 142–46.

Helstein, Michelle T. "Seeing Your Sporting Body: Identity, Subjectivity, and Misrecognition." *Sociology of Sport Journal* 24, no. 1 (2007): 78–103.

Herman, Barbara. "A Cosmopolitan Kingdom of Ends." In *Reclaiming the History of Ethics: Essays for John Rawls,* edited by Andrews Reath, Barbara Herman, and Christine M. Korsgaard, 187–213. Cambridge: Cambridge University Press, 1997.

Herzog, Don. *Cunning.* Princeton: Princeton University Press, 2006.

Herzog, Don. *Happy Slaves.* Chicago: University of Chicago Press, 1989.

Herzog, Don. *Poisoning the Minds of the Lower Orders.* Princeton: Princeton University Press, 1998.

Hey, Richard. *A Dissertation on Duelling.* Cambridge: Cambridge University, 1784.

Heywood, Colin. *A History of Childhood: Children and Childhood in the West from Medieval to Modern Times.* Cambridge: Polity, 2001.

Hobbes, Thomas. *Leviathan.* Edited by Edwin Curley. Indianapolis: Hackett, 1994.

Hoberman, John. *Mortal Engines: The Science of Performance and the Dehumanization of Sport.* New York: Free Press, 1992.

Hoberman, John. *Testosterone Dream: Rejuvenation, Aphrodisia, Doping.* Berkeley: University of California Press, 2005.

Hobsbawm, Eric. "Mass-Producing Traditions: Europe, 1870–1914." In *The Invention of Tradition,* edited by Eric Hobsbawm and Terence Ranger, 263–307. Cambridge: Cambridge University Press, 1983.

Hume, David. *A Treatise of Human Nature.* Revised and annotated by L. A. Selby-Bigge and P. H. Nidditch. 2nd ed. Oxford: Clarendon, 1978.

Ikegami, Eiko. *The Taming of the Samurai: Honorific Individualism and the Making of Modern Japan.* Cambridge: Harvard University Press, 1995.

Ingham, Alan, and Stephen Hardy. "Sport: Structuration, Subjugation and Hegemony." *Theory, Culture and Society* 2, no. 2 (1984): 85–103.

International Paralympic Committee. "Classification." 2005. Available online at http://www.paralympic.org/release/Main_Sections_Menu/Classification (accessed May 3, 2005).

International Paralympic Committee. "Paralympic Games." 2005. Available online at http://www.paralympic.org/release/Main_Sections_Menu/Paralympic_Games (accessed May 7, 2005).

Jacyna, L. S. "The Physiology of Mind, the Unity of Nature, and the Moral Order in Victorian Thought." *British Journal for the History of Science* 14, no. 47 (1981): 109–32.

John, Hans-Georg. *Politik und Turnen: Die Deutsche Turnerschaft als nationale Bewegung im deutschen Kaiserreich von 1871–1914.* Ahrensburg: Czwalina, 1976.

Jones, Stephen G. *Sport, Politics, and the Working Class: A Study of Organised Labour and Sport in Inter-War Britain.* Manchester: Manchester University Press, 1988.

Jost, Kenneth. "Sports and Drugs: Are Stronger Anti-Doping Policies Needed?" *CQ Researcher* 14, no. 26 (2004): 613–36.

Kant, Immanuel. *Correspondence*. Edited and translated by Arnulf Zweig. Cambridge: Cambridge University Press, 1999.

Kant, Immanuel. *Gesammelte Schriften*. 29 vols. Berlin: Preußische Akademie der Wissenchaften, 1902–.

Kant, Immanuel. "Hauptwerke." 1998. Available online at http://pastmas ters2000.nlx.com/ (accessed 2003).

Kant, Immanuel. *Lectures on Ethics*. Edited by Peter Heath and J. B. Schneewind. Translated by Peter Heath. Cambridge: Cambridge University Press, 1997.

Kant, Immanuel. *Practical Philosophy*. Translated and edited by Mary J. Gregor. Cambridge: Cambridge University Press, 1996.

Kant, Immanuel. *Religion and Rational Theology*. Translated and edited by Allen W. Wood and George Di Giovanni. Cambridge: Cambridge University Press, 1996.

Karst, Kenneth L. *Belonging to America: Equal Citizenship and the Constitution*. New Haven: Yale University Press, 1989.

Kessler, Suzanne J. *Lessons from the Intersexed*. New Brunswick, N.J.: Rutgers University Press, 1998.

Kiernan, V. G. *The Duel in European History: Honour and the Reign of Aristocracy*. Oxford: Oxford University Press, 1988.

Kirkland, Anna. "Representations of Fatness and Personhood: Pro-Fat Advocacy and the Limits and Uses of Law." *Representations* 82, no. 1 (2003): 24–51.

Kolata, Gina. *Ultimate Fitness: The Quest for Truth about Exercise and Health*. New York: Farrar, Straus, and Giroux, 2003.

Koppelman, Andrew. *Antidiscrimination Law and Social Equality*. New Haven: Yale University Press, 1996.

Koselleck, Reinhart. *Preußen zwischen Reform und Revolution: Allgemeines Landrecht, Verwaltung und soziale Bewegung*. Stuttgart: Klett, 1967.

Krammer, Reinhard. "Austria: 'New Times Are with Us.'" In *The Story of Worker Sport*, edited by Arnd Krüger and James Riordan, 81–95. Champaign, Ill.: Human Kinetics, 1996.

Krause, Sharon. *Liberalism with Honor*. Cambridge: Harvard University Press, 2002.

Krüger, Arnd. "The German Way of Worker Sport." In *The Story of Worker Sport*, edited by Arnd Krüger and James Riordan, 1–25. Champaign, Ill.: Human Kinetics, 1996.

Krüger, Arnd. "'Once the Olympics Are Through, We'll Beat up the Jew': German Jewish Sports 1898–1938 and the Anti-Semitic Discourse." *Journal of Sport History* 26, no. 2 (1999): 353–75.

La Cava, Giuseppe. "The Use of Drugs in Competitive Sport." *Bulletin du Comité International Olympique*, no. 78 (1962): 52–53.

Laine, Leena. "TUL: The Finnish Worker Sport Movement." In *The Story of Worker Sport*, edited by Arnd Krüger and James Riordan, 67–80. Champaign, Ill.: Human Kinetics, 1996.

Langley, Russell. "WADA Decides against Hypoxic Chamber Ban." 2006. Available online at http://www.uksport.gov.uk/news/wada_decides_against_hypoxic_chamber_ban/ (accessed February 27, 2008).

LaVaque-Manty, Mika. *Arguments and Fists: Political Agency and Justification in Liberal Theory.* New York: Routledge, 2002.

LaVaque-Manty, Mika. "Kant's Children." *Social Theory and Practice* 32, no. 3 (2006): 365–88.

LaVaque-Manty, Mika, and Robert W. Mickey. "Ring of Truth: Johnny Cash and Populism." In *Johnny Cash and Philosophy: Ring of Truth,* edited by John Huss and David Werther, 59–73. Chicago: Open Court, 2008.

Lay, Taimour. "Olympic Dream over for 'Blade Runner' Pistorius." *The Guardian,* (London), July 19, 2008, 13.

Leal, Joseph. "Disabled Athletes in Training." *Olympic Review,* no. 291 (January 1992): 26–27.

Leo [pseud.]. "Ueber Zweikämpfe und ihre Schädlichkeit." *Deutsches Museum* 2 (1787): 15–22.

Litsky, Frank. "Wheelchair Athletes File a Complaint." *New York Times,* September 29, 1999, D7.

Littwin, Mike. "Now Everyone's Talking about Boulder Bolder." *Denver Rocky Mountain News,* April 29, 1998, 2C.

Longman, Jeré. "An Amputee Sprinter: Is He Disabled or Too-Abled?" *New York Times,* May 15, 2007, A1.

Longman, Jeré. "Athletes Embrace Size, Rejecting Stereotypes." *New York Times,* February 8, 2007, A1.

Longman, Jeré. "East German Steroids' Toll: 'They Killed Heidi.'" *New York Times,* January 26, 2004, D1.

Longman, Jeré, and Marjorie Connelly. "Americans Suspect Steroid Use in Sports Is Common, Poll Finds." *New York Times,* December 16, 2003, D1.

Lowerson, John, and John Myerscough. *Time to Spare in Victorian England.* Hassocks: Harvester, 1977.

MacIntyre, Alasdair. *After Virtue.* 2nd ed. Notre Dame, Ind.: Notre Dame University Press, 1984.

MacKinnon, Catherine. *Toward a Feminist Theory of the State.* Cambridge: Harvard University Press, 1989.

Mangan, J. A. *Athleticism in the Victorian and Edwardian Public School: The Emergence and Consolidation of an Educational Ideology.* Cambridge: Cambridge University Press, 1981.

Mangan, J. A. *The Games Ethic and Imperialism: Aspects of the Diffusion of an Ideal.* Harmondsworth: Viking, 1986.

Mascagni, Katia. "Paola Fantato: Sports as a Means of Social Integration." *Olympic Review* 26, no. 10 (1996): 75–77.

McAleer, Kevin. *Dueling: The Cult of Honor in Fin-de-Siècle Germany.* Princeton: Princeton University Press, 1994.

McCarthy, Colman. "Wheelchair Marathoners Deserve a Chance to Compete." *Washington Post,* May 13, 1979, F10.

McCloskey, John, and Julian Bailes. *When Winning Costs Too Much: Steroids, Supplements, and Scandal in Today's Sports.* Lanham, Md.: Taylor, 2005.

McIntosh, Peter. *Fair Play: Ethics in Sport and Education.* London: Heinemann, 1979.

McKinley, James C., Jr. "No Stop Signs on the Course; Also, No Prizes at the End of It." *New York Times,* November 8, 1999, F3.

Mendelssohn, Moses. "On the Question: What Is Enlightenment?" In *What Is Enlightenment? Eighteenth-Century Answers and Twentieth-Century Questions,* edited by James Schmidt, 53–57. Berkeley: University of California Press, 1996.

Mill, John Stuart. *On Liberty.* Indianapolis: Hackett, 1978.

Mimiague, Marie-José. "The Doping Problem in Comparative Penal Law." *Olympic Review,* no. 80–81 (July–August 1974): 313–19.

Mitchell, George J. *Report to the Commissioner of Baseball of an Independent Investigation into the Illegal Use of Steroids and Other Performance Enhancing Substances by Players in Major League Baseball.* New York: Office of the Commissioner of Baseball, 2007.

Mommsen, Wolfgang J. *Max Weber and German Politics, 1890–1920.* Translated by Michael S. Steinberg. Chicago: University of Chicago Press, 1984.

Monestier, Martin. *Duels: Les combat singuliers des origines à nos jours.* Paris: Sand, 1991.

Montesquieu, Charles Louis de Secondat, Baron. *Persian Letters.* Translated by C. J. Betts. London: Penguin, 1973.

Montesquieu, Charles Louis de Secondat, Baron. *Persian Letters.* Translated by George Healy. Indianapolis: Hackett, 1999.

Moretti, Franco. "Homo Palpitans: Balzac's Novels and Urban Personality." In *Signs Taken for Wonders: Essays in the Sociology of Literary Forms,* 109–29. London: Verso, 1983.

Mosse, Werner. "Nobility and Bourgeoisie in Nineteenth Century Europe: A Comparative View." In *Bourgeois Society in Nineteenth-Century Europe,* edited by Jürgen Kocka and Allen Mitchell, 70–102. Oxford: Berg, 1993.

Muthu, Sankar. *Enlightenment against Empire.* Princeton: Princeton University Press, 2003.

Neilson, George. *Trial by Combat.* Glasgow: Hodge, 1890.

Neuendorf, K. G. "Fragmente über Basedow." *Deutsche Monatschrift* 3 (1790): 281–316.

Nozick, Robert. *Anarchy, State, and Utopia.* New York: Basic Books, 1974.

Nussbaum, Martha C. "Human Functioning and Social Justice: In Defense of Aristotelian Essentialism." *Political Theory* 20, no. 2 (1992): 202–46.

Nussbaum, Martha C. *Women and Human Development: The Capabilities Approach.* Cambridge: Cambridge University Press, 2000.

"The Olympics Meets the War on Drugs." 2006. Available online at http://stopthe drugwar.org/chronicle/424/olympics.shtml (accessed February 24, 2006).

O'Quinn, Robert P. *The Americans with Disabilities Act: Time for Amendments.* Cato Policy Analysis 158. Washington, D.C.: Cato Institute, 1991.

O'Neill, Onora. *Constructions of Reason.* Cambridge: Cambridge University Press, 1989.

Orlie, Melissa A. "Political Capitalism and the Consumption of Democracy." In *Democracy and Vision: Sheldon Wolin and the Vicissitudes of the Political,* edited by Aryeh Botwinick and William E. Connolly, 138–60. Princeton: Princeton University Press, 2001.

Ortner, Sherry B. *Making Gender: The Politics and Erotics of Culture.* Boston: Beacon, 1996.

Orwell, George. *The Road to Wigan Pier.* San Diego: Harcourt, Brace, Jovanovich, 1958.

Orwell, George. "Such, Such Were the Joys . . ." In *A Collection of Essays,* 1–47. San Diego: Harcourt Brace Jovanovich, 1970.

Paddick, Robert J. "Drugs and Sports: A Review Article." *Sporting Traditions* 9, no. 2 (1990): 64–72.

Pålbrant, Rolf. "A Vital Period in Swedish Worker Sport: 1919–1936." In *The Story of Worker Sport,* edited by Arnd Krüger and James Riordan, 117–29. Champaign, Ill.: Human Kinetics, 1996.

Park, Roberta J. "A Decade of the Body: Researching and Writing about the History of Health, Fitness, Exercise and Sport, 1983–1993." *Journal of Sport History* 21, no. 1 (1994): 59–82.

Park, Roberta J. "'Embodied Selves': The Rise and Development of Concern for Physical Education, Active Games and Recreation for American Women, 1776–1865." *Journal of Sport History* 5, no. 2 (1978): 5–41.

Park, Roberta J. "Physiologists, Physicians, and Physical Educators: Nineteenth Century Biology and Exercise, *Hygienic* and *Educative.*" *Journal of Sport History* 14, no. 1 (1987): 28–60.

Park, Roberta J. "Sport, Gender and Society in a Transatlantic Victorian Perspective." In *From "Fair Sex" to Feminism: Sport and the Socialization of Women in the Industrial and Post-Industrial Eras,* edited by J. A. Mangan and Roberta J. Park, 58–93. London: Cass, 1987.

Pateman, Carole. *The Sexual Contract.* Stanford: Stanford University Press, 1988.

Peltonen, Markku. *The Duel in Early Modern England: Civility, Politeness and Honour.* Cambridge: Cambridge University Press, 2003.

Pestalozzi, Johann Heinrich. "Ein Gespräch über Volksaufklärung und Volksbildung." In *Politische Schriften,* 358–76. Basel: Birkhäuser, 1991.

Pingree, Amanda. "The Development of the Paralympic Games." *Olympic Review* 26, no. 20 (1998): 58–60.

Pinker, Steven. *The Blank Slate: The Modern Denial of Human Nature.* New York: Viking, 2002.

Porritt, Arthur. "Doping and the Use of Chemical Agents to Modify Human Performance in Sport." *Bulletin du Comité International Olympique,* no. 90 (1965): 49–50.

Porter, Roy. *Flesh in the Age of Reason.* New York: Norton, 2004.

Power, Chris. "Pistorius Clocks in World Record and Eyes the Treble." *London Mail on Sunday,* Sept. 14, 2008, 92.

Putnam, Robert D. *Bowling Alone: The Collapse and Revival of American Community.* New York: Simon and Schuster, 2000.

Putnam, Robert D., Robert Leonardi, and Raffaella Nanetti. *Making Democracy Work: Civic Traditions in Modern Italy.* Princeton: Princeton University Press, 1993.

Raevuori, Antero. *Paavo Nurmi: Juoksijain kuningas.* Helsinki: WSOY, 1997.

Rawls, John. "The Idea of an Overlapping Consensus." *Oxford Journal of Legal Studies* 7, no. 1 (1987): 1–25.

Rawls, John. *Justice as Fairness: A Restatement.* Cambridge: Harvard University Press, 2001.

Rawls, John. "The Law of Peoples." In *On Human Rights: The Oxford Amnesty Lectures 1993,* edited by Stephen Shute and Susan Hurley, 41–82. New York: Basic Books, 1993.

Rawls, John. *Political Liberalism.* New York: Columbia University Press, 1993.

Rawls, John. *A Theory of Justice.* Cambridge: Harvard University Press, 1971.

Reid, Douglas A. "Beasts and Brutes: Popular Blood Sports, c. 1780–1860." In *Sport and the Working Class in Modern Britain,* edited by Richard Holt, 12–28. Manchester: Manchester University Press, 1990.

Review of Guts Muth's *Gymnastik für die Jugend. Neue allgemeine deutsche Bibliothek* 21, no. 2 (1796): 459–61.

Richelieu, Armand Jean du Plessis, duc de. *The Political Testament of Cardinal Richelieu.* Translated by Henry Bertram Hill. Madison: University of Wisconsin Press, 1961.

Richelieu, Armand Jean du Plessis, duc de. *Testament politique.* Edited by Françoise Hildesheimer. Paris: Société de l'Histoire de France, 1995.

Riess, Steven A. "From Pitch to Putt: Sport and Class in Anglo-American Sport." *Journal of Sport History* 21, no. 2 (1994): 138–84.

Riordan, James. Introduction to *The Story of Worker Sport,* edited by Arnd Krüger and James Riordan, vii–x. Champaign, Ill.: Human Kinetics, 1996.

Riordan, James. "Worker Sport within a Worker State: The Soviet Union." In *The Story of Worker Sport,* edited by Arnd Krüger and James Riordan, 43–65. Champaign, Ill.: Human Kinetics, 1996.

Roberts, Selena. "Fear of Disability the Same on a Course or a Track." *New York Times,* July 18, 2007, D1.

Robinson, Joshua. "Study Suggests That Amputee Holds an Unfair Advantage." *New York Times,* January 10, 2008, D1.

Rousseau, Jean-Jacques. "Letter to M. d'Alembert on the Theatre." In *Politics and the Arts,* 1–137. Ithaca: Cornell University Press, 1968.

Rousseau, Jean-Jacques. *Social Contract and Discourses.* Translated by G. D. H. Cole. London: Dent, 1973.

Ruskin, John. *Unto This Last, and Other Writings.* London: Penguin, 1985.

Rutledge, Wilmuth S. "Dueling in Antebellum Mississippi." *Journal of Mississippi History* 26 (August 1964): 181–91.

Sabine, Lorenzo. *Notes on Duels and Duelling.* Boston: Crosby, Nichols, 1855.

Sassoon, Siegfried. *Memoirs of a Fox-Hunting Man.* London: Folio Society, 1971.

Schama, Simon. *The Embarrassment of Riches: An Interpretation of Dutch Culture in the Golden Age.* New York: Vintage, 1997.

Schapiro, Tamar. "What Is a Child?" *Ethics* 109, no. 4 (1999): 715–38.

Schiller, Friedrich. *On the Aesthetic Education of Man.* Translated by Elizabeth M. Wilkinson and L. A. Willoughby. Oxford: Clarendon, 1967.

Schmidt, James. "What Enlightenment Project?" *Political Theory* 28, no. 6 (2000): 734–57.

Schuld, Kimberly. "A Flawed Interpretation of Title IX Is Keeping Male Students from Playing Sports." *Chronicle of Higher Education,* March 31, 2000, B3.

Selden, John. *The Duello or Single Combat from Antiquitie Deriued into this Kingdome of England, with Seuerall Kindes, and Ceremonious Formes Thereof from Good Authority Described.* London: Helme, 1610.

Sen, Amartya. "Capability and Well-Being." In *The Quality of Life,* edited by Martha Nussbaum and Amartya Sen, 30–53. Oxford: Oxford University Press, 1993.

Sen, Amartya. *Inequality Reexamined.* Cambridge: Harvard University Press, 1992.

Sen, Amartya. "Rational Fools: A Critique of the Behavioral Foundations of Economics." *Philosophy and Public Affairs* 6, no. 4 (1977): 317–44.

Sen, Amartya. "Rights and Capabilities." In *Morality and Objectivity,* edited by Ted Honderich, 130–48. London: Routledge and Kegan Paul, 1985.

Shapiro, Dana Adam, Jeffrey Mandel, and Henry Alex Rubin. *Murderball.* THINK-Film, 2005.

Sherrill, Claudine. *Adapted Physical Activity, Recreation, and Sport: Crossdisciplinary and Lifespan.* 5th ed. Boston: WCB/McGraw-Hill, 1998.

Simmel, Georg. "The Web of Group Affiliations." In *Conflict and the Web of Group Affiliations,* 125–95. New York: Free Press, 1955.

Sokolove, Michael. "From Pastime to Naptime." *New York Times Magazine,* February 5, 2006, 24–25.

Spencer, Herbert. *Education: Intellectual, Moral, and Physical.* London: Routledge/Thoemmes, 1993.

Spirn, Ann Whiston. "Constructing Nature: The Legacy of Frederick Law Olmsted." In *Uncommon Ground: Rethinking the Human Place in Nature,* edited by William Cronon, 91–113. New York: Norton, 1996.

Stanley, Arthur Penrhyn. *The Life and Correspondence of Thomas Arnold.* Vol. 1. London: Fellowes, 1845.

Stone, Deborah A. *The Disabled State.* Philadelphia: Temple University Press, 1984.

Suggs, Welch. "Foes of Title IX Try to Make Equity in College Sports a Campaign Issue." *Chronicle of Higher Education,* February 4, 2000, A55.

Suggs, Welch. "Poll Finds Strong Public Backing for Gender Equity in College Athletics." *Chronicle of Higher Education,* July 7, 2000, A40.

Sunstein, Cass R. "The Anticaste Principle." *Michigan Law Review* 92, no. 8 (1994): 2410–55.

Sunstein, Cass R. "On Analogical Reasoning." *Harvard Law Review* 106, no. 3 (1993): 741–91.

Suomen Työväen Urheiluliitto. "Esittely." 2001. Available online at http://www.tul.fi (accessed August 6, 2002).

Süstermann, A. U. L. "Ist es eine so gleichgültige Sache, dem großen Haufen Freyheit zu predigen? Ein kleiner Beytrag zum Für und Wider die Freyheit." *Der neue Teutsche Merkur,* no. 3 (1793): 188–99.

Taylor, Charles. *Multiculturalism and the Politics of Recognition.* Princeton: Princeton University Press, 1992.

Taylor, Charles. *Sources of the Self: The Making of the Modern Identity.* Cambridge: Harvard University Press, 1989.

Tocqueville, Alexis de. *Democracy in America.* Translated by Henry Reeve and Francis Bowen. Edited by Phillips Bradley. 2 vols. New York: Random House, 1990.

Toll, Thomas (?). *The Female Duell; or, The Maidens Combate.* London: Clarke, 1672.

Tomkins, Calvin. "The Tennis Artist." *New Yorker,* September 4, 2000, 52–60.

Trollope, Anthony. *British Sports and Pastimes.* London: Virtue, 1868.

Trollope, Anthony. *The Prime Minister.* London: Penguin, 1994.

Truman, Ben C. *The Field of Honor: Being a Complete and Comprehensive History of Duelling in All Countries.* New York: Fords, Howard, and Hulbert, 1884.

Twin, Stephanie L., ed. *Out of the Bleachers: Writings on Women and Sport.* Old Westbury, N.Y.: Feminist Press, 1979.

Ueberhorst, Horst. *Frisch, frei, stark und treu: Die Arbeitersportbewegung in Deutschland, 1893–1933.* Düsseldorf: Droste, 1973.

Ungerleider, Steven. *Faust's Gold: Inside the East German Doping Machine.* New York: St. Martin's, 2001.

Vamplew, Vray. *Pay Up and Play the Game: Professional Sport in Britain, 1875–1914.* Cambridge: Cambridge University Press, 1988.

Vamplew, Vray. "Sport and Industrialization: An Economic Interpretation of the Changes in Popular Sport in Nineteenth-Century England." In *Pleasure, Profit, Proselytism: British Culture and Sport at Home and Abroad, 1700–1914,* edited by J. A. Mangan, 7–20. London: Cass, 1988.

Veblen, Thorstein. *The Theory of the Leisure Class.* Boston: Houghton Mifflin, 1973.

Villaume, Peter. "Über die Gewalt der Leidenschaften in den Jünglingsjahren." *Deutsche Monatschrift* 2 (1790): 153–75.

von der Lippe, Gerd. "Landmarks in the History of Norwegian Worker Sport." In *The Story of Worker Sport,* edited by Arnd Krüger and James Riordan, 131–42. Champaign, Ill.: Human Kinetics, 1996.

von Humboldt, Wilhelm. *The Limits of State Action.* Translated by Joseph Coulthard. Edited by J. W. Burrow. Indianapolis: Liberty Fund, 1993.

Voy, Robert. *Drugs, Sport, and Politics.* Champaign, Ill.: Leisure, 1991.

"War on Doping in Switzerland." *Bulletin du Comité International Olympique,* no. 80 (1962): 62–63.

Weber, Marianne. *Max Weber: Ein Lebensbild.* Heidelberg: Lambert Schneider, 1950.

Weber, Max. "Economic Policy and the National Interest in Imperial Germany." In *Selections in Translation,* edited by W. G. Runciman, 263–68. Cambridge: Cambridge University Press, 1978.

Weber, Max. "National Character and the Junkers." In *From Max Weber: Essays in Sociology,* edited by Hans H. Gerth and C. Wright Mills, 386–95. New York: Oxford University Press, 1958.

Weber, Max. "Politics as a Vocation." In *From Max Weber: Essays in Sociology,* edited by Hans H. Gerth and C. Wright Mills, 77–128. New York: Oxford University Press, 1958.

Williams, Gareth. "From Popular Culture to Public Cliché: Image and Identity in Wales, 1890–1914." In *Pleasure, Profit, Proselytism: British Culture and Sport at Home and Abroad, 1700–1914,* edited by J. A. Mangan, 128–43. London: Cass, 1988.

Wilson, Adrian. "The Infancy of the History of Childhood: An Appraisal of Philippe Ariès." *History and Theory* 19, no. 2 (1980): 132–53.

Wilson, John. *Playing by the Rules: Sport, Society, and the State.* Detroit: Wayne State University Press, 1994.

Wood, Gordon S. *The Radicalism of the American Revolution.* New York: Knopf, 1992.

Wordsworth, William. "Kendal and Windermere Railway: Two Letters." In *The Prose Works of William Wordsworth,* edited by W. J. B. Owen and Jane Worthington Smyser, 321–41. Oxford: Clarendon, 1974.

Wordsworth, William. "Speech at the Laying of the Foundation Stone of the New School in the Village of Bowness, Windermere, 1836." In *The Prose Works of*

William Wordsworth, edited by W. J. B. Owen and Jane Worthington Smyser, 291–96. Oxford: Clarendon, 1974.

World Anti-Doping Code. Montreal: World-Anti Doping Agency, 2003.

Yack, Bernard. *The Longing for Total Revolution: Philosophic Sources of Social Discontent from Rousseau to Marx and Nietzsche.* Berkeley: University of California Press, 1992.

Young, Iris Marion. *Justice and the Politics of Difference.* Princeton: Princeton University Press, 1990.

Zimbalist, Andrew. "Backlash against Title IX: An End Run around Female Athletes." *Chronicle of Higher Education,* March 3, 2000, B9.

Zupan, Mark, and Tim Swanson. *Gimp.* New York: HarperCollins, 2006.

Index

About the Author

Trained as a philosopher, Mika LaVaque-Manty is an associate professor of political science at the University of Michigan, where he teaches political theory. His research has focused on political action and agency in both historical and contemporary contexts. He is the author of, among other works, "Food, Functioning and Justice: From Famines to Eating Disorders" (2001), *Arguments and Fists: Political Agency and Justification in Liberal Theory* (2002), and "Bentley, Truman, and the Study of Groups" (2006).

DATE DUE

GAYLORD			PRINTED IN U.S.A.